CONTENTS

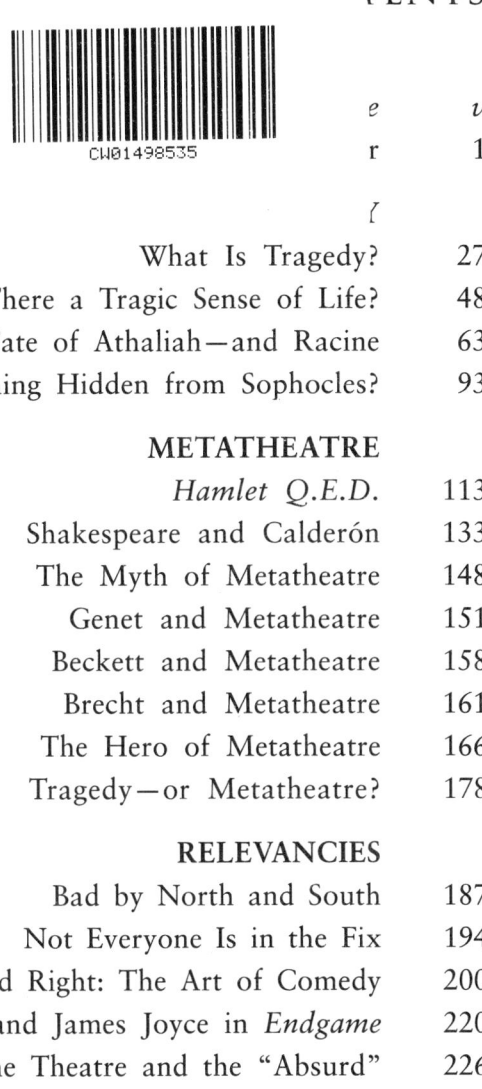

TRAGEDY AND METATHEATRE

ESSAYS ON DRAMATIC FORM

Lionel Abel

HOLMES & MEIER
New York/London

Published in the United States of America 2003
by Holmes & Meier Publishers, Inc.
160 Broadway • New York, NY 10038
www.holmesandmeier.com

This book has been printed on acid-free paper.

Designed by Brigid McCarthy

Library of Congress Cataloging-in-Publication Data

Abel, Lionel.
    Tragedy and metatheatre : essays on dramatic form / Lionel Abel.
        p. cm.
    Includes bibliographical references and index.
    ISBN 0-8419-1352-8 (cloth : alk. paper) — ISBN 0-8419-1353-6 (paper : alk. paper)
    1. Drama—History and criticism. I. Title.

PN1623.A37 2003
808.82'512—dc21   2003050851

Manufactured in the United States of America

10   9   8   7   6   5   4   3   2   1

PREFACE

This new work, *Tragedy and Metatheatre,* presents some of my more recent essays on modern theatre, together with the most often discussed and debated pieces from *Metatheatre* (1963).

Before *Metatheatre* went to press, good friends advised me to change the title, which they felt no one would comprehend. Instead of which, from that time on, the word has been constantly used, not only here but around the world. *Metatheatre,* at the very least, has added a word to the language with which we now talk of theatre.

At the time that *Metatheatre* first appeared, I attempted to do two things: one, to explain why tragedy is so difficult, if not altogether impossible for the modern dramatist, and two, to suggest the nature of a comparatively philosophic form of drama which I had then designated as *metatheatre.*

Four of the essays in this new volume focus on tragedy as distinct from metatheatre. I see tragedy as dealing with the real world and metatheatre as dealing with the world of the imagination. I understand that I should clarify precisely what tragedy is and explain why it is impossible to have what has been called "a tragic sense of life." In addition, I explore the possibility that in his writing of tragedy Sophocles might have had something hidden from himself which he did not want to bring to light.

I myself have been criticized by eminently responsible and authoritative critics for what they consider my ever loose and sometimes erratic definition of metatheatre. Such critics have spurred me on to offer a more definite and perhaps a clearer explanation of this dramatic form.

Some of the plays I refer to in this book can be classified as instances of the play-within-a-play, but this term suggests only a device, and not a definite form. I designate a whole range of plays as metatheatre, some of which do not employ the play-within-a-play, even as a device. The plays I point to as metatheatre have one common character: all of them are theatre pieces about life seen as already theatricalized. By this I mean that persons appearing on the stage in these plays are there simply because they were caught by the playwright in dramatic postures as a camera might catch them, and because these characters already knew they were dramatic. They are aware of their own theatricality.

In my essay "Genet and Metatheatre" I ask the question: "Why have Western dramatists, bent on writing tragedy, been unable to do so successfully?" My answer is summed up in one word: *self-consciousness*. I mean the self-consciousness of our modern dramatists as well as their protagonists.

Also, in describing the nature of tragedy, I maintain that one cannot treat tragedy without accepting implacable values. Here again, our modern dramatists have difficulty with such acceptance. Thus, instead of tragedy, we now have *metaplay*, a dramatic form for revealing characters whose self-consciousness creates their dramatic situations. This dramatic form is actually not really a modern invention. I show that Calderón, Cervantes, Shakespeare, as well as Genet, Beckett, and Brecht, have contributed their own kinds of metatheatre. These great dramatists have turned tragic situations into metaplays, in which the comic and the tragic are brought together under a single unified form.

INTRODUCTION

by Martin Puchner

FOR ANYONE WHO has seen Shakespeare or Calderón, Pirandello or Genet, the word *metatheatre* defines itself. Hamlet's advice to the players and the play-within-the-play signal undeniably that we are watching a play about theatre. The blurring of play and reality, and the confusing passage from one to the other, also supply the stuff from which the plays of Pirandello are made. Pirandello delights in our bewilderment as we watch one layer of theatricality and illusion give way to the next as if they were so many Russian dolls stacked into one another. And Genet's characters like nothing more than dressing themselves in various costumes and assuming different roles as if the world offstage were even more theatrical than what we see onstage. The term *metatheatre,* coined by Lionel Abel, is so indispensable that it has acquired a life of its own. It is not always used with reference to its originator, especially when applied to new areas such as postcolonial theatre or postmodern performance.[1] One reason for the present, and sadly posthumous, publication of old and new texts by Lionel Abel is to reconnect metatheatre to its originator and thus to use Abel's work as a point of departure for rethinking the term *metatheatre* as a powerful tool for understanding the history of theatre.

When we contemplate *metatheatre* today, forty years after it was coined, we may wonder how it relates to a host of other terms using the prefix *meta,* such as *metalanguage, metanarrative, metahistory,* and *metatheory.* The most recent coinage is probably

---

1. See, for example, Joanne Tompkins, "'Spectacular Resistance': Metatheatre in Post-Colonial Drama," *Modern Drama* 38 (Spring 1995).

1

Jean-François Lyotard's *metanarrative* (1979), which designates the modern tendency toward grandiose stories such as the progress of science in the search for truth or the progressive emancipation of humans from oppression.[2] A similar interest in the "grand stories" we tell ourselves motivated Hayden White's magisterial study *Metahistory* (1973), which argues that the way we think about history has itself a history.[3] In a related vein *metatheory* describes the project of thinking theoretically about different types of theories. However, the term most closely related to Abel's metatheatre is *metalanguage*, popularized by the linguist Roman Jakobson.[4] *Metalanguage* describes those moments when language is used not to communicate, but to talk about the act of communication, when language does not refer to the world "outside," but only to itself. In this it corresponds to Abel's definition of *metatheatre* as a theatre not concerned about the world "outside" the theatre, but only with the theatre itself.

The fact that *metacritique, metalanguage,* and *metatheatre* came to prominence in the late fifties and early sixties is no coincidence. The particular self-awareness, self-reflexivity, and self-knowledge which Jakobson and Abel describe have correlates in other disciplines and genre, even if they do not always rely on the prefix *meta*. For this is the moment when the literature, painting, music, and theatre produced in the first half of the twentieth century are canonized, when prominent scholars engage the often hermetic, puzzling, and complex works of high modernism, introducing and explaining them to the academy and to a wider public. The formulation they commonly use is that these difficult works do not seek to represent the

---

2. Jean-François Lyotard, *The Postmodern Condition: A Report on Knowledge* (Minneapolis: University of Minnesota Press, 1984).
3. Hayden White, *Metahistory: The Historical Imagination in Nineteenth-Century Europe* (Baltimore and London: Johns Hopkins University Press, 1973).
4. Roman Jakobson, "Linguistics and Poetics," originally presented at a conference on style at Indiana University in the spring of 1958, then revised and published in *Style in Language*, ed. Thomas A. Sebok (Cambridge: MIT Press, 1960). Jakobson also refers to the use of the notion of *metalanguage* in the field of logic, for example by Alfred Tarski (1933).

world, but are rather "about" art itself. This change occurred most clearly in abstract painting, which patently did not try to represent the world. And so, when Clement Greenberg began to argue in the fifties that modernist painting was only and exclusively "about" the flatness of the canvas—his argument dominated the art world for decades.[5] The other arts have since followed suit: hermetic poetry from Stéphane Mallarmé through Ezra Pound to William Carlos Williams has long been presented as poetry-about-poetry, or *metapoetry;* and more recently the term *metacinema* has appeared as well. There existed no art form in the twentieth century that did not acquire, sooner or later, the prefix *meta,* and often these *meta* terms were coined without knowledge of one another: Abel does not refer to Jakobson, for example, although he was aware of Greenberg. From the mid-century onward, then, *meta* was in the air and was used specifically to make sense of the arts of modernism.

If Abel's term *metatheatre* thus participates in a larger attempt to explain modernism, it must nevertheless also be related to the more particular context of writings on theatre, in particular those of Abel's contemporaries Eric Bentley and Martin Esslin, whose works he engaged constructively, if not uncritically. Abel took issue, for example, with Esslin's own attempt to explain modernist theatre as "absurd theatre," arguing convincingly that the label "absurd" only named the apparent confusion caused by modernist theatre, but did little to solve it.[6] *Metatheatre* is an attempt to come up with a better alternative to "theatre of the absurd," to attempt a positive explanation of modernist theatre. Abel's dedication to modernism can be measured by his resistance to looking back at past epochs, such as Greek tragedy, with nostalgia. Even Susan Sontag, who criticized Abel on other counts, praised this refusal of nostalgia (in fact Abel responded to one of Sontag's critiques, namely, that he had not included an account of comedy in *Metatheatre*, and the present

---

5. Clement Greenberg, *Art and Culture: Critical Essays* (Boston: Beacon Press, 1961).

6. Martin Esslin, *The Theatre of the Absurd* (New York: Anchor Books, 1961).

collection therefore includes Abel's later work on that genre).[7]

The name of Susan Sontag also indicates another context of Abel's work, namely New York intellectuals and artists. Like Bentley, Abel belongs to a generation of New York critics who crossed the borders between theory and practice, writing a considerable number of plays, many of which were produced and one of which won him an Obie award for Best Dramatic Play. In addition, Abel did important work in translation (Jean-Paul Sartre, Camille Pissarro, and Arthur Rimbaud), and he often engaged in heated discussions outside the subject of theatre, for instance, in those surrounding Hannah Arendt's *Eichmann in Jerusalem*. At an early age, Abel collaborated with André Breton on editing the influential Surrealist journal *VVV*. His intellectual life spanned the larger part of the twentieth century and his intellectual autobiography, *The Intellectual Follies*, is one of the most fascinating accounts of intellectual life in New York from the thirties to the eighties.[8]

Even though Abel's metatheatre is part of the interpretation and canonization of modernism, it cannot be reduced to this attempt, for metatheatre not only describes modernist theatre, but Renaissance and baroque theatre as well, in particular the theatre of Shakespeare and Calderón. Abel's characterization of metatheatre as being based on the double belief that "the world is a stage and life is a dream" (163) is a combination of Shakespeare and Calderón, and it is in a discussion of these two baroque playwrights, and not of Pirandello or Genet, that the term metatheatre emerges for the first time. Indeed the baroque seems to be an even clearer example of metatheatre than modern drama is. The visual arts of the baroque are dominated by visual tricks: mirrors; painters painting themselves painting; *trompe l'oeil*, the art of creating illusions, and consciously fake marble dominate the decorative arts and architecture.

---

7. Susan Sontag, "The Death of Tragedy," *Partisan Review* 30 (1963), 122–28.
8. Lionel Abel, *The Intellectual Follies: A Memoir of the Literary Venture in New York and Paris* (New York: W. W. Norton, 1984).

The most important literary work of the period, however, is *Don Quixote*, whose protagonist lives in the world of literature, having suppressed reality in favor of medieval chivalric romances. The artificial, affected, self-conscious, and sophisticated rule over the naïve, simple, and straightforward.

It is not so remarkable, perhaps, that Abel would single out Don Quixote as the single most important figure of metatheatre, even though he appears within a novel and is misled by the reading of medieval romance. "The world is a stage and life is a dream" really designates—more than just a particular form of drama—a general baroque attitude. Don Quixote can be said to "stage" the world around him: he assigns "roles" to everyone he meets and takes great care to live up to the "script" he has chosen for himself, namely, that of a knight errant. Metatheatre is not simply something that occurs in the theatre, but also something that encompasses an understanding of the world as theatre, of "life seen as already theatricalized," (134) Abel says, even before it is brought onto the stage. This theatricality of life is expressed in the way people interact, dress themselves up, and perceive themselves. And this fundamental sense of the theatricality of social life can then be presented in paintings or novels, even as it might be most appropriately expressed in the theatre, from which it is derived.

The understanding of the baroque as artificial, self-conscious, and sophisticated implies that there must have been a preceding period that was authentic, naïve, and simple. The dramatist who developed such a scheme was Friedrich Schiller, contrasting what he called "naïve" art to a second art that he called "sentimental" art.[9] The latter term is slightly awkward, for it does not designate melodramatic, heart-throbbing plots, but rather the consciousness of being belated, sophisticated and artificial, and no longer authentic and originary; it describes the consciousness of a period that is looking back at its putative origins with nostalgia and, in Schiller's term, *sentimentalism*. Along with the same distinction goes a value judgment, for Schiller

---

9. Friedrich Schiller, *On the Naïve and Sentimental in Literature* (Manchester: Carcanet New Press, 1981).

imagines that the true artistic genius works only during the period of "naïve" art, unconsciously creating great works, which are then consciously imitated by later and belated periods, periods that are doomed to contemplate their predecessors with envy and nostalgia.

Structurally, if not in terms of value, Abel presents a similar understanding of the theatre. He presumes that there must have existed a period of drama that was about the real world, not about itself, that was concerned with the moral and ethical questions of society and not narcissistically engaged only with itself. This necessary counterpart and precursor to baroque metatheatre is tragedy. Tragedy, in particular Greek tragedy, and metatheatre are, for Abel, two sides of the same coin; they define each other, both conceptually and historically. For in keeping with Schiller's distinction, naïve art is always the original, and artificial art the later and belated; metatheatre emerges precisely when tragedy declines. On many occasions, Abel therefore defined the term metatheatre as that which happens when it has become impossible to write true tragedy, almost as if metatheatre were another form of failed tragedy. I say "almost," for Abel does not subscribe to Schiller's value judgment in favor of the naïve over the self-conscious. The entire project of metatheatre attempts to demonstrate what is specific and compelling about baroque and modernist theatre, to persuade us that we should not understand the plays of Shakespeare and Genet as "insufficient" tragedies, when they are in fact superb examples of metatheatre. It is for this reason that the present collection of essays begins with Abel's discussion of tragedy before moving on to metatheatre, for the former is both the historical and the critical prerequisite for the latter. Before we can hope to understand metatheatre, we must understand tragedy.

The 2002 New York theatre season produced what must be one of the most striking examples of the necessary relation between metatheatre and tragedy as it was conceived by Lionel Abel in 1961: Edward Albee's twenty-seventh play, *The Goat or Who Is Sylvia?* Albee's plays have always been about the theatre but his latest play takes metatheatre to an extreme. It is based on the conceit that a successful and happily married architect falls in love with a goat. This love, predictably, creates havoc in the happy domestic world of the nuclear family. When taken at face value, Albee's play can be seen as an attempt to write a modern tragedy. The goat, however, is more than the force that wrecks the happy family; it is also the presumed origin of Greek tragedy itself: the sacrificial ritual of Dionysus, the killing of a scapegoat. And indeed, the play's last scene has the wife return to the stage with a bloody bag containing the killed, "sacrificed" goat. Albee's play was originally sub-titled "a commentary on tragedy," to signal, no doubt, that this play is not so much an attempt to write modern tragedy as a commentary on it. The attempt to write tragedy invari-ably turns into a commentary on tragedy, the failure of tragedy into metatheatre.

All this corresponds rather nicely to Abel's understanding of tragedy and metatheatre. *The Goat* can almost be seen as a play about the process by which failed tragedy turns into meta-theatre. A successful architect gets caught in an insoluble dilemma caused by his inexplicable love for a goat. We can find here all the classical ingredients of tragedy: the fall of the hero; the tragic dilemma. Only destruction can result from this setup. The play, however, does not stop there, at the tragic plot, but also shows us the sacrificed goat as if trying to return Greek tragedy to its origin. This programmatic return indicates that this play is more a play *about* tragedy—about the attempt at modern tragedy—than it is a straightforward example of modern tragedy. The sacrificed goat may be the origin of Greek tragedy, but the origin is nowhere visible in regular tragedy. It is of interest to Aristotle, the commentator on tragedy, but not to the author or the audience of a tragic play. *The Goat* is thus closer to Aristotle than it is to Aeschylus—it is, as the original subtitle indicates, a commentary about tragedy, and not tragedy itself.

Unlike Albee, however, Abel is less interested in the origin of Greek tragedy than in its finished form, as it was detailed by Aristotle. Arguing vehemently against common expressions such as "tragic" events or even a "tragic" philosophy of life, Abel opts for a much more narrow and precise notion of tragedy that is restricted to a certain type of play. "Life is not tragic, plays are," could be his slogan against common parlance, and this first specification is followed by a second one: what is tragic is first of all that which inspires fear and pity in the audience. Like Aristotle, Abel's definition of tragedy takes the form of a *reception* theory, a theory of how plays affect the audience. In testing whether a given play corresponds to the definition of tragedy, Abel therefore tends to investigate his own reactions while watching the play, determining whether he was indeed moved to fear and pity. Following Aristotle, he singles out Sophocles' *Oedipus* as the paradigmatic tragedy, the one that meets the fear and pity test most thoroughly; there is no moment in the play that does not move us to these two emotions. For Abel, even more so than for Aristotle, tragedy describes a rare species. The only tragedy Abel allows Shakespeare is *Macbeth*, Jean Racine's *Athalie* counts as well, and the dramatized version of Herman Melville's *Billy Budd* comes close, but in general tragedy ends pretty much with Greek tragedy. Even here, Abel tends to restrict the term to the two earlier playwrights, Aeschylus and Sophocles, and excludes most of the plays by the later Euripides, the *Bacchae* being one of the only exceptions.

This master list of true tragedies is based on Georg Hegel as much as on Aristotle. What Abel borrows from Hegel is an understanding of tragedy that is not satisfied with having the tragic hero fall through forces larger than human; Hegel also demands that a true tragedy catches the hero in a double bind of two competing and mutually exclusive values. Hegel's chief example, also quoted by Abel, is *Antigone*, which has become the preferred tragedy for philosophers and theorists from Hegel through Jacques Lacan and Judith Butler.[10] *Antigone* does not pit right against wrong, but, as Abel put it, "right against right," (37) being based, as it is, on the unsolvable conflict between the right of kinship and the right of the state. A different version of such a moral double bind occurs in Pierre Corneille's *Le Cid*:

---

10. Judith Butler, *Antigone's Claim: Kinship Between Life and Death*. Wellek Library Lecture Series at the University of California, Irvine (New York: Columbia University Press, 2000).

the very qualities that make Chimène love Rodrigue are those that make him kill her father; and the very values that make her worthy of his love also drive her to demand revenge for her father's murder. It is Abel's adherence to Hegel that leads him to reject so vehemently the so-called tragedies whose conflicts are merely accidental, and not necessary, determined by circumstance and not by what he calls "implacable values." (41) Along with the accidental comes another danger, namely melodrama. *Othello*, for example, is not a tragedy because the villain Iago is simply a villain from the beginning, a mere schemer, and thus not worthy of appearing in a tragedy. The murder of Aegisthus and Clytemnestra in Euripides' *Electra*, on the other hand, is melodramatic because it is not the product of conflicting values, but of personally motivated revenge. Melodrama, sentimentality, circumstantial and accidental conflicts—these are the qualities that led to the decline and fall of tragedy after its early Greek climax in *Oedipus* and *Antigone*.

Traces of Schiller's idea that the naïve and original tragic genius who creates half-unconsciously in contrast to the sentimental and self-conscious one can be seen elsewhere in *Tragedy and Metatheatre*. One example is the speculation that Sophocles must not have been "aware" of all aspects of the plays he was writing. Abel here calls for a "new theory of the hidden," (100) one that would account for the lack of the author's control over his own creation. Abel here responds also to the first wave of Freudian interpretations of literature, and he is rightfully skeptical about them, since they, unlike the later and much more sophisticated psychoanalytical interpretations of the eighties and nineties, are merely attempts to put characters on the couch. Abel's theory of the hidden imagines a hidden that is not explained by individual psychology, traumata, and repression, but rather by the fact that we may be capable of perceiving things in hindsight that were hidden from Sophocles. While proposing an alternative to fifties Freudianism, Abel's notion of tragedy exhibits vestiges of the unconscious genius, who does not always know what he is doing, and who thus stands in contrast to the self-aware creator of metatheatre. "In a true tragedy one is beyond thought" (180)—we can see here Schiller's

genius lurking in the background, the genius who creates unconsciously rather than by careful calculation. At the same time,
however, it is possible to tease out a more progressive meaning from this theory of the hidden, for that which we can perceive
more clearly than the author, Abel says, are the ethical and
political implications of a given play. Indeed, Abel here comes
close to anticipating Fredric Jameson's notion of the "political
unconscious" of literature, calling upon the critic to articulate
those ethical and political consequences that must remain unknown even and especially to the author.[11]

Abel's last and most consequential definition of tragedy is
that tragedy gives us the effect of the real. Even though tragedy
is a property not of the world but of plays, these tragic plays
do "thrust one against the ultimate real." (180) Concerned with
moral values, unsolvable dilemmas, and necessary conflicts,
tragedy expresses what is most intractable about the world;
without the recognition that the tragic conflicts presented on
the stage could one day involve us, there would be no fear,
and perhaps also no pity. This does not mean that tragedy is
realistic in the technical sense of the word. On the contrary,
life in and of itself is not tragic, since, as Abel observes, life
tends toward unflinching optimism. Tragedy extracts from the
optimism of life whatever unsolvable nodes and double binds,
contradictory values and forms it can find and distills them
into highly formalized, even formulaic, tragic structures. And
yet, however stylized and improbable, tragedy achieves its peculiar effect only by touching the nerve of its audience.

One of the central ways in which metatheatre differs from
tragedy is that metatheatre has no such commerce with the
real. In fact, its very definition is that there be no reference to
the real world, however indirect and formalized. "Tragedy
glorifies the structure of the world," metatheatre deals with the
"imagination," (183) Abel observes, thus designating metatheatre
not only as the historical inheritor of tragedy, but also as its
logical counterpart. The same polarization between tragedy and

---

11. Fredric Jameson, *The Political Unconscious: Narrative as a Socially Sym-
bolic Act* (Ithaca, N.Y.: Cornell University Press, 1981).

metatheatre stands behind the second feature of metadrama, its self-awareness. While tragedy is "beyond thought" and therefore demands a "theory of the hidden," metatheatre is self-conscious and self-aware. However, even though the two central features of metatheatre—a lack of concern for the real and a self-awareness—are precisely what tragedy is not, Abel avoids joining the chorus of those who bemoan the death of tragedy. For metatheatre's lack of concern for the real and its self-awareness also imply an affirmation of the theatre as an art form, an unprecedented self-confidence of the theatre. The theatre no longer has to worry, so to speak, about morals, and it does not need to express consciously or unconsciously the underlying conflicts of society. Instead, the theatre, as if it were suddenly freed from a moral and political burden, can celebrate itself, and this means celebrating actors, costumes, directors, and even the audience. In one of the later essays included in the present collection, Abel observes that the term *metatheatre* is a subset of what should be called theatricality.[12] And so we can say that metatheatre marks the moment when the theatre must no longer justify itself through reality effects, by "thrusting the audience against the real"—it can step forward and, for the first time, be just itself.

Abel's discussion of Shakespeare and Calderón foregrounds the celebration of theatricality. Even the most excruciating moments in these attempted tragedies, such as the third act of *King Lear*, are also meditations on costume and nakedness, the necessity of fulfilling roles, while the scenes furthest from mean deceit are those in which the characters disguise themselves in false costumes and appear under assumed names. We can see here metatheatrical elements everywhere invading tragedy. And these are only what Abel called the "failed" (147) tragedies, the plays that Shakespeare unfortunately tried to turn into tragedies instead of writing metadramas, as he did in such successful plays as *Hamlet* and *The Tempest*. In these metadramas, the

---

12. For a longer discussion of this problem, see my *Stage Fright: Modernism, Anti-theatricality and Drama* (Baltimore and London: Johns Hopkins University Press, 2002).

power of the theatre is beyond all bounds. With the help of his stagehands Caliban and Ariel, Prospero creates a realm of breathtaking learning and beauty, whose only fault seems to be that it cannot last forever. And in *Hamlet*, the revenge plot is postponed at least long enough for Shakespeare to show the whole repertoire of theatrical techniques, from the advice to the players and their effect on the audience all the way to the endless confusions between madness and reality. In the plays of Calderón, finally, this obsession with all things theatrical has thoroughly infiltrated the worlds in which the plays are putatively set. *Life Is a Dream* (*La vida es sueño*) is the title of Calderón's most paradigmatic play, but the whole conceit of the dream is itself only a theatrical technique to allow the play to move from one layer of "reality" to the next. The protagonist Sigismund is thrown back and forth between alternate realities, the grim prison of the secluded tower and the exuberance of the court. Ultimately we cannot say which world is real and which is only a dream—it is so many stage sets, roles, and plays superimposed on one another. *Life Is a Dream* consists of several plays; Sigismund assumes alternatively the role of a prisoner and the role of a prince, and it does not matter which is the final one. Once Calderón has demonstrated that whatever we are doing, we are playing a role and that wherever we are, we are surrounded by stage sets, the theatre has become a ubiquitous condition from which there is no escape. Whatever else these metaplays of Shakespeare and Calderón may be about—from the discontents of colonialism to the decadence of politics—they have managed to relegate these political, ethical, tragic, or comic plots to the second tier in order to glorify the theatre itself, the theatricality of the theatre. Metatheatre, we might be tempted to conclude, is the pure essence of the theatre, the theatre relieved from all other obligations except for celebrating itself.

We are approaching here the reason why for Abel *tragedy* is an extremely restrictive term, while *metatheatre* is an extensive one. In order to be tragedy, theatre must essentially suppress its own nature or at least it must press its exuberance into strict forms. But the tragic form and the lack of self-knowledge cannot last forever; in fact, they do not last long at all. Almost as soon as tragedy is born, it turns into metatheatre. This process moves perhaps even faster than Abel thought. The best example here is Euripides' *The Bacchae*, which Abel considered to be one of the (last) Greek tragedies. But *The Bacchae* is a perfect example of metatheatre as well. Its protagonist, the God Dionysus, is the God of Greek theatre, and all of the Greek tragedies we know were performed in his name in the Dionysus theatre just below the Akropolis. But this is only the most external hint that Euripides is celebrating Athenian theatre. The entire play revolves around the fact that Dionysus appears in various disguises; only toward the very end will he enter undisguised to pass judgment on his opponents. Throughout the play, however, he changes costume, constantly disappearing and reappearing— to the great distress of Pentheus, who cannot get a firm hold on Dionysus, even when he is put in chains. What's more, this dressing and cross-dressing catches on, and not only among the Bacchantes who have decided to follow Dionysus. Even the most antitheatrical character of the play, Pentheus, who does everything to arrest Dionysus and to return Thebes to order, ends dressed up in women's clothes, and he is finally torn apart when caught secretly watching the spectacle of the Bacchantes' dance. Without a doubt, *The Bacchae* is a play about the theatre, a play about the impossibility of escaping the theatre, and also a revenge of the theatre against its enemies.

If we understand metatheatre as the moment when theatre comes to itself, it is no longer surprising that it is almost impossible for the theatre not to become metatheatre. For how could any theatre not know, somehow, and show that it knows, somehow, what it means to be theatre? Following the case of *The Bacchae*, it is possible to find traces of self-conscious theatricality in almost all the Greek tragedies: Orestes disguises himself skillfully in *The Libation Bearers* and Agamemnon's body is displayed theatrically at the end of the play bearing his name. It is not my purpose here to demolish the distinction between tragedy and metatheatre, but rather to show the proliferating tendency of metatheatre, in contrast to the contracting one of tragedy. It takes relatively little to push the theatre into metatheatre; a bit of histrionics and ostentation, a moment of self-awareness—and how could that be avoided—and the theatre becomes theatrical, the stage becomes, in Abel's own words, "stagy." With slight exaggeration one could say that tragedy has little to do with the essence of the theatre; it is only a very particular, but at the same time rare, form of Greek theatre that, for better or worse, has held Western theatre hostage. If only Shakespeare and Corneille, Racine and Eugene O'Neill had not tried, anachronistically, to write tragedies, we would have many more of the plays that celebrate the theatre as theatre and that are adequate for modernity, namely metaplays.

What does it mean for Abel's understanding of modern drama that his key term, *metatheatre*, is defined in terms of Shakespeare and Calderón? Can we conclude that modern drama is merely a repetition of the baroque? That there is an affinity between these two periods has been remarked by many, most prominently, perhaps, by Walter Benjamin, whose study of baroque theatre, with its preference of allegory over symbol, artificiality over the natural, is also a study of modernism.[13] But how does the relation between baroque and modern drama present itself through the lens offered by Abel? To what extent does the category of metaplay highlight a kinship between those two different periods? And how can we account for the glaring differences between baroque theatre and modern drama?

While baroque drama develops, however indirectly, in response to Greek tragedy (even though it fails to live up to Greek tragedy, as Abel would say), modern drama thinks mostly about its relation to late nineteenth-century realism and naturalism. Abel constructs something of a parallel relation here, for Greek tragedy, we remember, is as deeply concerned with the real—"it thrust[s] one against the ultimate real"—as late nineteenth-century realism. Nineteenth-century realism and naturalism thus are for modern drama what Greek tragedy is for baroque drama, namely, the "realist" precursor of the later self-absorbed metatheatre. For this reason, Abel devotes con-

---

13. Walter Benjamin, *Der Ursprung des deutschen Trauerspiels*, ed. Rolf Tiedemann (Frankfurt am Main: Suhrkamp, 1955).

siderable attention to realism. Henrik Ibsen for him is the playwright who precisely sought to marry Greek tragedy with realism.
Ibsen's mistake, if that is the word, was to have tried to trans-
plant the rigorous formulas of Greek tragedy into the modern
bourgeois world, as if the drawing room could ever become a
place in which conflicting "implacable" values collided, evok-
ing the emotions of fear and pity. Albee's *The Goat* is a perfect
illustration of Ibsen's dilemma, for what does the architect do
after the unimaginable occurs, after he has fallen in love with
a goat? He goes to the nearest therapy group, discovered on
the Internet, of human beings who have all fallen in love with
an animal. There is no conflict, it seems, that we do not deem
solvable—we have support groups for everything. The one exception Abel grants Ibsen is *Peer Gynt*, Ibsen's most exuberant
and nonrealistic play, which was influenced by Goethe's *Faust*
and not by Greek tragedy. But as far as Ibsen's other plays are
concerned, the attempt to write a modern bourgeois tragedy
fails. It fails because there are no implacable values that could
be set in conflict with one another—not in the liberal, skeptical world of the nineteenth century. It fails in seeking tragedy
in everyday life when tragedy would have to be constructed in
a mode that is no longer a credible dramatic form. What is
left for Ibsen is the fascination with the real, which becomes
the source of legitimization in his plays. They are franker than
other plays, they describe human passions without piety, and
they are not afraid to confront the audience with unpopular or
controversial ideas. But Ibsen's fault remains, and it was to
have failed to recognize that instead of reviving tragedy he
should have written commentaries on tragedy.

Ibsen's influence on modern drama cannot be overestimated,
and Abel knows this well. However, what makes his understanding of Ibsen so interesting is that he sees in Ibsen's "false
tragedies" a line of influence that has distracted modern drama
from coming into its own, namely, from becoming metadrama.
Greek tragedy, the desire to turn Greek tragedy into a modern
form, is the specter haunting modern drama, and the real struggle
in modern drama is to exorcise that specter. It is almost as if
Ibsen had revived that specter, seducing writers, in particular

the great American dramatists of the twentieth century—O'Neill, Tennessee Williams, and Arthur Miller—into trying to write tragedies when they would have been much better served trying to write metatheatre. The dangerous influence of Greek tragedy returns in the form of Ibsen, and modern drama can only realize itself to the extent that it can distance itself from Ibsen. This is an unusual account of what otherwise seems only as a conflict among different styles. That Alfred Jarry, Vsevolod Meyerhold, Bertolt Brecht, and Samuel Beckett somehow had to "break" with Ibsen in order to establish their respective styles is a common and uncontroversial claim. Ibsen is so often seen as the beginning of modern drama because the writers of the late nineteenth and early twentieth centuries had to struggle so hard against him. What Abel gives us is a deeper analysis of this anxiety of influence. Ibsen was not so much the beginning of modern drama, as a false beginning, and modern metatheatre could emerge only once this false beginning was corrected, once Ibsen's ghosts were banished.

Yet even if we take Ibsen as representing the dangerous example of false tragedy in order to construct a parallel between Greek and modern tragedy and thus between baroque and modern metadrama, even if we accept the fact that both baroque and modern drama represent a turn from reality effect to self-awareness, we may be tempted to find as many differences as similarities between the two pairs: Greek tragedy/baroque metadrama and modern tragedy/modern metadrama. Ibsen, after all, is not Christopher Marlowe or any of the other Elizabethan revenge tragedians, and Pirandello and Beckett are a far cry from Shakespeare and Calderón. These differences are worth pursuing, not in order to question their common identity as metatheatre, but rather to gain a more differentiated understanding of the various forms that metatheatre can take.

When we contemplate Beckett and Eugène Ionesco, Brecht and Genet, our first impression is probably not that we are faced with playwrights and directors who exuberantly celebrate the pleasures of theatricality. Almost all actors who ever worked with Beckett complained that they were not allowed to "act" and that Beckett merely used them like a puppeteer pulling strings. Beckett put his actors in ash cans and controlled every one of their movements with obsessive fastidiousness. At times one has the impression that his stage directions are as important as his dialogue and that he really preferred his plays to be read rather than seen, as so many other modernist dramatists, from Mallarmé to Maurice Maeterlinck and from Hugo von Hofmannsthal to Gertrude Stein had done at various points in their careers. Brecht, on the other hand, admitted to being driven by a continual "mistrust of the theatre," and he, too, wanted his actors to stop acting, recommending that they imagine themselves as witnesses or narrators instead. The theatre, for Brecht, was a dangerous art form, "culinary" as he put it, catering to the masses; his own "epic" theatre was an attempt to make the theatre less theatrical and more like the novel, which he mentions repeatedly as the paradigm for a new theatre. In Genet as well as in Pirandello, finally, role playing and quasi-rituals always end in blood. It is true that neither Shakespeare nor Calderón had shied away from violence, and *Life Is a Dream* in particular shows the terrible consequences that can result from a malignant confusion of theatre and reality. But in Brecht and Pirandello violence seems to be the only means by which to break the artificiality of the theatre. I think that there can be no doubt that these plays are "about" the theatre, that their primary frame of reference is not the world but their own theatricality. Their important difference from their baroque relatives, however, is that far from celebrating the theatre, these modernist playwrights view the theatre with mistrust and suspicion. Modernist art does not delight in the *trompe l'oeil*, in mirrors and the power of illusion, the way baroque art does. On the contrary, illusionist spectacles are often exposed as empty and meaningless tricks. Modernist playwrights are still self-aware, but what this means for them is that they are all too aware of how problematic theatre really is.

The theatre's self-awareness, it turns out, can mean rather different things. The term *metatheatre* tells us that the theatre reflects on itself, but it does not yet tell us anything about the spirit in which this self-reflexivity occurs; in other words, it does not tell us whether the theatre is viewed with approval or suspicion. It may be that the theatre is simply delighted with itself, but it might also be that the theatre is rather self-critical, and self-critique is precisely the mark of much of modernist metatheatre. Modernist metatheatre very often assigns a negative value to the theatre and for this reason it can be called anti-theatre. Even though Abel did not use this term himself, he did refer, in one footnote, to the description of Ionesco as "anti-play," and the differentiation within the category of metatheatre between a protheatrical metatheatre and an antitheatrical one is in the spirit of his thought.[14] This distinction also accounts for the historical difference between baroque and modernist metatheatre, and it foregrounds the fact that there is a historical development in the genre of metatheatre.

Another way of specifying this difference between protheatrical theatre and antitheatrical theatre is by examining the spirit in which these plays engage in their gestures of self-reflexivity. While the baroque theatre multiplies itself, delighting, as it does, in the play-within-the-play, masks and deceptions, and a general sense of the theatre as a world, the modernist metadrama seeks to keep the theatre under control. While the baroque theatre piles theatre upon theatre as if to replicate the famous baroque mirror hall at Versailles, the modernist theatre engages in self-critique, and this self-critique is enacted through various modes of interruption. Modern theatre becomes metatheatre when there is an accident in the machinery of the play, when something goes wrong, or when the play simply no longer progresses. Even Pirandello's metadramas, which are perhaps closest to the baroque, start with such interruptions. In Beckett, the inability of a proper drama to unfold is perhaps most clearly accentuated, for his plays become the waiting for an event that will never occur; everyone is more or less immobile, lame, buried in mounds, and always out of energy. Interruptions, moments of hesitation, and tableaux are ubiquitous in Beckett, but they

---

14. For a discussion of Abel and theatricalism, see also Elinor Fuchs's "Clown Shows: Anti-Theatricalism in Four Theatricalist Plays (1960–1990)," in *Modern Drama: Special Issue on Modernism and Anti-theatricality*, ed. Alan Ackerman and Martin Puchner (Fall 2001).

also characterize Brecht's dramaturgy. Here the "epic" acting style requires that the theatre's illusionist power be constantly broken and interrupted, that the play be structured around a series of vignettes arranged in a loose stop-and-go manner. Characters say something, then they sing, then they comment on their actions, and each of these switches happens without transition or mediation. Brecht never wants us to get enraptured in the play, and for this reason he builds into his theatre as many interruptions as possible, be it on the level of the plot, dialogue, or acting.

Even Ibsen, this most ambiguous figure in the history of metatheatre, was described by George Bernard Shaw as representing an interruption of the standard nineteenth-century melodrama.[15] However, as in the case of the other antecedent form, tragedy, Ibsen's plays also exhibit moments of metatheatre. *The Wild Duck* is probably the best example here, for one of its scenes is the pseudo-wilderness re-created in the attic of the Ekdals, a wilderness in which the old Ekdal can play at going a-hunting. So even though Ibsen is for the most part the realist antecedent to modernist metatheatre, his work also anticipates this modernist metatheatre. As in the case of the distinction between Baroque metatheatre and Greek tragedy, we find metatheatre expanding and its tragic predecessor contracting until it seems that almost any play, no matter how much it may resemble a tragedy, exhibits at least small moments of metatheatre.

The difference between protheatrical metatheatre and antitheatrical metatheatre, between a theatre reflecting endlessly upon itself in a hall of mirrors and a theatre permanently interrupted, is already prefigured in the two paradigmatic baroque metadramas, *Life Is a Dream* and *Hamlet*. While *Life Is a Dream* takes the confusion between life and dream, theatre and reality, as far as it possibly can, giving expression to the belief that the world is indeed a theatre, *Hamlet* assumes a different, and more negative, attitude toward the theatre. For Hamlet, as has been pointed out by T. S. Eliot, refuses the one category on

---

15. George Bernard Shaw, *The Quintessence of Ibsenism* (New York: Brentano's, 1904; reprint, New York: Dover, 1994).

which all theatre depends: action. The action in *Hamlet* is endlessly postponed and interrupted. When judged from the point of view of theatricality, this interruption of action is a bad thing, and Eliot was perhaps right to say that *Hamlet* is insufficient as a theatrical event. But when we approach this interruption from the point of view of the modernist antitheatrical metatheatre we can see in it a precursor of precisely the kinds of interruptions at work in modern drama. This speculation is borne out when we remember that Hamlet is the single most important figure hovering over modernist antitheatrical theatre. Mallarmé considered him a precursor of his own closet dramas, Maeterlinck admired Hamlet's inaction, which he incorporated into his own antitheatrical symbolist texts, and Beckett's debt to the same inaction and postponement has been pointed out many times. We might say then that protheatrical metadrama is expressed most directly in *Life Is a Dream*, while the antitheatrical metadrama of modernism was already prefigured in *Hamlet*.

But why would modern drama, inspired by *Hamlet*, turn upon itself with so much suspicion? What made the theatre doubt itself so much that its self-awareness would become so intensely self-critical? A couple of factors might have played a role. For some—Brecht among them—it was the decadent state of the theatre itself, the fact that theatre signified a debased and complacent form of bourgeois entertainment, rather than critical thought, that made them suspicious of the theatre. This aversion to the "official" theatre, in particular the opera, was exasperated by the long shadow cast by Richard Wagner, who had propagated an aesthetically and politically suspect form of total theatre.

An additional development that is somewhat more difficult to describe is what one might call the theatricalization of politics. Theatricality has always been part of politics, of course, from the spectacle of the court to that of the revolution, but it had been perhaps less pronounced in the established and emerging democracies of the nineteenth and early twentieth centuries. Fascism, by contrast, relied on various forms of mass spectacles, from the Roman-inspired rallies of Mussolini to the Nuremberg rallies of the Nazis, while the young Soviet Republic celebrated the anniversary of the October revolution with mass stagings of *The Storming of the Winter Palace*. And a later generation of socialists, Abel among them, had to witness the spectacle of the Moscow trials. All of these movements have vastly different political implications, but they share a dedication to the use of theatricality on the scene of politics. One might describe this communality as the twentieth century's own understanding of the *theatrum mundi*—the theatre of the world—a *theatrum*, however, that is decidedly more problematic and suspect than anything the baroque was thinking of when that word gained currency. To simplify this distinction: modernist metatheatre is antitheatrical because the theatricalization of modern life is seen as ambiguous at best, and as morally suspect at worst. We may hold onto Abel's definition of metatheatre as being based on the idea that life is already theatricalized and add that this theatricalization can take very different forms and thus lead to very different forms of metatheatre.

After having examined Greek tragedy, then baroque metatheatre, and finally modernist metatheatre, we may wonder to what extent a still different notion of metatheatre might emerge from the theatre of the last decades. Even a cursory survey of contemporary theatre and performance suggests that the modernist self-awareness of the theatre has not gone away. The plays of Caryl Churchill and Heiner Müller, Harold Pinter and Tom Stoppard are nothing if not metatheatre. Pinter, for example, works more or less directly in the tradition of Beckett, and Caryl Churchill makes excessive use of cross-dressing as well as cross-racial, cross-age, and cross-gender casting. Her plays are roles and costumes thrown together—it doesn't matter whether or not they fit. Heiner Müller's *Hamletmachine* and Tom Stoppard's *Rosencrantz and Guildenstern Are Dead* are metatheatre also in the most literal sense that they are plays about *Hamlet*, one of the paradigmatic examples of metatheatre. If anything, metatheatre seems to have increased as the century wore on, and it also seems to have become less antitheatrical. It is almost as if we had forgotten our reservations about theatre and once more become exuberant in our understanding of the theatre.

There is another factor that has had a profound impact on

the history of metatheatre throughout the centuries including
our own, and that is the struggle between the theatre and the
other arts and media. The literary genre against which the
theatre increasingly had to define itself after the baroque era
was undoubtedly the popular novel. Abel was well aware of
the rivalry between novel and drama, but he did not, as is
typically done, simply "defend" drama against the novel. Instead, he enlisted the novel in the project of metatheatre and
thus singled out Don Quixote as the most theatricalized character of the baroque era. Don Quixote is even more theatrical
than either Sigismund or Hamlet because Don Quixote actively
chose to theatricalize the world and himself rather than being
forced to do so by the manipulation of others, whether they be
ghosts or humans. And the most theatrical nineteenth-century
writer, according to Abel, was not a dramatist at all, but Feodor
Dostoevsky. A continuation of these reflections is represented
in the present collection by a previously unpublished piece on
the "novelization" of the theatre. Here Abel takes issue with
Mikhail Bakhtin, the critic who had the nerve to describe the
novel in theatrical terms without feeling the need to engage
the theatre in a serious manner. Abel points to the significance
of Ibsen for James Joyce, for example, or of Anton Chekhov
for modernism in general, but he also argues that theatricality
is a more capacious category than the novel. We can think of
life as being dramatized, Abel observes, but we cannot novel-
ize it in the same way, for novelization requires the active
presence and intervention of a narrator. While all the novel
can ever hope to be is a particular artistic genre, theatricality
possesses the particular ability to become a general condition
or feature of life outside the theatre.

While the modernist metatheatre borrows from and competes
with the novel, the postmodern metatheatre borrows from and
competes with other genres and media, in particular film, radio,
television, or even the Internet—media that are characterized
by their ability to record and reproduce endless copies of themselves. As in the case of the novel, these media have been seen
as both a threat and a blessing in the eyes of theatre practitio-
ners and theorists. Only a few modernist directors, such as

Erwin Piscator, actually incorporated film into their theatre, and as a rule, the early film was more dependent on and afraid of the theatre than the other way around. When synchronized sound was introduced into film, many directors and theorists objected to it, some on aesthetic grounds, arguing that the silent film, in its absence of sound, was a more abstract and therefore purer medium than sound film.[16] Others, however, argued that sound film would be too much like the theatre and thus only a shallow, two-dimensional replica of the three-dimensional, live theatre.[17] For many decades, now, the same anxiety has been reversed, and the theatre has felt threatened by film and television. One reaction has been to emphasize the extent to which theatre is unlike prerecorded, reproducible film, and how thrilling the theatre's liveness is in contrast to film's dead copies. At the same time, the latest trend on Broadway makes musicals out of classic films, such as *The Producers, The Graduate, The Sweet Smell of Success,* and *Thoroughly Modern Millie.* Whether this be called *metamusical* or *metafilmmusical*, it represents yet another way in which film and theatre have become aware of each other and also more intertwined. In yet another crossing of film and theatre, the theatre of Laurie Anderson or the Wooster Group has incorporated recorded media, be they sound or visual media, into its live performances. Often, when we hear the actor's voices, what we hear is amplified and prerecorded, and sometimes the actor's bodies are hidden behind flat screen monitors that depict their recorded doubles.

This new type of theatrical performance art allows for a different mode of metatheatre. In a staging of Gertrude Stein's *Dr. Faustus Lights the Light*, for example, the Wooster Group shows excerpts from a B-movie, displayed on several monitors on the stage. At various moments, the actors onstage imitate the movements executed by the actors in the film, including the montage with which the film breaks up the integrity of

16. Béla Balazs, *Theory of the Film: Character and Growth of a New Art,* trans. Edith Bone (New York: Dover, 1970).
17. Rudolf Arnheim, "A New Laokoön: Artistic Composites and the Talking Film," in *Film as Art* (Berkeley: University of California Press, 1957), 199–230.

scenes and acting. The effect was an alienation of both film and theatre. When reenacted on the stage, the cut from one scene to the next—necessitating sudden change of pose and gesture—seemed surprising and artificial; and it serves as an estrangement of and therefore a commentary on the relation between the difference between film and theatre. Metatheatre, these days, most likely involves the commentary of a recorded medium on the liveness of performance, so that this liveness can be taken for granted.

One more conclusion can be drawn from the history of metatheatre. Since metatheatre is based on an unshakable belief in the power of the theatre, the mere existence of contemporary metatheatre belies the fears of those who worry that the theatre might be on its last legs, about to be swallowed by film or the Internet. Metatheatre has always implied an interest in a changing world, rather than an insistence on inherited forms. In this sense, metatheatre also signals an optimistic program, a belief that if contemporary theatre manages to make use of the new media, just as modern drama had made use of the novel, it will create new forms of metatheatre. For this reason, Abel's term *metatheatre* will remain a central category for understanding not only modernist but also contemporary theatre, and for the same reason, the present collection of essays should be greeted as a timely and important event.

New York City, January 2003

TRAGEDY

WHAT IS TRAGEDY?

Also the when, the where and the wherefore

I

THERE ARE THOSE who will object to the question in my title on the ground that it is probably impossible for me—or anyone else, for that matter—really to answer it.

Those who take this view will probably assert in any one of three different language games that no set of events in life or on the stage can be indisputably seen as "tragic." Of the three language games, one may be that employed by journalists, media pundits, and the generally vulgar. These are people who can refer to catastrophes like earthquakes or floods as "tragedies," as if there were no difference between the "tragic" and the "catastrophic" and as if Miguel de Unamuno had not pointed up the difference denoted by these different terms. Supporting the view of the journalists, media pundits, and vulgarians are the professors in our English departments in whose special language game definitive traits are denied to any dramatized set of events that might compel us to call it a "tragedy." And if nothing compels us to call certain dramatic works "tragedies," then nothing forbids us to designate as "tragedies" those dramatic works that are in no sustainable sense "tragic." The third group backing up the vulgarians and the English department professors are certain contemporary philosophers. These guys and gals are opposed to anything that smacks of essentialism, and here is what they all will say: Since there are no essences of anything, there can hardly be an essence of tragedy. Thus the language game of the journalists and the vulgar and that of the English department professors is supported in the main by the language game of those in our academies who have a professional claim to be clearheaded.

It might be argued that essentialism of some kind is finally inescapable and if one looked deeply enough one could find a trace of essentialism even in Ludwig Wittgenstein and his followers, but I do not propose to give that kind of argument here. But I will approve a modern notion of essence, the one proposed by the phenomenologists based on a procedure they call "the eidetic reduction." According to phenomenology, in order to find the essence of an object one has only to vary it in the imagination so as to discover just which of its features can be eliminated without damaging or destroying the object's identity. Relying on this view I would suggest that in trying to formulate a general idea of tragedy, Aristotle's thinking had more in common with that of the phenomenologists than with that of the British empiricists. The latter, with the general idea of red firmly in mind, claimed to discover it by isolating a common element in shades as different as the most fulsome crimson and the most hesitant redness in russet, a shade which from time to time says it is brown.

Aristotle (who has been praised by Sören Kierkegaard for the "inwardness" of his views on tragedy) did not have to look for something common to all of the grave and violent plays on the Athenian stage. He was able to acquire his model for tragedy from a single play whose effect on him was clear enough for its nature to be definable. And it was thus, I believe, that he came to describe as tragedies only those plays, which in his judgment, could stimulate their audiences to feel pity and fear.

James Joyce further developed Aristotle's model. He told us that pity will unite us with the suffering victim in a dramatic action and that fear will unite us with the secret cause of the victim's suffering. If we apply this test rigorously, we can exclude from our list of genuinely tragic works those melodramas our academics are perfectly willing to regard as tragedies.

Let us be clear about this: evidence of tragedy is not to be found in facts of any kind, however dismal or frightening, like the twisted bodies of passengers after a train wreck or the heaps of corpses on a battlefield. That the stories of many victims of war or of natural disasters may be found on examination to be judged as "tragedies" will not be evident from the mere facts of their suffering or their demise. What counts as evidence for tragedy is something we find in ourselves on hearing their stories told. Evidence for the tragic is, as Aristotle held, our experience of pity and fear during the *recounting* of a story that unfolded in life or was invented for the stage. Evidence for tragedy is not publicly confirmable, as according to our pragmatists evidence that is responsibly held must be: we happen to be the only ones who can say whether we have experienced pity and fear in responding to a dramatic work. The effort of Sidney Hook in the titular essay of his book, *Pragmatism and the Tragic Sense of Life*, to show that John Dewey's philosophy involved a deep consideration of what is tragic in human life, is obviously wrong and should have been repudiated by his pragmatist colleagues. (I mean: Wake up Richard Rorty!) Would it not be strange and even scandalous for a view of things which regards successful action as the reward for intelligent calculation to be in harmony with a description of events in which the consequence of high-minded effort can result in torment, frustration, and death? Now I am not claiming that the tragic is consistent with some general view of life that is opposed in important ways to pragmatism. What I am arguing is only this: the evidence for tragedy is not like the evidence provided by experiment, proving or disproving some hypothesis; though Albert Einstein seems to have thought that Feodor Dostoevsky's novels were indeed like experiments, and brought out the basic consequences of holding particular moral views. Certainly this is closer to the mark than Hook's notion that the spirit of tragedy is in harmony with Dewey's philosophy. All the same, Einstein's notion of moral experimentation could only be held of those novels of Dostoevsky which do not end tragically. When Prince Myshkin loses his sanity, weeping over the dead body of Nastasya, killed by her lover, we do not feel that a moral hypothesis has been sustained or disproved; we feel pity for Nastasya, for the Prince, and for

Nastasya's murderer too, and we feel fear, for we realize that the murder was not the result of some impulse to aggression but a consequence of something quite different and of an altogether higher order: the murderer's fear—a fear we ourselves might have—of someone far nobler; in Roghazin's case, fear of Myshkin's gentle strength, fear even, if you like, of the Christian God; for fear, as Kierkegaard pointed out, is always, fundamentally, fear of the good.

Sidney Hook's essay also has this major fault: we never know, in his writing on tragedy, whether he is writing about events in real life or of dramatic constructions in novels, in narrative poems, or on the stage. Let me state the difference clearly: "tragedies" are dramatic works in which catastrophic events are so recounted as to give us a very peculiar kind of pleasure not found in other works and certainly not to be found in real life. Let me point this up: suppose we were present when Oedipus, his eyes torn out, exiled himself from the city of Thebes where he once ruled. Is it conceivable that we could have felt any kind of pleasure witnessing the event, the very same event, whose overwhelming pathos is so pleasurable when we see Sophocles' play? There are indeed many occasions in life when, as Hook has noted, the right is in conflict with the right or the good, and the consequences of such collisions of value are often catastrophic, but without the author of tragedy to describe these events in adequate dramatic form, recounting them in such a way as to give us pleasure, these events in real life would give us nothing but pain. We could be revealed as sadists were they merely pleasurable. Painful events were not infrequent in Athenian public life, which is perhaps one reason they created the Dionysian festivals and gave awards for the tragic poets who could place such events on the stage.

One reason the professors in our English departments are against a strict definition of tragedy is that if any such standard is applied to Shakespeare, it would be difficult to maintain that *King Lear, Hamlet,* or *Othello* can be shown to be authentic tragedies. Certainly in these works we feel united with suffering victims. The question is this: do we feel terror? For this we would have to accept and even identify ourselves with whatever caused the victims' suffering. Of the three plays of Shakespeare I've mentioned is there even one in which we can identify ourselves with whatever has caused the suffering of its protagonist? The plight of King Lear is due to the machinations of his daughters. We are quite unable to identify ourselves with their villainy. Othello's sufferings are due in part to the vile insinuations of Iago and in part to his own stupidity. We certainly cannot want to identify ourselves with either Iago's deceitfulness or Othello's weakness of mind. Let us turn to Hamlet now. Certainly we identify ourselves with the suffering prince, but the cause of his suffering is his inability to act, as he himself says. And we cannot identify ourselves with that inability, for we hardly understand it any better than Hamlet does. Were his inability to act before returning from England due to the guilt of his mother, then why should her guilt not have continued to inhibit him when he returned to Elsinore? Clearly, the kind of analysis I am making would lead one to withhold the term of tragedy from these major plays of Shakespeare taken as tragedies by the public, by theatre directors, and by the English department worthies who regularly comment on Shakespeare's works.

The one "tragedy" of Shakespeare which may stimulate us to both pity and fear is *Macbeth*, though we are not frightened by the weird sisters (we know that people called witches did exist and were feared during the sixteenth century); and we see them invite Macbeth to a course of action which will destroy him. He yields to their promise that he will be "king hereafter," and then, our fear for Macbeth is further intensified when we hear Lady Macbeth's prayer to be unsexed so that she can convince him to plot the death of their sovereign. After which there is Macbeth's speech when he sees an imaginary dagger, and summons up all the reasons not to kill Duncan even as he resolves to do the deed. It is interesting that throughout this part of the play, Macbeth's conscience is always alive, and as long as it is, we pity him. It is only in the latter part of the play, when Macbeth has usurped the throne and succeeded in frightening or killing most of those who opposed his reign, and when he calmly plans the death of his friend Banquo and Banquo's son—it is only then that we lose our feelings of pity for him and begin to await his downfall, which we are by then aware is sure to come. Nevertheless, in this play, the Shakespeare play closest to a Greek tragedy, we do experience the emotions tragedy is meant to stimulate in us.

There is indeed a moment of terror in *Antony and Cleopatra* when a friend and supporter of Antony, his comrade in arms, Enobarbus, disgusted with Antony because of his lack of military toughness, has turned traitor and deserted the leader he once adored. Enobarbus then discovers that Antony in his will has left a fortune to him. The discovery causes Enobarbus to fall on his sword. We can identify here with the cause of his suicide—remorse—and yet pity the man. We feel here a pity and terror that we do not feel at the fate of the main characters of the play.

There is also such a moment of pity and terror in *King Lear*, when the old king, stripped of many of his knights by his daughter Regan, thinks he can get better terms from his other daughter Goneril, who is just then coming on the stage. We feel for the king, for we do know what it is like, when in need and rejected by someone, not necessarily a relative, from whom we expected aid, we turn to another who in his or her turn may not help us either. But we cannot identify ourselves with the cause of Lear's suffering. "There is something in nature," he observes, "which makes these hard hearts." But we do not identify ourselves with any such force in nature, so that while we feel pity for the king, we do not feel the terror which the tragic poet ought to induce along with it.

It might be well here to point out just why the catastrophic is not necessarily tragic, as our journalists often assume it to be. Let's take the California earthquakes as an example: there was one in the Bay Area. When we heard of it, those of us who live in the eastern part of our country certainly felt pity for the earthquake's victims. But we did not feel terror, for such quakes have not to our knowledge occurred in the eastern part of the United States. But those of the Bay Area who escaped harm during the earthquake were indeed able to feel both pity for victims' suffering and terror insofar as their own lives are more connected with the area of the country in which earthquakes often take place. So one must be in a certain geographical relation to a catastrophic event to feel a tragic significance in it, and those journalists who describe a catastrophic event in the press or over television are not always in just that relationship to the event, which would make it possible for them to feel it as tragic. The English department professors who regard Shakespeare's dramas as tragedies keep themselves as distant, in my opinion, from the events in the plays of Shakespeare they comment on as East Coast journalists often are from an earthquake in California.

I turn now to the Athenian tragedies. Do we feel terror in those plays which were the models for the Elizabethan, the French, and the Spanish playwrights? Let us first of all take the *Agamemnon* of Aeschylus. Is there a point in the development of the action when we do in fact feel terror? We feel it, I think, in the ambiguous judgment of the chorus, which describes the victories of Agamemnon but also dwells on the crime he committed to achieve them, namely the sacrifice of his daughter Iphigenia. They also describe the atrocities committed against the Trojans by the Greeks when they entered Troy. The fear we yield to on hearing the judgment of the chorus becomes more powerful when Clytemnestra asks Agamemnon to cross over to her on the red carpet she has laid out for him, just the kind of carpet the Greek gods considered it *hubris* to tread upon. Agamemnon at first refuses and then we begin to fear that he will agree and offend the gods again as he did when he took the life of his daughter and, as Martha Nussbaum rather brilliantly pointed out, *rejoiced* in sacrificing her. Will he walk lightheartedly over the red carpet and deliver himself to the net Clytemnestra has prepared for him? But this moment of dramatically induced fear is fear for Agamemnon, and not yet tragic fear: we do not as yet fear for ourselves. Tragic terror comes with the speech of Cassandra, who describes the killing of Agamemnon even as the murder is taking place, and then prophesies her own death, and exulting all the while in the retribution being visited upon the house of Atreus for the family's past crimes. Exulting with her, we feel the rightness of retribution, thus identifying ourselves with the forces which will make a victim of Cassandra along with Agamemnon. We may even foresee that Orestes, thus far innocent, will finally be a victim also. Certainly we feel pity, but tragic terror, also. We identify ourselves with Agamemnon and with Cassandra, and also with the force of retribution which Cassandra herself hailed.

Oedipus the King was Aristotle's preferred model for a work of tragedy, and in this work we feel terror for Oedipus throughout, beginning with the moment the seer Teiresias urges him not to continue his search for the murderer of Laius. From then on the evidence mounts that it may be Oedipus himself, Oedipus the investigator of the crime, who is the culprit he is seeking, and from then on, every effort of Oedipus to locate some further fact which will show that the deed was committed by someone else points, when revealed, precisely to him: so our fear for him mounts along with our pity until he reveals the truth and tears out his eyes which failed to see the true, horrifying facts. My point here is that in *Oedipus* there is not just one moment of terror, and certain moments of pity, but a continuous development of both pity and terror, even as the action proceeds. Probably it would be a mistake to make of this play a model for all tragedies, for we cannot expect a similar continuity of terror and pity in other works. This model, chosen by Aristotle, has one unfortunate effect: it exposes what is deficient in every other tragedy, not only the plays of Shakespeare, but of all other playwrights who have tried to write tragedies.

What about the *Antigone,* which Georg Hegel put above *Oedipus* as the finest of all tragedies? We feel real terror in the *Antigone,* and more than once. Let me recall what happens early in the play. Creon, in command of Thebes, announces to the chorus the victory obtained by Thebes against the assault on it by an army led by Polyneices. The city had been defended by his brother Eteocles, and both brothers have fallen in battle, each by the other's hand. Eteocles is now to be remembered as a hero, but what about his brother Polyneices, who had attacked the city? Creon announces that Thebes will bury Eteocles with honor, but in order to distinguish patriotism from treason, will leave the body of Polyneices unburied, exposed to wild creatures and birds of prey. When he makes this announcement, we are inclined to agree with him, but then someone in the chorus asks, "Why strike a dead man?" and we become aware that our initial agreement with Creon is perhaps less justified than we at first thought, and this becomes clearer in Antigone's scene with Creon, when she asserts her right as the sister of Polyneices to bury her dead brother. Creon, for his part, holds that he cares nothing at all about family feeling, and acts only for the city's good; here he weakens rather than supports his own case. Then he condemns Antigone to death, and attacks his son Haemon, who defends her. Notice, too, the manner in which he orders the execution of Antigone. She is to be buried alive, for he wants to show contempt for her assertion that we live longer with the dead than with the living. After this, Teiresias comes onstage. He is blind and has to be led by a boy and he tells the triumphant Creon, you have sinned against all the gods, you have ordered the burial of a living person and refused to bury the dead. With this remark we suddenly see Creon, whose judgment we initially almost agreed with, at least in part, transformed into a criminal against the order of the world, the object of the gods' hatred. And Creon who ordered Antigone's death finally asks someone to relieve him of his life. The terror we feel at this point has to do with the fact that a drastic action may be so close to an act of outright madness, that the difference can be quite indiscernible by one who has to act. We are suddenly aware of the danger inherent in *any* violent deed and we feel the terror of *doing as such*, having seen the result of Creon's behavior. And in fact, we feel more pity for Creon than we may have felt for Antigone.

When I lectured on this play, I used to ask my students: Would you bury your brother or sister if the act was forbidden by the authorities and you were told you would die if the deed were found out? My students always replied that they would want to act as Antigone did, but would not do so if it were forbidden by law. Here we see one reason why the play may not have the same force with a modern audience that it had in Athens. We are less pious nowadays and have less respect for family values. On the other hand, it cannot be denied that in any civilized community, ancient or modern, there has to be respect for the dead.

But what I want to emphasize here as my main point is this: In *Oedipus the King* and in *Antigone* we feel terror as well as pity, though I would not claim as much for all the other plays of Sophocles, or for many of the plays of Euripides; from which it must be clear that genuine tragedy is quite rare, hardly ever achieved in Athens, and perhaps only once by Shakespeare.

II

There has to be adequate motivation for drastic action so I want to consider next the motivations of the characters both in the plays I have indicated as genuinely tragic and in some others that have been judged to be tragedies, and here I shall indeed take up a suggestion from the phenomenologists which I find valuable in considering the formal side of motivation as they have dealt with it. I have in mind especially the late Alfred Schutz who taught in New York City in the late thirties and forties at the New School for Social Research. According to Schutz, motivation, whatever it be materially, falls under two headings formally: we act *in order to* achieve some purpose or *because* we have been tutored by some past experience. Sometimes the *because* motive is confused with the *in order to*. Sometimes they can be clearly separated. If it is raining and I pick up my umbrella before going out, this is *in order to* keep my head and clothing dry, but also *because* I've experienced, unpleasantly, the effect of being without an umbrella when caught in the rain. Now my claim is this: taking an umbrella before going out in the rain is a casual act, hardly requiring a double motivation, but for a drastic act—for such a thing as murder or revenge—both a *because* and an *in order to* motivation are required, and if one of these motivations is missing from someone's drastic action, we will have difficulty believing in or yielding to its inevitability. If we look at the motives of Antigone and Creon in Sophocles' tragedy, we see immediately that Antigone has both an *in order to* and a *because* motive for burying her brother. Antigone's *in order to* motive is to be found in the promise she made to him when he set out to attack Thebes; she said she would honor him if he died in the struggle he was set upon. And she had a *because* motive of the strongest kind, one made sacred by custom. For it was the custom in the Greek cities for families to be in charge of the funeral of the family dead. On the other hand, Creon had only an *in order to* political motive for prohibiting the burial of Polyneices: a felt need to distinguish after their deaths a hero from a traitor; but there was no *because* motive for Creon's action, and the act is, I claim, too drastic to be solely motivated by a political intent; I believe, too, that this is one of the reasons audiences will always be on the side of Antigone and unable to side with Creon. It is often said that both of them violated the law: Creon, the law of the family, and Antigone, the law of the city. And it has been said that both were equally right, and both equally wrong, and that the tragedy, as Hegel understood it, was a conflict of right against right. But while there is some truth in this discussion of the matter, there is something important which has been left out of such considerations and that is the element of motivation. Creon is unable to cite any prior case in which the rights of a family to dispose of the body of one of its members has been set aside by the city. He only speaks of what seems to him politically important for the future. He never justifies his action by looking even once into the past. Antigone looks backward and forward in time as she asserts the rightness of her deed, and that is why she strikes us as so powerful. Creon in the end is weak, first of all in motivation, and finally when, facing the consequence of his action, he asks for someone to take his life.

Oedipus has a *because* and an *in order to* motive for pursuing his search for the killer of Laius. The *because* motive is his past success, he successfully resolved the riddle of the Sphinx; his *in order to* motive is to obey the injunction of the oracle and stop further pollution of the city. No one else has both an *in order to* and *because* motive in urging him to desist, and thus Oedipus is able until the very end to disregard all the admonitions given against his course of action.

If we turn now to Shakespeare's *Hamlet* we can see at once that the Bard, who probably never once gave thought to these conceptual matters, was intuitively in line with the notion of motivation I have set forth. Hamlet has no *in order to* motive for killing Claudius. He is strictly limited to a *because* motive; to the motive of revenge for his father's death, required of him by the ghost. He does have some doubts about the authenticity of the ghost, and he never thinks of the necessity of killing Claudius as a step toward becoming King of Denmark. I said that Shakespeare was sensitive to the formal side of motivation. Let me give another instance from *Othello*. What is the motive of Iago in poisoning Othello's mind with falsehoods about his wife? He does have an *in order to* motive, to destroy the commander honored by everyone, but should he not have, Shakespeare may have wondered, a *because* motive also? And the Bard suggests that Iago *thinks* he has a *because* motive; Iago *thinks* Othello may have been in bed with his wife. But the whole matter is brought up in what seems to be an afterthought of Shakespeare's. Iago never seriously addresses the matter. He suggests that an act of infidelity may have occurred, and this partly accounts for his determination to bring Othello down. What I see in all this is an indication of Shakespeare's profound grasp of motivation, since he may well have penetrated to the formal side of motivation before it had ever been set forth by anyone.

I come now to the question of motive in *Macbeth*. Leo Tolstoy for one dismissed the play saying that Macbeth had no motive for killing Duncan. And George Bernard Shaw agreed with Tolstoy, saying that Macbeth was a literary man who would never have done what Shakespeare tells us he did. Our Shakespeare scholars on the whole have tended to ignore these judgments by writers who certainly knew their trade, and if we ignore Shaw's remark, which was made partly in jest, we have to keep in mind that Tolstoy was one of the greatest psychologists. And his judgment that Macbeth had no motivation for his action needs to be answered if we are to take the play seriously. My answer is this: Macbeth does not have a genuine *because* motive, he has an artificial *because* motive, one given him fantastically by the weird sisters, who tell him that he is destined to be king. They give him this *because* motive in the following sense: if he is going to be king, this can only be because the murder has already been accomplished. It is already known and, in that sense, is now in the past. His *in order to* motive, also partly unreal, is provided him by his wife, who wants him to be king; thus he finally has both motives, but both are partly unreal. And so it is that his final statement about life is that it is a tale told by an idiot and signifies nothing. This could only be said by a character who had unreal motives for his real and also horrible deeds.

The dramatic need for both a *because* and an *in order to* motive for a drastic action becomes clear when we consider the problem of making credible the deed of suicide, either in a play or in a novel. I happen to think the most moving instance of suicide in a novel is that of Gustave Flaubert's Emma Bovary, whereas I have always had some doubts about the suicide of Anna Karenina in Tolstoy's novel. I find something to substantiate my doubt in the fact that Tolstoy himself considered ending the novel differently, and wrote an ending in which Anna does not take her life, but he finally opted for the ending we now have in which she throws herself on the tracks in the path of an oncoming train. The problem of suicide is as follows: It cannot have an *in order to* motive. It can only have a *because* motivation. You do not kill yourself to accomplish anything, but simply because you cannot bear to go on living. Another instance of the difficulty of credibility in presenting suicide may be found in one of Henrik Ibsen's masterpieces, *Hedda Gabler*. In this play, Hedda shoots herself with one of her father's pistols. We know that Ibsen in writing a play always set down a complete biography of all the characters prior to constructing his plot. And in the biography of Hedda he mentions the fact that her father, General Gabler, committed suicide with one of his pistols. This fact is not introduced into the play itself. We know of it only from the biography of Hedda which Ibsen wrote prior to writing his play. But it suggests to me that Ibsen had some doubts about Hedda's need to commit suicide, and because he wanted the play to end with a suicide he tried to make the deed more credible to himself by mentioning the suicide of her father in his biographical notes. Suicide is only completely convincing when the *because* motivation is overwhelming and there is no possibility of a character being moved by anything else. Thus once again, I insist on the importance of both an *in order to* and a *because* motivation for a drastic action to be completely believable.

III

I have already noted that not every one of the Greek dramas Aristotle accepted into his canon of tragedy can pass the rigorously applied test of pity and terror. Aristotle himself severely criticized the *Medea* of Euripides on the ground that the terror evoked in it by Medea's assault on her own children was objectionable and unnecessary. On the other hand, it is to be assumed he accepted as adequately tragic those plays of Euripides and of Sophocles which could not pass the test he himself provided, so that the inability of Shakespeare and, I think, of Euripides, and even of Sophocles to fulfill the model set by *Oedipus* is not a sign of incompetency but rather, of the extreme difficulty and rarity of tragedy. What Shakespeare was not able to achieve more than once, what no other Elizabethan playwright could do, and Sophocles himself not more than two or three times, what Jean Racine contrived to put on the stage in maybe four of his dramas tells us simply that tragedy is very rare and not easily achieved. I think Albert Camus was perfectly right in asserting that tragedy is only possible in certain periods when there is a developing humanism, with a religious background receding perhaps, but still real enough. I think he assumed that this was true of fifth-century B.C. Athens and sixteenth-century England, as well as seventeenth-century France, but while I think that Camus was right about the historical conditions necessary for the appearance of tragedy, he did not go on to take up the difficulties in the way of a modern construction of tragedy.

Even looking back at the Greek works, I think we can see that what is required for tragedy is the operation of what I would call implacable values, and it is such values that modern feeling tells us are false. We tend not to believe in values which can be described as implacable, and they must be present in any work which is to have tragic consequences. The one modern writer who has produced what I would consider to be tragedies equal to the Greek works was not a playwright but a novelist—namely, Dostoevsky. It is interesting to note that Bakhtin, who has written so brilliantly on Dostoevsky, tells us that there are no death scenes in Dostoevsky's novels, indicating that he was not interested in death—which so interested Tolstoy—but tragedy does not require scenes of dying, which in the Greek dramas always took place offstage.[1] Tragedy requires the torment of the protagonist and our identification with the cause of his torment, impossible unless we accept implacable values of some kind. In Dostoevsky, the implacable values come from Christian conscience. Thus it is that Dostoevsky's characters are pushed around by moral ideas. Raskolnikov kills the pawnbroker and her sister to prove that he is capable of taking the lives of others, and has not yielded to the promptings of his conscience, but once the deed is done his conscience, which is not extinct, inexorably demands that he confess his crime, and he finally does. The Christian conscience of Ivan Karamazov causes in him a violent, though brief, period of insanity after the murder of his father, to which he has assented, and the sight of Ivan, stricken with remorse for having agreed to his father's death, causes Smerdyakov, his half-brother, the one who actually committed the crime, to hang himself. In Bakhtin's general argument about the value of the novel as the most powerful medium in modern literature, he could have made the point that in his novels, especially *Crime and Punishment, The Idiot,* and *The Brothers Karamazov,* Dostoevsky has written genuine tragedies such as have not been achieved since the seventeenth century by any

---

1. It will be recalled that Racine, in defending his tragedy *Bérénice*, argued that the death of an important and valued character is not indispensable to the desired effect of a tragedy.

writer for the stage. Bakhtin's motives for failing to notice Dostoevsky's power as a writer of tragedy are very complicated. When his great book on Dostoevsky appeared in Soviet Russia, Anatoly Lunacharsky, the most intelligent of the Bolshevik literary critics, pointed out that the special merit Bakhtin saw in Dostoevsky, that is, that in his novels his characters had the same rights and privileges as their author, was in fact true of Shakespeare. Did the Bard *order* Iago to swear by Janus? Can we not think that Iago decided to swear by Janus on his own? One might even think that Shakespeare overheard him swear by Janus; my point here is that Iago was indeed free to think as he pleased, he was not under strict orders from Shakespeare to think in accordance with the author's formula for his thought. According to Bakhtin, a playwright could not allow a character of his to think as freely as Dostoevsky's characters do, the novel being the only literary form in which characters can be free from the instructions, or devices, or prejudices of the author. I don't think this is a complete judgment of the matter; it seems to me that Shakespeare's major characters often seem to speak different languages, and who could have shown a preference for such languages if not the characters themselves? Bakhtin refers to the "word of 'The Double'" in Dostoevsky's story of that name, but we could certainly speak of the "word of Hamlet," the "word of Othello," and the "word of Iago." The interesting point here, though, is that Dostoevsky was successful in elaborating dramatic actions of a kind that eventuate in tragedy, in a way that even Shakespeare was not, and the ability to do this by Dostoevsky was due I maintain to the hold on him of the Russian faith in Christ, and in the implacable consequences in dramatic action of Christian conscience, felt not only as valid, but necessary for the moral life.

Now does the importance I attribute to Dostoevsky imply that a background of religious belief is necessary for the construction of a tragedy? This question is of course related to those operational values in tragedy which I have characterized as implacable. So let me put my question this way: Is religious belief in some way necessary to the postulation of implacable values?

My test case will be Pierre Corneille's wonderful play, *Le Cid*, which for all its unquestionable merit as a dramatic work has to be called a pseudo-tragedy, and I call it that not just because it ends happily. Aristotle did concede that some tragedies may end happily—I am not so sure of this. Would not happiness at the close of a tragedy destroy "the majestic sadness" Racine thought we should take with us after experiencing the tragic in the theatre? I only want to make the following point: A supposed tragedy that somehow ends happily has to be called a pseudo-tragedy if the so-called implacable values operating in it lose in the course of the action their inexorable power and yield to pragmatic exhortation and compromise. This is what happens in *Le Cid*. Moreover, the implacable values in the drama are not religious but secular, although they were maintained in the Spanish court with a fervor which may be characterized as religious.

In *Le Cid*, Rodrigue is compelled for reasons of honor to call out the father of Chimène, the woman he loves. In the duel that follows Rodrigue kills his opponent, and Chimène we realize would not have loved him at all had he failed to challenge her father. Similarly, Rodrigue would not have continued to love Chimène if after the duel she had not sought his death, in other words, if she had failed to seek an honorable revenge. There are few other tragedies in which implacable values are so clearly the motivations that charge the plot with feeling. But on the other hand, the play comes to a close with a maneuver by the king, who succeeds in attenuating the implacability of those values for the sake of which Chimène sought Rodrigue's death. After some argument with her the king orders Chimène to discontinue plotting the death of the man she loves and in fact to accept his offer of marriage. Ordered by the king to obey, Chimène yields.

I have just reread *Le Cid*, which I saw many times at the Comédie Française, and noted once again the zest and rapidity, the verve and flash of the rhyming verse. French scholars have remarked that Corneille was seldom afraid of being able to find a suitable rhyme, and for the most part wrote the first line of his alexandrines before the second, while Racine, who did not feel the need to privilege speed in his poetic exchanges, often can be found to have come by the first line of his alexandrines after having made sure of the word ending the second. And Corneille's speedy verses are perfect for a drama of love and swordplay privileging romantic honor and the necessity of revenge, but at the close the implacable has been placated by sensible reasoning. This is why I do not think this play is genuinely tragic; it ought to be called a pseudo-tragedy, though a very brilliant one.

There is one more thought we may derive from examining *Le Cid*. Religious thought is very likely to sustain the implacability of those values on which a tragedy may depend, while secular values are seldom powerful enough to withstand the attack of skeptical or pragmatic thought. Modern thinking has looked for and found remedies for the irremediable, in which William Faulkner, according to André Malraux, tried to wrap himself so as to be able to write *Light in August* and *The Sound and the Fury*.

Camus, as I noted, situated tragedy historically between a diminishing power of religion and the advancing power of humanist thought, and very similarly, the greatest contemporary French classicist Jean Vernant has judged the daemonism evident in certain tragic protagonists as an ambiguous mixture of the human and the divine. Many years back when I first published *Metatheatre*, I took a somewhat similar view of the daemonic in an essay titled "Daemons True and False." The only point I want to make about this here, though, is that Shakespeare, who may have been without religious belief of any kind, felt it necessary to connect his protagonists, even his villains, in some way with an order of things conceived religiously. Iago swears by Janus, the two-faced god, but yet let us not forget, Janus is a divinity. Moreover, Iago says, "I am not what I am," reversing the Old Testament God's description of Himself. These strategic touches are hardly accidental. Note, too, that Hamlet, having had conversations with the ghost of his father, judges his own acts and failures to act in the light of orders from someone from another world, and finally, Macbeth is inspired by the predictions of the weird sisters, all of whose predictions are in fact confirmed in the course of the play.

Daemonic, Macbeth is invulnerable to the attack of anyone but Macduff, also daemonic as a result of Macbeth's having murdered his wife and all his children. When Macduff is told of his wife's death and the death of all his children, he asks, "Did you say all?" The word *all* is very important. There is now no tie in Macduff to any moral purpose in life except revenge against Macbeth. My interest in making these points is that the religious, let's say that element of religion that is present in tragedy, is not unrepresented even in Shakespeare, though the Bard was in all probability skeptical about religious belief and probably held to no religious dogma of any kind; still he must have felt the need to introduce an element of the religious in connection with those of his characters whose fate was to touch, even tangentially, on the tragic. As Hegel noted, in a period when religion is dominant, even a nonbeliever will paint religious paintings. My variant on this remark will be the following: even a nonbeliever who intends to write a tragedy is likely to connect his protagonist, insofar as he can become daemonic, with otherworldly powers. The French philosopher Philippe Lacoue-Labarthe, commenting on Friedrich Hölderlin, has said that tragedy may be found in the caesura of the speculative. I would rather say it might be found in the caesura of the naturalistic, as expressed in the daemonic.

IV

Stimulating us to feel pity and terror, tragedy induces us to undergo what Aristotle called a catharsis. Now what is a *catharsis?* In an intelligent and learned book, *Tragic Pleasures*, Elizabeth S. Belfiore has argued, and I think convincingly, for what she calls an *allopathic* interpretation of catharsis, and against, again in her terminology, the *homeopathic* version of it which seems to have prevailed since the Renaissance What is the difference between these two interpretations of catharsis? In the first, in the homeopathic—made influential, as Belfiore notes, by Jacob Bernays—the notion is that the effect on us of a tragedy is to stimulate and purify our feelings of pity and fear. This view is called homeopathic because the assumption is that the like affects the like, and not its contrary, though no one has made it clear just how the pity we feel in witnessing a tragedy purifies the pity that may have been in us before we saw the play, or how the fear induced in us by a tragedy purifies the fear that may have already been there. And a final question: In what sense is all this pleasurable? I am convinced by Belfiore's argument that in catharsis pity is stimulated so as to overcome lack of concern for others, and terror is stimulated so as to overcome feelings of pride. In other words the emotions stimulated by tragedy replace the *opposite* feelings, rather than purify feelings already present in us. Belfiore quotes John Dryden on this, and I find his comment utterly convincing. Here is Dryden: "Rapin, a judicious critic, has observed from Aristotle, that pride and want of commiseration are the two most prominent vices in mankind; therefore, to cure us of these two, the inventors of Tragedy have chosen to work upon two other passions, which are, fear and pity."

As I noted before, I am convinced that the allopathic notion is the right one, but neither Dryden nor Rapin, whom he cites, nor Belfiore, has explained what is pleasurable about pity and fear, why being temporarily cured of self-concern and pride should be pleasurable. That we are better morally if we are interested in others and have curbed our native arrogance is not something I want to contest, but all that this would prove is that tragedy has a moral value; yet the last thing that Aristotle was interested in asserting when he wrote his *Poetics* was to prove the moral validity of tragic poetry. His concern was rather to protect the tragic poets from the moral criticism made of them by Plato. All the same, it is true he did not give a clear exposition of what it was about tragedy that makes it pleasurable. Now I cannot speak here as a trained psychologist. I can only offer, with a special effort to understand it, my own experience of pleasure in witnessing those tragedies I have seen on the stage, and as I recall the experience, I find it must be similar to that of someone who has escaped from a flood, a shipwreck, or an earthquake, who finds himself or herself intact afterward and yet, unlike the survivors of some natural catastrophe, has no feeling of guilt for being a survivor where another perished, for during the action on the stage which led to the torture, the execution, even the death of the protagonist, I suffered with him or her; I *was* the protagonist, I endured his or her agonies, I can have no possible feeling of guilt for not having ventured further with the hero or heroine finally to his or her death. I emerged from a catastrophe to another or to others without guilt and perhaps morally improved, elated at being better in many ways than before I entered the theatre and the tragedy began.

IS THERE A TRAGIC SENSE OF LIFE?

WE SET A particular value on those writers of plays—sometimes of novels—who give expression to what has been called the "tragic sense of life." Do we overvalue them? The truth is, I think, that we value them in a very special way, for we see demonstrated in their works the possibility of viewing life other than with optimism or pessimism. And for ourselves, when we reflect, the only possible choice lies with one or the other of these extremes, so that it is not only the art of the writer of tragedy we admire, but some special insight which we feel that we can achieve only through his intervention and which he—for that is our assumption—enjoys by some peculiar privilege of rare wisdom, or intelligence, or some yet more mysterious endowment. He seems more *philosophic* than other writers of equal art or scope, so that by a kind of tacit consent philosophers have honored authors of tragedy as the most *philosophical* of writers. In this estimate of the writer of tragedy I think there is a misunderstanding of his very special achievement, hence also a misunderstanding of what he achieves, namely, tragedy. If we can correctly think out what we are right to admire the author of tragedy for, we may correct some wrong notions of what tragedy is.

Our Dissatisfaction with Optimism and Pessimism

Now it should be clear why optimism as an attitude toward life cannot satisfy us. It should be clear, too, that our dissatisfaction with it is mainly *intellectual*. For we are quite naturally optimis-

This essay originally appeared in *Moderns on Tragedy*, Lionel Abel, ed. (New York: Fawcett World Library, 1962).

tic insofar as we are active beings, living in time and planning the future which our very life structure requires us to think of as being capable of yielding to our purposes. But when we reflect, when we remember "things said and done long years ago," and also the things we did not say or do, as well as those said and done by others, we realize—we have to—that there are a great many negative facts. Only a few of these, and there are a great many of them, would be enough to invalidate any optimistic hypothesis that the world as it is can be truthfully described as *good*. Instances of such negative facts may be remote or local: the unjust sentence passed on Socrates, or the fact raised by André Malraux at a congress of Soviet writers during the thirties about a man run over by a trolley car.[1] Such negative facts are able to render void all optimistic *generalizations* about the world, just as a few tiny facts which remain obdurate to explanation are sufficient to refute a whole scientific theory accounting for a multitude of others. So those who live by optimistic beliefs are like bad scientists, clinging, despite the evidence, to refuted theories.

But what about the negative facts? Do they at least justify pessimism? Not as a hypothesis, not as a generalized view. For the negative facts comprise merely one set of facts, and the world is such that no one set of facts is able to speak for it. We know that having heard one set out, we must listen to very different facts. Alas for the heartbreak of the defeated and the dead: if we do not straightway share their fate, we are forced to think of something else.

The Russian thinker Leon Chestov—I will not call him a philosopher—repeated again and again in his writings that the injustice done to Socrates was a fact he could not endure. He thought, too, that a fact of this sort should make us suspicious of any facts we ordinarily think of as positive. But even if the positive facts were far fewer than the negative, they could still

---

1. The reply made to Malraux was that the Soviet authorities would see to it that accidents of that sort decreased annually. The argument of the Soviet writers was for optimism, to them obligatory; the greater relative safety of future generations would more than make up for the absolute harm which had befallen one individual.

not justify our electing for pessimism. (For Arthur Schopenhauer a preponderance of negative facts did justify pessimism; his argument lacks subtlety.) The positive facts remain, and they prevent us from resolving without artificiality in favor of a pessimistic view. A very few positive facts can make pessimism unacceptable. This is illustrated, I think, in the biblical story of Abraham's debate with God when the Lord was intent on destroying the wicked cities of Sodom and Gomorrah. Abraham argued that if there were even ten good men in those cities, the Lord's proposed action would be unjust. And God finally conceded Abraham to be the better philosopher, admitting that if there were even fewer than ten good men in Sodom and Gomorrah, His pessimism about the two cities would be unjustified, notwithstanding all the wicked in them.

That the positive facts stand in the way of a resolve for pessimism is not in any sense an argument for being optimistic. Far from it! It is a sad fact indeed that sadness will bring us no closer than lightness of spirit to the heart of things.

What argues for optimism is that it is required by our life structure. If we plan to be optimistic, then at least we are not contradicting ourselves; but if we plan to be pessimistic—and since we live in time, to be pessimistic means to plan to be pessimistic—then we are contradicting ourselves; we are placing our trust in the view that things will be untrustworthy; we are reasoning that Failure cannot fail, and so, in a sense, can be depended on. Then, too, except in cases of present or permanent distress, optimism is natural and spontaneous, while pessimism is inevitably theatrical. Life requires optimism; but optimism leaves out of account and quite disregards pain, frustration, and death. Such disregard is, of course, intellectually shallow. So we are back with our dilemma: we can be optimists or pessimists; but can we want to be either?

The remedy is a fantastic one: it is a vision of the irremediable. We go to the theatre to see a tragedy. We see human action in the clearest light the mind can cast on it, and behold, we see the human person at his best. We do not disregard pain or frustration or death; in fact we give them our whole attention, and they do not make us pessimistic, they give us joy. As Aristotle said, we feel pity and terror, the very emotions pessimism threatens us with and optimism would have us avoid. We see life tragically; we have for the duration of the play at least and perhaps for some time afterward the tragic sense. Would that it were more lasting!

Can we make it so? Can we not make permanent the view of life we enjoyed in the theatre and in recollection afterward for however short a time? Can we not acquire or develop a sense of life such as the playwright himself must have had? Of course, we cannot be Sophocles, Shakespeare, or Racine. The question then is: can the tragic sense be acquired without the special genius of the writer of tragedy, and if so, how?

Why We Cannot Acquire the Tragic Sense

Suppose, though, for I think this true, that what we call the tragic sense does not form part of the playwright's genius and does not involve superior capacities of mind; then it must be the result of experience. Of what experience? The answer to this question is obvious; we should have thought of it immediately: The experience which leads to the tragic sense of life is the experience of sense. Or rather, the word *arrives* is misleading here, for one does not acquire or develop the tragic sense; it is not realized but imposed; one never possesses it, one has to be possessed by it.

We cannot add the tragic sense to our present sense of life, be that present sense optimistic or pessimistic. And without our present sense we have neither terms nor criteria with which to decide whether the tragic sense is worth what it will cost us. And from this it follows that no reason can ever be given for recommending the tragic sense, however good or great a thing the tragic sense may be.

Herbert J. Muller, in *The Spirit of Tragedy*, has had the temerity to urge on us the acquisition of the tragic sense for reasons which he himself does not deny are frankly utilitarian. He writes: "We might not continue to get along as a free, open society without more of the tragic sense of life." I think the error he has fallen into is expressed in his use of the word *more*. If we had *some* of the tragic sense of life then perhaps we could get still *more* of it, but it would not be the drastic thing it is if that were the way it could be come by. The prospect we would face, if we did not get just "more" of the tragic sense but enough of it to have it, would be one of all or nothing.

So we cannot urge the tragic sense on ourselves or on others. To try to attain it or to recommend it is comical and self-refuting, tragedy being real only when unavoidable. There would be no such things as tragedy if a tragic fate could be rationally chosen.

The Writer of Tragedy and the Philosopher

But what about the writer of tragedy? Must he not possess the tragic sense of life since he is able to make it available to us at least for the time we spend under his spell? Is there not reason for thinking that the writer of tragedy must have a more permanent relation to the tragic view than those who receive it from him? Does he have a special philosophy, a tragic philosophy if you please, permanently his, and which through his art he is able to share with us in some small measure? Now I do not think the writer of tragedy has to have any view of life drastically different from our own.

Supposing he were a philosopher, what difference would that make? He could not by means of philosophy resolve the question of optimism or pessimism, which we who are not philosophers face. For philosophers are also either optimistic or pessimistic. (Some philosophers are neutral, but this last attitude is finally comprised under pessimism. Neutrality to life really means pessimism about it.)

When the vision of a writer of tragedy is stated philosophically, it is always converted (I submit, necessarily) into a form of optimism or of pessimism. I shall give two examples. The first is taken from Matthew Arnold's famous poem *Dover Beach*. Arnold, looking out at the sea from Dover Beach and hearing in the cadence of the waves the "eternal note of sadness," thinks of Sophocles:

> Sophocles long ago
> Heard it on the Aegean, and it brought
> Into his mind the turbid ebb and flow
> Of human misery;

And the image of Sophocles hearing the note of "human misery" leads Arnold to this pessimistic declaration:

> Ah, love, let us be true
> To one another! For the world, which seems
> To lie before us like a land of dreams,
> So various, so beautiful, so new,
> Hath really neither joy, nor love, nor light,
> Nor certitude, nor peace, nor help for pain . . .

The view of life expressed here is not one that I, or any one else, could derive from seeing a performance of *Oedipus Rex, Oedipus at Colonus,* or *Antigone.* Perhaps Sophocles had such thoughts when he looked at the Aegean, but these are not the thoughts we think when witnessing his tragedies. And from the reports about Sophocles by his contemporaries, we are scarcely justified in calling to mind an individual contemplating human misery. The tragic poet was said to have been charming, gracious, genial, and with no better opinions about politics or life than other cultivated Athenians.

The wonderful Spanish writer and thinker Miguel de Unamuno, who is actually responsible for the phrase "the tragic sense of life," trying to state this "tragic sense" as a philosophical attitude, converts it, I think, into a refined and pleasing, though somber, form of optimism. Unamuno's tragic sense is even a misnomer; there is little tragic about it, for he is not urging us to set something above life; rather what he does urge us to set above life is nothing other than life, immortal life, the immortality of the soul, on which immortality he asks us to gamble the existence we are certain of. That this violently optimistic Christianity should attract us with its death-splashed Spanish cloak is due, of course, to our obscure recognition, even if we have not thought the matter through, that optimism presented simply as optimism would offer us only what we are well acquainted and dissatisfied with.

A novel and, I think, quite wrong view that thought, even philosophic thought, can have and has had a tragic cast is presented by Lucien Goldmann in his much-praised book on Blaise Pascal and Racine, *Le Dieu Cadre.* According to Goldmann there are certain philosophers whose thought can be characterized as tragic. He cites as instances Pascal and Immanuel Kant. Why is their thought tragic? Because, says Goldmann, it expresses the conflict in them between alternative and exclusive worldviews, the worldview of mathematical science and the worldview of revealed religion. But surely no character on the stage would be convincing in the tragic hero's part if his torment were due to nothing more drastic than his inability to choose between or mediate conflicting views. In fact, Kant and Pascal did both. What I mean is this: Kant opted for religion in his metaphysics and for science in his epistemology. And I think Pascal did the same in his distinction between *l'esprit géométrique* and *l'esprit de finesse.*

I submit that it is not through any particular philosophy that the tragic writer is able to give expression to his tragic sense of life, although this tragic sense does have for us, the audience, a virtue which has been called philosophic. Then is it by art alone that the writer of tragedy affects us as he does?

The Writer of Tragedy Without the Philosopher

The very great probability is, I suggest, that the writer of tragedy is no more endowed with a tragic sense of life than are we to whom he makes it available. By which I mean that he, too, in his regular experience of life, is condemned to the same unsatisfactory choice between optimism and pessimism that we are, and that only in the act of writing a tragedy, only by making the tragic view available to us, is he himself enabled to envisage life in such terms. His creation then is a communion with us, in the experiencing of a view of things which we could not have without him, but which he in turn can only have insofar as he is capable of extending it to us.

Why could we not have the tragic sense without the *written* tragedy? Let us consider this point from a somewhat different angle. There is something we could have without the help of art, and which many people may confuse with the tragic sense, namely, the feeling of a *pessimism that is justified.* This is all we can get from the lesser masters of the art of tragedy, from Euripides, John Webster, and Cyril Tourneur at their best, and from Shakespeare in his unsuccessful tragedies such as *Troilus and Cressida, Coriolanus, Timon of Athens,* and *King Lear.* Moreover, this justified pessimism appears at times even in the greatest works but it is not this which makes them tragic. When Richard in Shakespeare's *Richard II* complains of the vulnerability of kings,

> ... for within the hollow crown
> That rounds the mortal temples of a king
> Keeps Death his court; and there the antic sits ...
> Allowing him a breath, a little scene ...
> ... and humour'd thus,
> Comes at the last, and with a little pin
> Bores through his castle wall, and farewell king!

he gives expression to a pessimism which in view of his situation he is certainly justified in feeling. And the greatness of the verse penetrates Richard's feeling completely; what he says seems all the more inevitable because expressed in lines of such power. Who can be secure if the best protected of men, the king, is not? It is to be noted that a negative fact, in this instance death, armed with so mean and trivial an instrument as a pin, is seen as rendering meaningless the highest state a man can aspire to, that of a king. Later in the play Richard will say:

> ... nor any man that but man is
> With nothing shall be pleas'd till he be eas'd
> With being nothing.

The feeling expressed here of life's meaninglessness we may all have felt, indeed must have felt, at some time or another and with some measure of poetry, too, for such feelings provide a verbal talent all by themselves. We would not need the art of tragedy to acquaint us with such a judgment of life or even with the necessity to pronounce it consummately.

A judgment of life similar in its pessimism to Richard's and equally justified is uttered by Macbeth:

> Life's but a walking shadow, a poor player,
> That struts and frets his hour upon the stage
> And then is heard no more. It is a tale
> Told by an idiot, full of sound and fury,
> Signifying nothing.

This judgment, too, we could form for ourselves without either the experience of tragedy or Shakespeare's art. But what we could not get without actual or invented tragedy is the experience of resolution when nothing can follow from resolve, a resolution beyond optimism or pessimism, hope or despair. This we get from Macbeth's great words:

> Though Birnam Wood be come to Dunsinane,
> And thou opposed, being of no woman born,
> Yet will I try the last.

Richard's speech about the death of kings is a protest against the weakness and impotence of the most highly placed. Macbeth's lines of resolution express a much more complicated feeling, one in which are allied, to use Martin Heidegger's phrase, "utter impotence and super power." Richard's lines about the death of kings, justifying pessimism, point to the negative fact of death which renders optimistic notions of life invalid even for a king. Macbeth's lines of resolution refer to no negative facts at all, nor to anything common in human experience, not even to the common experience of kings, but exclusively to the withdrawal of their aid from him by those metaphysical beings, the weird sisters, who had for a time supported him. Macbeth's lines are thrilling; Richard's are merely sad. What has to be explained is why Macbeth's lines thrill us, and why he had to pass through the experience of tragedy in order to be able to utter them. The weakness of Richard is evident, so is Macbeth's. But whence comes Macbeth's power?

What Is Tragedy?

In tragedy it is not the negative facts, rendering optimism invalid, which finally cause misfortune. Such negative facts as commonly threaten all of us are even converted by the mechanism of tragedy into positive goods. Blindness is an evil, yet Oedipus deliberately blinds himself; death we would think is to be avoided at all costs, yet Antigone elects to die and denies her sister, Ismene, the same privilege. Ajax, when told that if he spends the day in his tent he will be allowed to live, deliberately leaves his tent and falls on his sword. In the tragic universe the negative facts of experience are finally unimportant. What might lead us in ordinary life to be pessimistic is never the cause of tragedy.

What is the cause then of tragedy? It is the opposition, as Hegel affirmed, of two conflicting goods. Tragedy is never caused by what is unambiguously evil. It is the sheerly positive in conflict with the sheerly positive that destroys the tragic protagonist. In the Greek world it was the collision of the values of the family with those of the state. Those contrary values, as Aeschylus and Sophocles understood them, could not be held to with equal fidelity in any superior experience of life. The superior man would inevitably violate the one or the other.[2] Perhaps it may be said that while this may have been true of the ancient Greek world, it was not true of the Shakespearean

---

2. It may be asked: Why is a collision of values different from a collision of worldviews? But a collision of views, even if we call them worldviews, takes place within consciousness and not within the *world*. Values such as the family and the state are not merely values; they are valued realities.

world. For in what sense can the witches who incite Macbeth to kill Duncan be called sheerly positive? In what sense can they be called representatives of the good? Are they not the expression of unmitigated evil?

If they were, *Macbeth* would not be a tragedy. It would be a melodrama, and Macbeth's story would merely be that of a villain defeated. But once again, in what sense can the witches be said to represent the good? In this scene: the witches in *Macbeth* are the only dramatic expression of the metaphysical. Duncan, the reigning king, is presented as kingly, just, morally right. But Macbeth and Banquo are the characters in the play who have direct contact with the representatives of the meta-physical, that is to say, the witches. Now in *Macbeth* the metaphysical does not coincide with the moral, but is at odds with it; yet both are to be valued. Since the justification for kingship was finally metaphysical—the Elizabethans believed in the divine right of kings as opposed to any merely moral right to kingship—how could an immoral deed of murder to attain kingship, when metaphysical forces, in this case, the witches, seemed to support that deed, be thought of as evil? And, in fact, we never feel Macbeth is evil. We think of him as suffering, suffering because he has violated moral values he cannot deny, in support of values neither he nor Shakespeare's age thought criticizable in moral terms. As in the Greek tragedies, we have in *Macbeth* good pitted against good, and the protagonist is the victim of their collision. What is dreadful then is never the mere negative facts ordinary experience fears. It is the good which is dreaded and has to be dreaded. Sören Kierkegaard, peculiarly sensitive to these matters, summed up what, I think, can be called the experience of tragedy when he said in his acute analysis of dread that it is fundamentally dread of the good.

I should like to point out here that one of the most interesting insights of Martin Heidegger—much more interesting than his remarks about anguish and guilt, which have become part of current twaddle—is his judgment that worldviews imply the absence of a world rather than a world's enduring pres-ence. Tragedy takes place in a world, not in a consciousness which is uncertain as to what the world is.

What Has the Writer of Tragedy Seen?

So the tragic writer has to have seen some collision of good with good in order to have been able to arrange the events he described into a tragedy. Was he predisposed to see some such collision of good with good? Not, I should say, if it were not there to be seen, even if only he saw it. For can we want to see what it is undesirable to see? Some of us may out of ambition or perversity, but not the writer of a proper tragedy. He sees what it is undesirable to see without desiring to see it. This is one of the things we admire him for. To be sure, there are other things. But in any case, what must be understood here is that the object of his vision was given by his age or epoch and not created by him alone. The collision of good with good which he witnessed had then to be given him along with others to see; his part was to take what he saw, and what others may have seen, and fashion it into art.

Thus the tragic view, properly understood, means to have seen the necessity for tragedy, to have recognized it rather than to have created it. That the tragic vision results from a direct act of seeing, and not from the holding of any particular view, or from any predilection for interpreting reality tragically, is something we must understand in order to evaluate that vision and judge it for its true worth. Just as in the tragedy he is going to write, the dramatist will set forth a sequence of events whose connections are necessary, so he himself can only be stirred to set forth such a sequence of events by the sight of a fatality that was thrust upon his view and which was necessarily, not accidentally, there before him.

Once again: What did he see? A collision of good with good. Is it desirable that such a collision come within our view? Not in life. No. Nobody can genuinely say that he wants to see a tragedy enacted anywhere but on the stage. For it is a misfortune to a society or to a culture if its main values contradict one another. On the other hand, tragedy, that art which expresses the collision and not the harmony of such values, is in itself a positive aesthetic good. But this good, this aesthetic good, is achieved through an appropriate description of the ultimate in human misfortune: that man's values should contradict rather than support one another.

Once Again "The Tragic Thinker"

Perhaps it is right to say of the writer of tragedy that his thought, since it had to be equal to what he saw—what he saw was tragedy—is a kind of "tragic thinking." But this can only mean that the writer of tragedy has not permitted any philosophy or ideology to impede or obstruct his vision. But what about those thinkers who have been called "tragic," as for instance Pascal? As I indicated before, I think the term "tragic" when used to designate the thought of anyone not the writer of a tragedy is always wrongly used. Nonetheless, there are in Pascal's *Pensées* many dramatic characteristics of experience which give us a kind of thrill comparable to the kind we get from tragedy. My contention is that in the case of such *Pensées*, Pascal has merely created an abstract replica of the kind of collision of values we find embodied with ever so much more concreteness in tragic poetry. Here is one of the most famous of Pascal's thoughts:

> Man is but a reed, the feeblest of Nature's growths, but he is a thinking reed. There is no need for the whole universe to take up arms to crush him; a breath, a drop of water, may prove fatal. But were the universe to kill him, he would still be more noble than his slayers; for man knows that he is crushed, but the universe does not know that it crushes him.

I think what we have here is an imitation in conceptual terms of the kind of event set forth in a real tragedy. It is to be noted that Pascal begins by saying men can be destroyed by a drop of water or a breath; but he chooses not to continue the thought that men can be destroyed by such small means. The drop of water, the breath, are tiny facts: acting negatively, they would be of no interest in tragedy. So in Pascal's thought they are expanded—in possibility, of course—into the universe. From the breath, the drop of water, Pascal goes to the whole universe, which he imagines in the act of overwhelming a man. Even then, says Pascal, the man would be nobler than his slayer. But, in any case, the slayer would be noble, being the universe. Insofar as Pascal's thought here may strike one as tragic, I should say that the event he has described was modeled on that structure of events always present in a true tragedy. For he who is destroyed in a true tragedy is always destroyed by something of worth. The drop of water, the breath, may be thought of, as I said before, as tiny facts behaving negatively but which Pascal had finally to forget about and obscure from his view in order to make a true judgment of man's nobility in misfortune.

What We Should Admire the Writer of Tragedy For

Let us turn from the "tragic thinker" to the writer of tragedy. Why do we admire him? Not for his philosophy, for he has none. If he does hold to one in his personal life, this is not pertinent to his achievement or to our judgment of it. Nor are we required to think of him as a master of experience, as wiser or more deeply human than ourselves. Let us admire him for his art; we should recognize, though, that what he gives us goes far beyond what art generally or regularly gives. And let us admire him for his luck, too, at having been given by his age the opportunity to see in his mind's eye certain paradigm instances of human adversity. Does not Pushkin say that the day after the flooding of Petrograd, "Khostov, poet, favorite of the heavens, already sang in verses never to die the griefs of Neva's shores"?[3]

Moreover, the effort the writer of tragedy makes has to be immense. He has seen the collision of the main values of his age or culture, he has seen the nonmeaning of meanings. Now

---

3. From Pushkin's poem *The Bronze Horseman* in Edmund Wilson's translation, *Triple Thinkers* (New York: Harcourt Brace, 1938).

the mind naturally seeks out meanings; the writer of tragedy has to deny and reverse this process in the very movement with which he yields to it.

His interest is, of course, an aesthetic one. May I speak for just one moment from a professional point of view? When you have written a play you are faced with this problem: What does this play mean? If it is meaningless, it is uninteresting. Suppose it does have a meaning, though. This is scarcely better. Have you not then reduced the action in your play to the illustration of an idea? Now illustrative art is scarcely better for many of us today than is meaningless art. Here the idea of tragedy exerts its fascination. For it is the kind of idea that attains to its truth only when represented in the work itself: the play, the tragedy. We are much more clear about what tragedy is when we see a tragedy enacted than when we try to reason about tragedy.

And let us not forget that what the writer of tragedy gives, he himself gets in the very act of giving: communion with us in a privileged view of human adversity. We admire him then for what he makes us see, a world in which the highest values collide and in which we know we could not live. We recognize this when the curtain comes down and we do not know where to go. We have to become optimists or pessimists again in order to think of going home.

THE FATE OF ATHALIAH—
AND RACINE

I

A FIGURE SHAPED to the purpose of tragedy—such is Athaliah, Queen of Judah, daughter of Ahab and Jezebel, even as she appears, set violent before us, strictly judged and summarily disposed of, in the Second Book of Kings.[1]

A faithful daughter and a monstrous grandmother, Athaliah fell victim to the only grandson whom she had failed to kill. Except for this grandson, Joash, and her father, Ahab, every male member of Athaliah's immediate family was either destroyed by God or slain by her. God, having avenged Himself on Athaliah's mother, Jezebel, encompassed the ruin of Athaliah's brothers, of her husband, Joram, and of all her sons, including Ahaziah, King of Judah. The Lord, not satisfied with vengeance on Jezebel, was interested, it seems, in wiping out the posterity of Ahab,[2] who were an offense to Him. But Athaliah, equal to her terrible Opponent, was ready to match Him murder for murder, life for life. She undertook to wipe out the posterity of David, though this meant slaughtering her own grandsons. In their veins the blood of David mingled with the blood of Ahab. To extirpate the one race meant to sacrifice the other. Before this atrocity, Athaliah, headlong and sanguinary, did not flinch. At the eleventh hour it was God who did. (From a theological

---

1. Athaliah's story is recounted with like brevity in the Second Book of Chronicles.
2. Ahab appears to have escaped God's wrath, which is undoubtedly why God was so vengeful toward his descendants. In any case, Ahab's escape from God's anger seems to have made his name the appropriate one for Herman Melville's impious hero in *Moby-Dick*.

view, had He not wavered, humanity would have lost. Was not the promised Messiah ordained to come from David's seed?) Suddenly the Lord bethought Him that He would have to save some of the blood of Ahab in order not to lose all of David's. Thus, from the cruel Queen's assault upon her grandsons, the infant Joash was by miracle preserved. The boy, found and hidden by Jehosheba, wife to the High Priest Jehoiada, was raised secretly by them, and in time was revealed to the people as David's descendant. After a palace revolution Joash assumed the throne. His grandmother was put to the sword.

These facts are sufficient to justify our judgment that Athaliah is tragic—to the most eminent degree. And in how many meanings of the word! First, for the greatness of her Opponent (could there be a greater?); then, for being even more uncompromising than He, and again, for the grandeur of the aim which she refused to compromise. And when we think about that aim, we see that she is tragic in still another and—to a modern mind—especially interesting sense: her aim was precisely tragedy; her purpose was to bring the epic history of the Jews to a bloody close. If it was God who began the tragedy, it was Athaliah who continued it from the point where He left off, so that He was finally forced to intervene and prevent her from accomplishing what had originally been His own design. Thus Athaliah's action, until the very end, is indistinguishable from God's. We may even say that God realized His vengeance by means of her: in her appeared the rigor He Himself had to renounce. So if the Queen was accursed, all of her acts were sacred.

II

Seen thus, Athaliah surely merits our respect; yet she does not appear to have greatly impressed the writers of the Book of Kings (or Chronicles). It is not surprising that this rebel against God elicited little admiration from those who wrote the Scriptures; but one wonders that the writers did not take some lyrical note of the Queen's quality. They had, after all, written wonderfully of her scarcely better mother, Jezebel, fashioning in their best rhythms an imperishable image of flaming iniquity. Jezebel's fate is prophesied: "In the portion of Jezreel shall the dogs eat the flesh of Jezebel, and the body of Jezebel shall be as dung on the face of the field in the portion of Jezreel, so that they shall not say 'This is Jezebel.'" This marvelous malediction—pronounced by a prophet with the oddly delightful name of Elijah the Tishbite—has surely helped to make Jezebel remembered. But Athaliah is scarcely depicted in the Book of Kings. We hear nothing that she says; she is never characterized; only her deeds are told. The only poetry she has comes from the facts of her story. The figure of Athaliah, as the Bible presents her, is purely, exclusively tragic. And for centuries the Queen remained imaginatively, poetically unknown. But in 1691, Jean Racine presented *Athalie*,[3] his last and one of his most original tragedies, at Saint-Cyr. This play may be said to do more than remedy the neglect suffered by the Queen at the hands of the writers of Kings and Chronicles. Charles-Augustin Sainte-Beuve called *Athalie* "as beautiful as *Rex Oedipus*, and with the true God to boot." Voltaire judged it "the masterpiece of the human mind."

III

Athaliah's epiphany, so long delayed, so perfect when it came, required, of course, some help from chance. I shall review briefly the favoring, well-known circumstances. Jean Racine, brought up at Port Royal, learned the Greek classics together with the Bible; his understanding of the Greek conception of fate blended with his awe at the implacable acts of the Old Testament God.

---

3. Georges Mongredian, in his book *Athalie*, claims there were no literary sources for Racine's play besides the Old Testament. But Professor Meyer Schapiro has shown me a brief text on Athaliah in Giovanni Boccaccio's book on the misfortunes of celebrated persons. Translated into French, Boccaccio's work appeared with a medallion of Athaliah by Fouquet. Racine must have read the book. Boccaccio's book contains texts on two other famous persons treated by Racine: Agrippina and Bérénice. However, the text of Boccaccio on Athaliah is quite brief, not especially penetrating, and tells us little not already known from the Bible.

Evidently the writing of *Athalie* required a sensibility formed both by Jansenism and the Greek dramatists; the very same sensibility, though, was essential for the writing of *Phèdre*. It would seem to me, too, that simply to compare Racine the orphan, brought up by the nuns at Port Royal, and the grandson of Athaliah, raised by the High Priest Jehoiada can tell us little about *Athalie* or the likelihood that Racine would write it. Let us note, instead, everything that might have prevented him from writing that play.

Racine began his career as a court poet. His subjects were taken from Roman history and Greek mythology, and while he was, no doubt, influenced in his bent for tragedy by the religious education he had received at Port Royal, still the themes of his first plays had been almost exclusively erotic. Nothing surprising in this: the new young court of Louis XIV was almost exclusively interested in erotic relations. However, in 1677, *Phèdre* failed, as the result of an intrigue against Racine. The dramatist had considered this play his greatest work. His judgment may be questioned; but certainly *Phèdre* contains the most wonderful poetry Racine was capable of writing. Had the play succeeded, it is likely that Racine would have continued to make dramatic poetry out of Greek and Roman stories; we might have had an *Alceste* by him and an *Iphigénie en Tauride*. We might not have had *Esther* or *Athalie*. But *Phèdre* failed, and Racine stopped writing plays, embarking on his new career as court memorialist. Twelve years later Madame de Maintenon asked him to write a dramatic poem to be played by the girls of Saint-Cyr. She specified that the work should be without erotic interest. Racine hesitated. Madame de Quellus, who knew of the affair, notes in her memoirs: "He wanted to please Madame de Maintenon. Refusal was impossible for a courtier, but the commission was a delicate one for a man who had a great reputation to maintain and who, while he had abandoned writing for the theatre, nevertheless did not want to diminish the reputation his works had gained." We know that Nicolas Boileau himself advised Racine against accepting. But Racine accepted, and *Esther* was presented before the King and court of Saint-Cyr in 1689. The play was a success and

Madame de Maintenon requested another. Racine wrote *Athalie*. It was produced in 1691, and did not find favor; in fact, Louis XIV is said to have left in a rage. Racine wrote no more plays. If *Esther* had not succeeded and if *Phèdre* had not failed, Racine would probably not have written *Athalie*.

Yet how could he not have written *Athalie?* What, from the facts, seems like a wonderfully lucky chance, appears as indispensable and necessary when we take into account Racine's special qualities as a writer of tragedy, and the value of his last work. Of all the authors of tragedy since Aeschylus, Racine, by temperament, training, and resolve, was probably the most gifted for making murder meaningful on the stage. Athaliah, in Racine's last play, is put to death more perfectly than any character in all dramatic literature, and I do not exclude the deaths of Agamemnon and Clytemnestra in the *Oresteia*, the death of King Pentheus in the *Bacchae*, the deaths of Anthony and Cleopatra, and of Macbeth. Yet before he wrote *Athalie*, Racine, with some six or seven dramatic masterpieces behind him, had not yet killed anyone on the stage adequately, let alone perfectly.

IV

Thierry Maulnier and Jean Giraudoux have underscored Racine's capacities as a killer of his characters; but they never saw how dependent this estimate of him is on what he achieved in his last work. Certainly their estimate is not justified by his prior works alone.

Andromaque, for example—which French critics from Jean-François La Harpe to Maulnier have regarded as a tragedy—is far too psychological and romantic a melodrama for the deaths of two of its main characters, at the climax, to strike us tragically. The loves of Orestes for Hermione, of Hermione for Pyrrhus, and of Pyrrhus for Andromache, are frankly presented by Racine himself as sentiments not quite worthy of persons of their rank and station. In fact, Racine's judgment of the sentiments of his own characters does not differ much from that of his rival, Pierre Corneille, who disliked *Andromaque,* nor from that of Madame de Sévigné, who liked it, but thought that it fell short of the sublimity Corneille had taught the French court to admire. The passions of Pyrrhus, Orestes, and Hermione are not to be admired, nor did Racine intend them to be.

Let us note, though, that these three characters are the children of the great figures whose exploits Homer had celebrated: Orestes is the son of Agamemnon; Pyrrhus the son of Achilles; Hermione the daughter of Helen. The one character in the drama who comes directly from Homer's *Iliad* is Andromache, the widow of Hector. Now her feeling for her dead husband *is* sublime. Andromache's passion, which we cannot but admire, is more natural than that exhibited by any character in any play by Corneille. She is the prisoner of Pyrrhus, Achilles' son. Achilles had killed her husband, and Pyrrhus, conqueror of Troy, had slain her father and brothers. Now Pyrrhus, who is in love with her, has the power of life and death over her son by Hector, the boy Astyanax:

> So young, so to be pitied, but yet the one link remaining between any still living Trojan and all the kings dead and buried under the ruins of Troy.[4]

If Andromache refuses Pyrrhus she will betray Hector, for Pyrrhus will kill Hector's son and heir. But if she accepts Pyrrhus' love in order to save Hector's son, she will be unfaithful to Hector. From this tragic dilemma no happy outcome is conceivable, except by chance. Racine in his play provided just that chance. The tragically conceived Andromache does not die, is not forced to marry Pyrrhus, and yet saves her son. The romantically conceived Pyrrhus dies at the hand of Orestes, and the equally romantic (and very modern) Hermione takes her own life. Certainly there is a tragic tonality in the play:

---

4.   *Astyanax, d'Hector jeune et malheureux fils,*
          Reste de tant de rois sous Troie ensevelis.

(*Andromaque,* Act I, scene 1); from my own translation of the play, published in *The Genius of the French Theater,* ed. Albert Bermel (New York: Mentor Book).

the events express the just revenge of Troy on Greece for the brutal excesses of the Greek victors; yet the one really tragic figure succeeds, and comes through the action safely. The pathetic, somewhat comical, and modernly complicated characters are ill-starred, and fail or die. This is an extraordinary work; it is not a true tragedy.

In *Bajazet*, which, too, has been called a tragedy, all the principal characters are killed at the end, strangled by the gigantic Negro executioner in the harem where the drama takes place. There are many deaths, but after reading and rereading the play, and after having seen it on the stage, one must agree with the seventeenth-century judgment: there is no reason for so much butchery. Racine, in this play, does demonstrate his temperament for killing, but he does not reveal himself as one with the *right* to kill, which, on the stage, means the ability to inflict death tragically.

No, *Bajazet* is no tragedy. Roxanne, the favorite of the absent Sultan, whom she is planning to depose, orders Bajazet to marry her. He, being in love with Atalide, after much hesitation, finally refuses. Roxanne brutally sends him to the strangler. But had Bajazet accepted Roxanne's offer of love, his end would have been the same, for Acomat, the Sultan's grand vizier, returning to take charge of the harem, would certainly have meted out the same fate to Bajazet that he does to Roxanne. Moreover, there is something commonplace in Bajazet's character, and something comical about his trying to be heroically true to his sentiment for one woman while living in a harem.

One character is indeed touched by tragedy: Atalide. She loves Bajazet, and knowing Roxanne will be unmerciful if he refuses her, implores him to accept her rival's offer. The scene in which she makes this plea is touching and beautiful, perhaps all the more so because Atalide, urging her own lover to be unfaithful to her, is realistic, not idealistic. Bajazet, as I have already noted, in preferring death to infidelity, seems, given the circumstances, not to know where he is. The movement of the play is pure melodrama; nothing great is at issue, and Bajazet is not really a romantic lover. Some French critics have called him a Christian gentleman who had wandered by chance into a harem; this judgment, far from justifying the play, makes it seem, for all its brilliance, somewhat absurd.

Neither *Britannicus* nor *Mithridate* need be considered at length. In the latter play there is a lovely woman, Monine, whom Voltaire thought a great creation. With her, he said, Racine "introduced taste into heroism." It is a fine remark. Yet Voltaire did not consider the play a tragedy. How could he have? It ends happily. Voltaire, however, did think *Britannicus* a tragedy. In this drama, Nero begins his career as a monster by killing his half-brother, Britannicus, in order to defeat the political intrigues of his mother, Agrippina. Evil is triumphant in the beautifully structured and eloquent drama. The true antagonists are Nero and Agrippina, between whom there is no moral issue, only a question of power. The young Britannicus and Junie, who love each other, are children. Whether they live or die, the fate of Rome will be unaltered. Britannicus is killed and Junie escapes from Nero by becoming a vestal virgin. Rome will be controlled by one or the other of the two evil persons in the drama, and it is hardly thinkable that Rome under Agrippina would be different from Rome under Nero. How can the death of Britannicus affect us tragically, then? The play, in its psychology and rhetoric, is "for connoisseurs," as Voltaire noted, but certainly not for connoisseurs of tragedy.

Consider Racine's first and probably most perfect tragedy, *Bérénice*. This is one of the most simply constructed and beautiful plays ever written. It is tragic throughout, yet it does not end with the death of its protagonists, Titus, Emperor of Rome, and Bérénice, the Jewish queen who loves him and is loved by him. They are unable to marry because Roman republican law, surviving under the Empire, forbids an emperor to marry a queen. As long as Vespasian, the father of Titus, lived, Titus and Bérénice expected to marry. When the play begins, Augustus has just died, and Titus realizes at last that he cannot defy the law of the state over which he hopes to rule. Titus sends Antiochus, a visiting king from the East, who also is in love with Bérénice, to inform her that the new Emperor of Rome cannot marry her. Antiochus is eager to bear the message; he sees a chance to plead his own case. But when he has told

Bérénice of the decision of Titus, she peremptorily dismisses him, forbidding him even to see her again. Antiochus is almost comical in this scene, and would indeed be, if Racine, with extraordinary finesse, had not saved him for tragedy by endowing him with a wonderful discretion. Racine also gave him one of his greatest, saddest, and most admired lines:

> In the desolate East
> How huge was then my grief![5]

At last Bérénice confronts Titus, and he tells her in his own words that he cannot marry her. Is he not the Emperor? she wants to know. He is the Emperor, and that is why he cannot obey his heart. Titus even considers giving up his empire for Bérénice, but would she love him if he were not the Emperor of Rome? They part forever, and the last word of the play, spoken by Antiochus, is "alas."

The movement of this play has the sureness of the very greatest tragedies. The mechanism is flawless. Rome, which decrees the separation of the lovers, is identical with the civilized world. It is the world at its best which denies what is best in the lovers: their feeling for each other. In the end they both recognize this. All the same, they choose to live. Moreover, the plot allows them to live, and we do not have to believe completely their protests that they would rather die than part. Racine himself, feeling that the absence of death from his play might be regarded as a fault, argued in his preface to it that death is not essential in tragedy. His argument is interesting:

> I grant that I did not push Bérénice to the point of a suicide like Dido's, for Bérénice was not bound as irrevocably to Titus as Dido to Aeneas; thus she was not obliged, like Dido, to refuse to live at all. Nevertheless,

---

5. *Dans l'Orient désert quel devint mon ennui!* (*Bérénice*, Act I, scene 4). Excerpt from *Jean Racine: Five Plays,* trans. Kenneth Muir (New York: Hill & Wang, 1960).

her final farewell to Titus, and her struggles to give him up, are not, I think, the least tragic moments of my play; I shall even go so far as to say that the emotion which the play had already excited is intensified in these moments. Blood and corpses are, after all, not essential to tragedy: enough if the action be great, the characters heroic, their emotions real; enough if the work provokes by its every detail, that majestic sadness wherein lies the whole pleasure of tragedy.

Racine's argument for not having pushed Bérénice to the point of a death like Dido's is not strong. It is conventional and one may doubt that it was written with full conviction. What is interesting about the passage—aside from the beautiful phrase explaining "the whole pleasure of tragedy"—is the fact that Racine, so praised as an *ange exterminateur* (angel of death), should here be arguing that death is not essential to the main purpose of the tragic poet.

In his *Iphigénie à Aulis*, there is death, blood is shed, but not the blood of Iphigenia. Death is meted out to Eriphilia, substituted at the last moment on the sacrificial altar for Iphigenia, and Eriphilia is too calculating and vicious for her death to touch us. As Racine noted in his preface, he chose that variant of the Greek story in which the daughter of Theseus and Helen is sacrificed, suffering the fate the gods demanded for Iphigenia, the daughter of Agamemnon. Racine argues that it would have been in bad taste to have Iphigenia sacrificed, since she was innocent and virtuous. According to Aristotle, he is right, and Racine understood Aristotle better than any other dramatic author of his time. It is, therefore, all the more surprising that Racine did not wish to see that the sacrifice of Eriphilia—in view of her character—was just as contradictory to Aristotle's conception of tragedy as the sacrifice of Iphigenia would have been. For while the Greek philosopher held that the death of a good person is untragic, causing the spectator to suffer too much, he maintained also that the death of a bad person is equally untragic, since it cannot but gladden the one witnessing it. The true tragic emotion is more complicated.

In fact, Racine's whole argument is disingenuous. Iphigenia, though virtuous, could die in a properly Aristotelian tragedy if she were not the protagonist of the play—if, for instance, this role were reserved for her father, Agamemnon, who, in every variant of the story, agrees to her sacrifice so that the winds can blow and the Greek fleet sail. Like Georg Hegel, Sorën Kierkegaard understood that the protagonist in any tragedy about the sacrifice of Iphigenia would have to be Agamemnon. And when Kierkegaard resolved to oppose a hero of religion to a hero of tragedy, he elected for Abraham, intent on sacrificing Isaac, as against Agamemnon, prepared to kill his daughter.

The truth is that Racine wanted Iphigenia as his protagonist because he wanted a play with erotic interest. In *Iphigénie à Aulis*, Eriphilia is the rival of Iphigenia for the love of Achilles; Iphigenia gets Achilles and Eriphilia is sacrificed in her place. The winds blow, the ships sail, the evil character has been punished, the good girl saved, and what makes this consummation so utterly untragic is that the army of Agamemnon can now head, without a pang of conscience, for the brutal ten years of carnage on the plains of Troy.

The art of inflicting tragic death on the stage is a difficult one, and even with his ninth play, Racine had not yet mastered it. Did he succeed in *Phèdre?*

This play is considered by most critics to be Racine's greatest. It is his most famous, the one most universally known, and the role of Phaedra is as prized by French actresses as that of Hamlet by actors on the English-speaking stage. I do not wish to examine this judgment here. Surely, the play is great; as certainly, it is faulty. But the point I want to insist on here is that with *Phèdre*, Racine for the first time in his career succeeds in constructing a tragedy that ends with tragic death. *Bérénice*, his first real tragedy, did not.

Yet as has been pointed out by French critics, Phaedra is almost dead at the moment the play begins. She loves her stepson Hippolytus, but she is not reconciled to the sinfulness of an adulterous and incestuous passion; she never forgets that she is the daughter of Pasiphaë, queen of the pure sky, and of Minos, king of Hades, who sits in judgment on the dead. Her first words on her entrance express her hatred for life and her desire to die:

> No, not another step. I need your arm.
> I can scarcely stand erect. My strength is gone.
> My eyes shut on that sun I have not seen so long.
> My knees give way. Oenone, stay. You be strong.

> N'allons point plus avant, demeurons, chère Oenone.
> Je ne me soutiens plus; ma force m'abandonne:
> Mes yeux sont éblouis du jour que je revoi;
> Et mes genoux tremblants se dérobent sous moi.
> > (*Phèdre,* Act I, scene 3, my translation)

Oenone, after long questioning, succeeds in making Phaedra confess to the cause of her torment and of her desire to die. When Phaedra finally admits to her passion for Hippolytus, she does so with a relentless exactitude. There is nothing comparable to the truthfulness of this confession by any character in Shakespeare:

> My ills began far earlier. Scarcely had I
> Pledged with Aegeus' son our marriage-tie,
> Secure in that sweet joy a bride should know,
> When I, in Athens, met my haughty foe.
> I stared, I blushed, I paled, beholding him;
> A sudden turmoil set my mind aswim;
> My eyes no longer saw, my lips were dumb;
> My body burned, and yet was cold and numb.
> I knew myself possessed by Venus, whose
> Fierce flames torment the quarry she pursues.
> I thought to appease her then by constant prayer,
> And built for her a temple, decked with care.
> I made continual sacrifice, and sought
> In entrails for a spirit less distraught—
> But what could cure a lovesick soul like mine?
> In vain my hands burnt incense at her shrine:
> Though I invoked the Goddess' name, 'twas he

I worshiped; I saw his image constantly,
And even as I fed the altar's flame
Made offering to a god I dared not name.
I shunned him; but—O horror and disgrace!—
My eyes beheld him in his father's face.
At last I knew that I must act, must urge
Myself, despite myself, to be his scourge.
To rid me of the foe I loved, I feigned
A harsh stepmother's malice, and obtained
By ceaseless cries my wish that he be sent
From home and father into banishment.
I breathed once more, Oenone; once he was gone,
My blameless days could flow more smoothly on.
I hid my grief, was faithful to my spouse,
And reared the offspring of our luckless vows.
Ah, mocking Fate! What use was all my care?
Brought by my spouse himself to Troezen, there
I yet again beheld my exiled foe:
My unhealed wound began once more to flow.
Love hides no longer in these veins, at bay:
Great Venus fastens on her helpless prey.
I look with horror on my crime; I hate
My life; my passion I abominate.
I hoped by death to keep my honor bright,

And hide so dark a flame from day's pure light;
Yet, yielding to your tearful argument,
I've told you all; of that I'll not repent
Provided you do not, as death draws near,
Pour more unjust reproaches in my ear,
Or seek once more in vain to fan a fire
Which flickers and is ready to expire.[6]

---

6. Excerpt from "Act I, scene 3" trans. Richard Wilbur in *Phaedra: Tragedy in Five Acts* (1677) by Jean Racine, (New York: Harcourt Brace, 1984).

Mon mal vient de plus loin. À peine au fils d'Égée
Sous ses lois de l'hymen je m'étais engagée,
Mon repos, mon bonheur semblait être affermi;
Athènes me montra mon superbe ennemi:
Je le vis, je rougis, je pâlis à sa vue;
Un trouble s'éleva dans mon âme éperdue;
Mes yeux ne voyaient plus, je ne pouvais parler;
Je sentis tout mon corps et transir et brûler:
Je reconnus Vénus et ses feux redoutables,
D'un sang qu'elle poursuit, tourments inévitables.
Par des voeux assidus je crus les détourner:
Je lui batîs un temple, et pris soin de l'orner;
De victimes moi-même à toute heure entourée,
Je cherchais dans leurs flancs ma raison égarée:
D'un incurable amour remèdes impuissants!
En vain sur les autels ma main brûlait l'encens:
Quand ma bouche implorait le nom de la déesse,
J'adorais Hippolyte, et, le voyant sans cesse,

Je l'évitais partout. O comble de misère!
Mes yeux le retrouvaient dans les traits de son père.
Contre moi-même enfin j'osai me révolter:
J'excitai mon courage à le persécuter.

Je pressai son exil; et mes cris éternels
L'arrachèrent du sein et des bras paternels.
Je respirais, Oenone; et, depuis son absence,
Mes jours moins agités coulaient dans l'innocence;
Soumise a mon époux, et cachant mes ennuis,
De son fatal hymen je cultivais les fruits.
Vaines précautions! Cruelle destinée!
Par mon époux lui-même à Trézène amenée,
J'ai revu l'ennemi que j'avais éloigné:
Ma blessure trop vive aussitôt a saigné.

Ce n'est plus une ardeur dans mes veines cachée:
C'est Vénus tout entière a sa proie attachée.

(Act I, scene 3)

Phaedra, resolved to die, is kept alive by the rumor that Theseus, her husband, is dead, which makes her love for her stepson, as Oenone interprets it, "not so extraordinary." Ferdinand Brunetière thought the action of the play invalidated by the fact that it is based on Phaedra's belief in a false rumor. But surely this is captious criticism. Phaedra wants to believe that Theseus is dead; a woman in her state of mind would believe such a rumor, especially when it is believed by others. Why should Brunetière have assumed that characters inflamed by passion generally act on sound assumptions? No, there is no flaw in Phaedra's acceptance of the report that her husband is dead. Taking counsel from Oenone, she confesses her passion to Hippolytus. It was not her intention to do so; she had meant, instead, to proclaim her continuing love for Theseus. But Phaedra's passion is more truthful than she wants to be. Her confession, heard on the stage, has an absolute magic. We see what is most inward in a character, expressed against the character's own wish. She says:

> PHAEDRA: Yes, Prince, I burn for him with starved desire,
> Though not as he was seen among the shades,
> The fickle worshiper of a thousand maids,
> Intent on cuckolding the King of Hell;
> But constant, proud, a little shy as well,
> Young, charming, irresistible, much as we
> Depict our Gods, or as you look to me.
> He had your eyes, your voice, your virile grace,
> It was your noble blush that tinged his face
> When, crossing on the waves, he came to Crete
> And made the hearts of Minos' daughters beat.
> Where were you then? Why no Hippolytus
> Among the flower of Greece he chose for us?
> Why were you yet too young to join that band

Of heroes whom he brought to Minos' land?
You would have slain the Cretan monster then,
Despite the endless windings of his den.

My sister would have armed you with a skein
Of thread, to lead you from that dark domain.
But no: I'd first have thought of that design,
Inspired by love; the plan would have been mine.
It's I who would have helped you solve the maze,
My Prince, and taught you all its twisting ways.
What I'd have done to save that charming head!
My love would not have trusted to a thread.
No, Phaedra would have wished to share with you
Your perils, would have wished to lead you through
The Labyrinth, and thence have side by side
Returned with you; or else, with you, have died.[7]

Oui, prince, je languis, je brûle pour Thésée:
Je l'aime, non point tel que l'ont vu les enfers,

Mais fidèle, mais fier, et même un peu farouche,
Charmant, jeune, traînant tous les coeurs après soi,
Tel qu'on dépeint nos dieux, ou tel que je vous voi.
Il avait votre port, vos yeux, votre langage;
Cette noble pudeur colorait son visage,
Lorsque de notre Crète il traversa les flots,
Digne sujet des voeux des filles de Minos.
Que faisiez-vous alors? Pourquoi, sans Hippolyte,
Des héros de la Grèce assembla-t-il l'élite?

Par vous aurait péri le monstre de la Crète,
Malgré tous les détours de sa vaste retraite:

---

7. Excerpt from "Act 2, scene 5" in *Phaedra: Tragedy in Five Acts* (1677) by Jean Racine, trans. Richard Wilbur (New York: Harcourt Brace, 1984).

Pour en développer l'embarras incertain,
Ma soeur du fil fatal eût armé votre main.
Mais non: dans ce dessein je l'aurais devancée;
L'amour m'en eût d'abord inspiré la pensée;
C'est moi, prince, c'est moi dont l'utile secours
Vous eût du labyrinthe enseigné les détours:
Que de soins m'eût coutés cette tête charmante!
Un fil n'eût point assez rassuré votre amante:
Compagne du péril qu'il vous fallait chercher,
Moi-même devant vous j'aurais voulu marcher;
Et Phèdre au labyrinthe avec vous descendue
Se serait avec vous retrouvée ou perdue.

(Act 2, scene 5)

Hippolytus is shocked, morally outraged by this avowal; he is himself in love with Aricia, Theseus' ward. Rebuffed, Phaedra has to endure, besides, the return of Theseus. She permits Oenone to tell her husband that his son has made advances to her. In a great scene, Theseus vents his rage on Hippolytus and calls on Poseidon to kill the youth. Poseidon obliges: Hippolytus is killed by a monster from the sea, whereupon Theseus realizes he had never completely believed Phaedra's story. He tells her, not without bitterness, of his son's death. She admits the truth and dies, a suicide, offstage.

Why diminish a work so splendid? But why praise, beyond its evident merit, a work so great? In *Phèdre* Racine created a true tragedy, and dealt death to two of his main characters. Nevertheless, the play is not without fault. First of all, as we have seen, Phaedra *wanted* to die from the beginning. Her death, when it comes, is therefore less pathetic and less terrible than would be the death of someone who had all along desired life. Another very serious fault: the gods are involved in the action but not in a way that is clear. As Phaedra says, she is the victim of Aphrodite. And it is Poseidon who executes on Hippolytus the curse pronounced by Theseus. A god and a goddess are involved, but there is no logical or ideological relation between them.

In the Euripides play, from which Racine took his story, Hippolytus was a worshiper of Artemis and Phaedra was submissive to Aphrodite: Artemis and Aphrodite were at odds, even at war. Hence, for Euripides, the deaths of Phaedra and Hippolytus followed from an irreconcilable dispute between two goddesses, one representing spiritual power against sex, the other the force of sex as such. Hippolytus refuses Phaedra, not because he loves another woman, but because he does not and cannot love at all, being vowed to Artemis. Racine's play is undoubtedly greater than the play of Euripides; yet its construction is less logical, its final meaning less clear.

Racine had finally killed a sympathetic character in a great but faulty tragedy.

V

In a novel, characters can grow old and die; on the stage a character, whose dying is to interest us, must be put to death. There is a most interesting recognition of this in Shakespeare's *Henry IV*, Part II. Henry IV is dying. He has fallen asleep. Prince Hal enters, thinks his father already dead, removes the crown from his head, and speaks as if he, Prince Hal, were already Henry V. Henry IV awakes, accuses Price Hal of wanting to kill him. In a subsequent scene we learn that Henry IV has died. The cause of death is, of course, old age and exhaustion; yet, Henry IV has been killed symbolically by his son, and thus has had a proper theatrical end.

The taking of a person's life is the most drastic, the most dramatic act there is. Obviously the most fundamental sanctions are involved. To kill—to destroy a life one has not created—is an *imitatio dei*, even when committed by an atheist. What about the infliction of death on an imaginary person, a fiction, a character in a play?

In my view—I am aware it may strike the reader as a paradox—it is as difficult to justify inflicting death on a character as to justify killing a real person. Perhaps the difficulty will be best understood if one thinks in purely rational terms of passing judgment on another life. One will then realize that no reason is sufficient. Also, there is this fact: The best and most convinced assassins have always been fanatics. Has one the right to kill without being fanatical? And does the dramatist who wants to bring his protagonist to a tragic end also have to be a fanatic in some sense?

In his fine book *Death in the Afternoon*, Hemingway pointed out that the best killers of bulls have never been the best or most skilled matadors. Those bullfighters whom Hemingway most admired as artists, he did not admire most for their manner of killing. On the contrary, he claims, the men who killed best were fairly simple, uncomplicated persons, rather unskilled in the earlier passes, and deft only when it came to the ultimate blow. May this hold, too, for the infliction of death on the stage? Does the great writer of a great tragedy have to be a fairly simple, rather religious fellow, to deliver with sureness the final and culminating stroke?

Or is it sheer skill in dramaturgy which justifies the playwright in putting a character to death when death is required by his plot? Yet Corneille, in so many ways a more skillful playwright than Racine, was inept at inflicting death. In fact, his plays, so well plotted, become disorganized once death occurs. Corneille, the dramatist of the rational will, thought he could clarify everything, but he could not impose death purposefully. Once *Le Cid* has killed the father of Chimène, the play collapses. Chimène, though she loves the man who has killed him, must avenge her father's death. If she does not, she is unworthy to be the wife of Rodrigue, or a heroine of Corneille. On the other hand, Corneille has plotted his play so that Chimène and Rodrigue must marry, and he is unable to resolve this contradiction. Something similar occurs in *Horace*. The younger Horatius has seen his two brothers die at the hands of the three Curiatii. He succeeds in killing the three, one of whom is the husband of his sister. She curses her brother and Rome. Whereupon Corneille's hero kills her. This was intended to be an exalted moment, expressing patriotic emotion. But one imagines that Corneille was a bit sickened by his own hero's action. In fact, the old Horatius, the hero's father, does not admire what his son has done. Nor do the Roman leaders, who have the problem of hailing the young Horatius as the savior of Rome, and of justifying his murder of his own sister. The play is never a tragedy, and it ends in what is very close to farce. The hero is acclaimed, but those who applaud him would prefer to try him for murder.

One needs something better than reasons to justify killing. This holds both in real and in imagined action.

What can justify killing on the stage? The feeling that the death of the character is destined. But what is meant by the word *destiny*?

If a rational meaning could be assigned to this term, there would be no such thing as tragedy. Yet how can the term *destiny* be understood, if not rationally?

Francis Bradley and Henri Bergson have pointed out that certain truths appear evident to consciousness when felt with a certain intensity, and that at a lesser intensity, these truths appear as contradictions. Does this notion apply here?

Let us take a play of Shakespeare, commonly regarded as a tragedy, but in which the death of each significant and appealing character disgusts us with life and with the play, too. In *King Lear*, the deaths of Gloucester, Lear, and Cordelia are all horrible and unjustifiable in aesthetic terms. There are two remarks in *Lear* which relate to destiny, and they contradict each other:

> As flies to wanton boys, are we to th' gods,
> They kill us for their sport.

and

> The gods are just, and of our pleasant vices,
> Make instruments to plague us.

Clearly, these remarks refute each other. The difficulty of thinking that both are true is the chief problem of Shakespeare's play and prevents it from being a true tragedy. We cannot accept or be exalted by the deaths of Gloucester, Cordelia, or Lear himself.

There is no destiny in any of these deaths, for in a true vision of destiny, the contradiction implied by the two views that (1) the gods are wanton in their treatment of us, and (2) the gods are just in their treatment of us, would be transcended. The deaths of Lear and Gloucester seem to follow from the proposition that the gods are just. The death of Cordelia—which Samuel Johnson found so objectionable, and which prompted him to suggest that Shakespeare was never at his best but always somewhat labored when it came to writing tragedy—seems to follow from the proposition that we are to the gods like flies to wanton boys. So that the deaths in *King Lear* follow from conflicting principles. The work is simply not unified. And this is one reason it tends to be ineffective on the stage.

Shakespeare did, of course, write *Macbeth*. When he wrote *King Lear* he did not, I think, have the single vision which tragedy requires. "Let your eye be single, and your body will be filled with light." Altered to our purpose, and addressed to the dramatist, these words of the New Testament would read: Let your eye be single and you will be able to bring the darkness of death tragically to the stage.

Shakespeare must have felt at some moment in his career that his interests were too varied, his skepticism too acute, for him to kill his own characters tragically. Even as the Duke of Vienna, in *Measure for Measure*, questions his fitness for punishing his subjects severely, so, I suggest, Shakespeare questioned his right to kill dramatically. He did not lack the technical means, to be sure; neither, of course, did Corneille. But Corneille, great playwright and poet though he was, did not have the kind of conscience we have a right to assume Shakespeare had, in giving up tragedy altogether to create an entirely new kind of drama.

The vision of the tragedian has to be single and simple. Are we back then with the thought that the tragic artist has to be an uncomplicated person? Religious if not devout? Or not unlike those men Hemingway described as the best killers in the bull ring? Now I would not altogether reject the notion, often held, that the great tragic artists have been religious persons. Feodor Dostoevsky was one of the most complicated of men;

perhaps he was not a believer, but certainly he wanted to believe. In his sophistication, he desired to be naïve. Though not a playwright, he was the most dramatic of all novelists—and the most tragic, too. In the *Brothers Karamazov*, Fyodor Karamazov is killed, in fact, by his illegitimate and epileptic son Smerdyakov. The real murderer, of course, is his eldest son Ivan, who has indicated by certain signs—though not in so many words—to Smerdyakov, who admires him, that he, Ivan, would be pleased by the old man's death. Can we say that Ivan killed his father knowingly? We cannot. Can we say he killed his father without knowing? We cannot say that either. The murder of the old Karamazov would have satisfied Aristotle completely. There is nothing more sophisticated in all of ancient or modern dramaturgy. No simple-minded dramatist could have brought off such an effect.

Dostoevsky was able to feel Fyodor Karamazov's death as wanton and yet as justified. From the outset of the novel, Dostoevsky had presented Fyodor as hated by his sons—all except the near-saint, Alyosha. The inability of Fyodor's sons to love him doomed him; they would have had to be saints for him not to have been murdered.[8] Thus his murder is inevitable, and yet his sons are responsible. This seems to us a paradox on reflection, not when we read the *Brothers Karamazov*.

Could Dostoevsky have so succeeded without being or wanting to be religious? It is doubtful. The desire for a simple faith can be the equivalent, in art at least, of faith itself. Of course, such desire must be genuine. In whom could it be more genuine than in a man tormented by his own complexity? There are many art forms which admit personal complexity as a value. The art of tragedy is quite different. Here complexity is of value only as something to be overcome.

To avoid any misunderstanding, I wish to make clear that religious belief is not the only kind of belief necessary for that

---

8. Alyosha tried to be a saint. His motive may have been to be capable of not killing his father. As matters turned out, though, his interest in the death of the saint, Zossima, prevented him from intervening when he might have saved his father and his brothers.

simplification and purity of vision that tragedy requires. Shakespeare, who we tend to think was not religious, did write *Macbeth*. (It is to be noted, though, that this play is the one work of his which projects a necessary order beyond nature's.) Let us put the matter this way: the single view necessary for the tragic poet cannot go without a certain humiliation of the mind, through its acceptance of an inflexible order. Such acceptance was not at all characteristic of Shakespeare. It would be surprising, though, if a man who sympathized with so many postures of consciousness did not, at some time in his career, yield completely to a feeling for fatality.

VI

Racine's life and career can be described as a voluntary yielding to different but always inflexible orders: first to that of the Jansenists, who educated him at Port Royal; then to that of classical Greek tragedy, which he never questioned, though his predecessor in the theatre, Corneille, had; finally to that of the court of Louis XIV. In his excellent book, *Racine and Poetic Tragedy*, Eugene Vinaver writes: "The classical doctrine left the poet the choice of sentiments. Yet, there again Racine forbids himself any boldness and, even in his predilection for certain moral states, does nothing but follow the tastes and tendencies of the century, accommodated to his manner." Vinaver denies that Racine was ever original in his understanding of classical tragedy, but insists that such originality as he shows—and at times this is very marked—was the inevitable result of a good mind yielding to an order which it had merely tried to understand, but not to change.

There was no criticism of the monarchy in Racine's plays—as there is in the works of Molière and Corneille. For most of Racine's life, no doubt, the authority of Louis XIV over Racine was absolute. There is a story that once Racine formulated a program to help the poor and presented it to the King, who is said to have replied: "Just because you're a great poet, don't think you can be a minister." Racine at once put his project aside and is not known to have ever again directly intervened in politics.

How are we to understand this voluntary submission of Racine to religious, classical, and royal authority? It is precisely what makes him exceptional in his own century; and among all the great dramatists of the age, taking into account those of England and Spain as well as of France, Racine was the only one who really tried to be faithful to Aristotle, who never criticized the figure of his king, and who never questioned the religion in which he was indoctrinated as a child. How different he was, not only from his contemporaries, Corneille and Molière, but from Christopher Marlowe and Shakespeare, and also from the great Spaniards, Lope de Vega and Pedro Calderón!

In the conduct of his life, Racine exhibits a conspicuous purposefulness in advancing his career. Was this dramatist of such poetic purity fundamentally a careerist? Why was there in him no feeling of rebellion, no violence against what was already canonized in religion, politics, and art? I would suggest that Racine concerned himself in the main with the perfect fulfillment of his role, which was to write tragedy. What did not help him in that role was inessential; he must have intuitively felt that the acceptance of the various orders to which he did submit—at times in the interest of his career—was helpful to him in his life task. There is something wonderfully adroit in his inner knowledge of what he needed in order to fulfill himself and to perfect the image we have of him. But we would not have had this image without his last play.

VII

Racine was writing *Athalie*. He had succeeded with *Esther*. His choice of a subject for the new work to be given at Saint-Cyr was the story of Athaliah, who had now found the perfect poet to describe her fate. It is interesting to consider how the two destinies, those of the poet and of the biblical Queen intersect. Athaliah, who had remained fairly insignificant for two thousand years, was now to express herself in one of the greatest tragedies ever written. Racine, who had trained himself to kill tragically on the stage, was to do so perfectly for the first time in his career.

But there were many practical reasons why Racine should not have chosen the subject. Had he been concerned at this point with Louis XIV's opinion of him, and not with faithfully completing his own image, he would surely have elected for some other story. As a courtier, Racine could not but have been aware that Louis XIV, having destroyed Port Royal and imprisoned the leading Jansenists—including the niece of the great Henri Arnaud himself—would not take kindly to a religious play based on the Old Testament, in which a ruling monarch was presented as the enemy of God and overthrown in a revolution led by a priest. Surely Racine knew this. Why then did he risk for the first time in his life the King's displeasure?

Racine was older now. He had a career behind him, one which the court had favored and finally frustrated. Without the support of the court, he would not have written *Andromaque* or *Bérénice*. But it was a court intrigue which had led to the failure of what he considered his greatest work, *Phèdre*. There is something else, too, to be considered. In *Iphigénie à Aulis*, which has been called Racine's "royal tragedy" but is no tragedy at all, Racine, the orphan, had made the villain an orphan, killed her off at the play's close, and thereby destroyed any chance of the work ending tragically. In writing *Athalie*, Racine again chose to deal with an orphan, Joash. This time an orphan would be the hero—backed by the greatest king of all: the Lord. So supported, Racine could risk displeasing Louis XIV. Though he was still submissive to authority, this time Racine would do the one thing which as a writer of tragedy he had thus far left undone.

He also felt free to violate the unities of time and place. In *Esther* he had violated the Aristotelian canon calling for a definite and single place; in *Athalie* both time and place are left undefined. Moreover, as in *Esther*, in *Athalie* he introduced a chorus. What is the reason for the Chorus in his last play?

As Aristotle pointed out, the Chorus must be functional. This is not always the case, even in the works of Sophocles. It is hard to see what function the Chorus has in *The Women of Trachis*. Greek scholars have noted, too, the purely conventional character of the Chorus in *Philoctetes*. Apparently Sophocles himself was not incapable of falling into neoclassicism. But in *Athalie* the Chorus, composed of young girls, in words taken from the Psalms and put by Racine into the very purest French, chants a continuous paean to the majesty, might, and love of the Old Testament God. Since it is fundamentally God who is the victor over Athaliah, the verses of the young girls, in adoration of His glory, have the further purpose of indicating how weak Athaliah is, how certain her destruction. I have the impression in reading the play that after each chorus—unheard by Athaliah; she is never present while the Chorus speaks—she bleeds a little. The verses are like the banderillas placed in the side of the bull by the matador to weaken and madden him, preparing him for death.

Athaliah begins to die with the first line of the play uttered by the slightly comical Abner, her military chief, who is faithful to the true God at the same time that he is loyal to Athaliah as the legitimate Queen of Judah. Abner does not suspect that a male descendant of David still lives. And, although he does not approve Athaliah's worship of Baal, he will not, for religious reasons, violate the monarchical principle. His first words are:

> Yes, I have come into this Temple now
> To adore the Everlasting; . . .[9]

The dropping in on God by Abner, the main support of Athaliah, sets the tone for each subsequent happening. Jehoiada, the High Priest, protests to Abner against the worship of Baal in the kingdom, which has the Queen's backing. Abner would like to be indignant, too, but does not think it proper to be critical of his sovereign. He suggests that the time of miracles is past and brings down on himself a ringing denunciation by the High Priest Jehoiada, who accuses him of lacking faith. However, the priest knows that there is a living male descendant of David;

9. *Oui, je viens dans son temple adorer l'Éternel;*

Abner does not. After their interview the High Priest confides to his wife, Jehosheba, that the time has come to reveal Joash to the people.

Athaliah has a premonition that Joash exists. She has had a dream, which she recounts to her advisers: her mother, Jezebel, has appeared to her

> In the dreadful deep of night
> My mother Jezebel rose up before me,[10]

and told her that she, too, is about to be overwhelmed by the cruel Old Testament God. Immediately afterward, Althaliah, still dreaming, sees a young boy in priest's dress. The sight of him raises her spirit; she admires his noble and modest air, his gentleness; whereupon the boy plunges a dagger into her breast. She dreams of the boy again and he repeats his action. Deeply troubled on awakening, she thinks of propitiating the God her mother's specter has warned her against. She goes to the temple and sees a young boy in every respect exactly like the boy who has killed her in her dream. Who is this boy? Neither Abner nor Mathan, the High Priest of Baal, know.

Athaliah has already foreseen her own execution. On the point of being destroyed by God, she seems to absorb, by a kind of divine contagion, God's mercy, even as prior to this she had absorbed God's wrath. She goes again to the temple, sees Joash, is again struck by his nobility, pride, and grace; and in an astonishing scene offers to take him to her palace and treat him as her son; she remarks that she has no son and suggests that he might become her heir. The boy rejects her overtures. The extraordinary thing about the scene is the fascination of Athaliah with the boy who, her dream has already informed her, is to be her executioner. Lucien Goldmann interprets Athaliah's attraction to Joash as springing from that uncertainty of judgment noted by most historians in ruling groups about to be

---

10. *C'etait dans l'horreur d'une profonde nuit.* Excerpt from *Jean Racine: Five Plays,* trans. Kenneth Muir (New York: Hill & Wang, 1960).

overthrown, and I think Goldmann is right in this observation—which points up the extraordinary realism of Racine. All the same, in tragedy, psychological acuteness has mainly a negative value. It aids the dramatist in avoiding error. In other words, Athaliah's weakness for Joash is psychologically plausible, but we are not touched because it is psychologically plausible; we are touched because she loves her grandson, not knowing him to be her grandson, and because his victory over her will mean her death.

She has already died four preparatory deaths by the end of scene seven of the second act: twice in her dream, again when she sees Joash in the temple for the first time, then again in the temple when he repudiates her offer to take him to her palace.

Of course, it is the High Priest who actually plots Athaliah's destruction. After her first two visits to the temple, he induces her to return a third time on the pretext of revealing to her David's "secret treasure." This is not, as Athaliah thinks, gold, but Joash, whose ascent to power will mean her death. She comes with Abner and finds that the assembled Levites have made obeisance to Joash: the High Priest has revealed him as their legitimate king. Abner turns against Athaliah, and her doom is sealed.

Some have questioned whether the High Priest is truly noble. If he is not, then, of course, my claim that Athaliah is killed perfectly, dramatically speaking, would be invalid. Voltaire, having praised the play above all other tragedies, finally elected to attack it as a piece of monumental superstition. He saw at once that the way to attack it was to diminish the character of Jehoiada, whom he called a "bloody, authoritarian priest."

If one has no sympathy for Jehoiada, then *Athalie* is no tragedy. For the form of tragedy requires that we sympathize with both the executioner and the victim. This was suggested by Aristotle when he said that tragedy relieves us of pity and terror, and made still clearer by James Joyce in *The Portrait of the Artist as a Young Man*, when Stephen Daedalus, commenting on Aristotle's *Poetics*, says that in tragedy pity unites us with the sufferer, terror with the cause of suffering. The difficulty of most dramatists trying to produce tragedy is not so much to create a sympathetic victim as to create a sympathetic executioner. After the Greeks, it was probably Racine who did this best, and I have said that he only did it perfectly in his last play, *Athalie*.

But *did* he in *Athalie*? Is Jehoiada ignoble or unsympathetic? One can answer by saying that he does nothing by himself, that all his actions are determined by God. Such was Sainte-Beuve's view:

> The great, or rather the only character in *Athalie*, from its first to its last line, is God. The Lord is there, above the high priest and the boy, and at every moment of this powerful and simple story they are controlled by Him. He Himself remains invisible and immutable; always His presence is felt, although hidden by that Holy of Holies to which Jehoiada goes once each year, always returning stronger because of Him whose strength cannot be measured. This unity, this omnipotence of the Eternal Character, far from destroying the drama, or reducing it to a continuous paean, becomes the dramatic action itself, and rising above all characters in the play, acts on everyone of them ...[11]

Nevertheless, Jehoiada must be justified in his human personality. He is a fanatic, and one can say against him that being fanatical he is incapable of moral experience. Jehoiada has of course dignity, courage, and faith. He belongs to an oppressed minority; and he is an instrument of God's purpose. But these facts are not sufficient, as Racine must have known, to make him sympathetic enough for us to accept him as the executioner of Athaliah. One of the most brilliant moments of the play occurs when the High Priest has a prophetic vision and sees that his own son will be put to death by Joash, when the latter is King. Because Jehoiada accepts the death of his son for the sake of God, we can accept him humanly as Athaliah's executioner.

---

11. Sainte-Beuve, *Port-Royal*.

Athaliah is caught in the temple. The Levites surround her. She sees Joash crowned. Abner deserts her. The Queen knows she is doomed, and dooms herself once again:

> So that this son reigns, Thy care
> And the work of Thy hands; so that to signalize
> His new gained empire, he will now be made
> To plunge the dagger in my breast.[12]

The Queen, about to die, foresees, though, that her grandson will eventually desert David and act as if he were Ahab's heir:

> Rebellious to Your wish, indifferent to Your will
> This grandson of Ahab shall confound You still!
> He'll flee Your law—I see it—even toward Hell!
> The avenger of Athaliah, Ahab, and Jezebel![13]

Athaliah, who grows weaker throughout the play wooing her own destruction, at the last foresees and boldly asserts the future treachery to the God of her destroyer. Having died so many times in her imagination, when she finally is about to be executed, she prophesies her future vengeance.

With Athaliah's last speech, Racine completed the old Queen's life in tragedy, and his own career as a tragic poet.

---

12.   *Qu'il règne donc ce fils . . .*
        Et que, pour signaler son empire nouveau,
        On lui fasse en mon sein enfoncer le couteau!

                                        (Act 5, scene 6)

13.   *Conforme à son aïeul, à son père semblable,*
        On verra de David l' héritier détestable
        Abolir tes honneurs, profaner ton autel,
        Et venger Athalie, Achab et Jézabel.

                                        (Act 5, scene 6)

WAS ANYTHING HIDDEN
FROM SOPHOCLES?

IT SEEMS THERE is much in the plays of Aeschylus that is still hidden from our scholars. Such is the conclusion of H. D. F. Kitto's *Poiesis*, in which the classicist singles out for special attack his British colleagues Sir Denys Page and Hugh Lloyd-Jones and the American scholars Richard Kuhns and Richmond Lattimore. Looking backward, he even takes on the respected Sir Richard C. Jebb, to whom we are indebted for a good, if Victorian, Sophocles.

Page thinks that the Zeus of the *Oresteia* was terribly, primitively vengeful, but Kitto thinks Page ought to have noticed that Orestes has a personal desire for vengeance, and in the *Choephori* he says so plainly. Page claims that Paris, who is referred to in the *Oresteia*, was "driven to his crime by supernatural powers against his better judgment." But where, asks Kitto, is the "better judgment" of Paris mentioned except in Page's note? Kitto writes: "Aeschylus himself was so remiss that he said not a word about it." Lloyd-Jones claims that Aeschylus was lacking in advanced conceptions. He does not see, replies Kitto, that the Erinyes of the *Oresteia* are strikingly like the Erinyes of that "advanced thinker, Heracleitus." Kuhns, in analyzing Cassandra's relation to Apollo, devotes several pages to Coronis, who is not mentioned, Kitto notes—not even once—by Aeschylus. Lattimore accuses the tragic poet of having grossly magnified in *The Persians* the importance of the battle of Psittáleia; he does, of course, concede that "there is some difference between a poet ... and ... [a] liar." To which Kitto replies that if Aeschylus had exaggerated to the degree Lattimore claims about a battle whose details were thoroughly known to his audience, we would have to call him a maniac, not just a

93

liar. The Athenian audience understood, as Lattimore does not, that the importance the poet attached to the battle was dramatic and not historical. And of Jebb's discussion of the trial scene in the *Eumenides*, Kitto asks: "Why did Jebb fail to see what the text says, on two points that directly bore on his argument?"

So even what the Greek text plainly says may be hidden from our scholars. How can this be? Kitto advances what I think the right—he calls it a simple—explanation: "We come to the play with settled convictions of our own, what F. M. Cornford called 'unchallenged and unsuspected presuppositions.' If there is a conflict between one of these and the text, it is the text that must give way." Obviously, the presuppositions of contemporary scholars are quite different from those that were held earlier in this century. On the history of our explanations of Greek tragedy, Kitto has this to say:

> Two generations ago the belief in Progress, in sweetness and light, was dominant; scholars fathered these *idées reçues* upon Aeschylus and tried to find in him an elevated Zeus-religion. Today, we can see clearly enough that this was a local aberration, sustained only by neglecting the evidence that did not suit. The time in which we are living now has no faith in continuous progress, but is fascinated by the primitive, the dark, the irrational. Punctually Greek Tragedy takes on the corresponding colour. One set of *idées reçues* takes the place of the other; that is all. The pendulum was bound to swing, no doubt; but need we stand directly in its path and get knocked flat? The new *idées reçues* can easily be fathered on Aeschylus if we can accept the assumptions just listed; they take away all our controls. If we can persuade ourselves that in no way was Aeschylus an intelligent artist, it is easy to conclude that he was not an intelligent thinker either.

I, for one, find this explanation quite convincing, but it has left me with a question that is not raised by Kitto: if we are so controlled by our presuppositions that what is plainly writ in the text of an author can remain hidden from our scholars, may there not be something in the text that was hidden from the author himself? Was not he, too, controlled by presuppositions? To point my question: could there be anything in the plays of Aeschylus not known to Aeschylus?

As I remarked, Kitto does not raise this question, and clearly he wants not to raise it; his whole effort has been to assert the competence of the Greek dramatists in the choice and disposition of the materials they used—that is to say, in their *poiesis*—and to back their *poiesis* against the confusion of commentators. The hidden, for Kitto, is what is hidden from critics and scholars.

Here, however, we may challenge Kitto's view with the judgment that Sophocles is said to have made of his predecessor. We have it from Athenaeus, a learned writer of the third Christian century, that Sophocles reproached Aeschylus with the remark that "even if he wrote as he should, he did it unconsciously."[1] If we can accept the report of Athenaeus as reliable—and to my knowledge it has not been questioned—then in the view of none other than Sophocles it was precisely the rightness of the *poiesis* of Aeschylus that was hidden from the dramatist. And since Athenaeus called the remark Sophocles made about Aeschylus a "reproach," we may assume that Sophocles thought he himself knew the rightness of his *poiesis* and practiced it, unlike Aeschylus, consciously.

Now, did he? This question is more radical than the one I raised about Aeschylus, since Sophocles was of course the more conscious artist. We may assume, however, that he could not have been artistically omniscient, despite the fact that this is the way Kitto tends to see him. So, on the one hand, there are the critics and scholars who, as Kitto points out, make the dramatist (Aeschylus or Sophocles) seem unintelligent; on the other hand, there is Kitto arguing against them, his assumption being that the dramatist (in this case, Sophocles) is flawless and that his *poiesis* can be justified in every respect. Kitto has written in his book *Greek Tragedy*, "Purely formal criticism of

---

1. According to Athenaeus, Aeschylus composed only when drunk.

Sophocles, by rule, is an impertinence." Now here I am not ready to follow the distinguished classicist. If, as the adage has it, a cat may look at a queen, then a critic of drama may look at the king of tragedians, but to look means to see whatever is there—the faults along with the virtues. Any other approach of the critic to Sophocles, I think, would lead to a mystique of the dramatist, like the mystique of Shakespeare in England and of Racine in France during the nineteenth century; the mystique surrounding these two was no doubt responsible for a great deal of unintelligent praise, which in turn led, I believe, to Leo Tolstoy's abusive rejection of both.

Do we have any reason, though, for thinking that Sophocles was unaware of certain elements in his own work, that he was not all-knowing in his *poiesis*? The fact is that there are difficulties in the plays of this dramatist which Kitto either ignores or does his best (and his best, I contend, is not good enough) to conjure away. I shall take up three of these difficulties, the first of which Kitto does not even treat. In the *Trachiniae*, Deianeira decides offstage to send the shirt with the centaur's blood on it to Heracles. This is the most important decision of her life. Why does not Sophocles have her make it on stage, even as his Antigone, in full view of the audience, decides to bury the body of Polyneices, even as the other protagonists of the dramatist—Oedipus, Electra, Ajax, and Philoctetes decide their fates before us? Any playwright who knows his craft—who is going to suggest that Sophocles did not know his?—will strive to have his characters make their decisions openly. So Sophocles' treatment of Deianeira has to be explained, though Kitto has chosen not to. However, he has faced up to two other problematic moments in the work of the dramatist that are raised by the following questions: Why does Ajax imply in his speech to Tecmessa that he has changed his mind and will not commit suicide? And why does Antigone, just before she is led to her death, assert that she would not have done for her husband or her child what she has done for her brother, justifying this remark with a sophism?

Let us first look at the problem raised by Antigone's speech and at Kitto's efforts to resolve it. In *Greek Tragedy*, Kitto points out that the sophism of Antigone was probably borrowed from Herodotus—what he calls one of the finest borrowings in literature. But he does not explain here why Antigone needed the sophism. In *Form and Meaning in Drama*, however, he gives this explanation: "Antigone is neither a philosopher nor a *dévote*, but a passionate impulsive girl, and we need not expect consistency from one such, when for doing what for her was her manifest duty she is about to be buried alive, without a gleam of understanding from anybody."

What is the sophism of Antigone? Having observed the funeral rites for her brother and just before being led to death herself, she makes this statement:

> I would not, if I had been the mother of children, nor if my husband, dead, lay rotting in death have taken this task on myself in defiance of my fellow citizens. In observance of what law do I say this? As for a husband, if he died, there could have been another, and another child from another man if I lost the first. But with my mother and father hidden in the realm of Hades, no brother could be born for me.

The problem of this speech is stated more powerfully by Bernard Knox than it is by Kitto, and obviously Knox is less sure of his solution.[2] Of the speech Knox writes in his book *The Heroic Temper*:

> Ever since Goethe, who found it *"ganz schlecht,"* expressed in his naïve and Olympian way the hope that scholars "would find it spurious," the argument has continued between those who find the lines intolerable and those who, most of them with various degrees of misgiving, defend the text. Opinions are still as divided as ever, and no conclusive proofs are likely to be forthcoming; every reader must make up his own mind. It must however never be forgotten that to attack the

---

2. From Knox I have taken the translation of Antigone's lines.

authenticity of the passage is in this instance an especially radical piece of surgery, almost a counsel of
despair. . . . On the other hand it is no use closing our
eyes to the difficulties the speech presents. Jebb, who
condemns it, states the case against it most eloquently.
"Her feet slip from the rock on which they are set; she
suddenly gives up that which, throughout the drama,
has been the immovable basis of her action—the universal and unqualified validity of the divine law." There
can be no doubt that she does exactly that; Hades desires the burial of a husband and a child just as much
as that of a brother. She has for the moment ceased to
speak as the champion of the gods below. Only for the
moment, for in her very last speech as she is led off to
her tomb she reasserts her claim. "See what I suffer . . .
for my reverent observance of reverence."

Knox concedes the illogicality of Antigone's sophism. He would
have it, though, that "the illogicality can be understood." How?

. . . for Antigone the distinction between living and dead
has ceased to exist. She has for some time now regarded herself as dead and she talks to Polyneices as if
he were alive; she is dead and about to be entombed
in the land of the living, he is alive in the world of
the dead.

I think this explanation even poorer than Kitto's; it is just a
piece of metaphysics. But at least Knox has not tried to blame
the critics and scholars for the problem presented by Antigone's
speech, whereas Kitto tends to blame everyone but Sophocles.
And clearly the objections of Goethe can hardly be disposed of
on the ground that the poet knew little of dramaturgy.

Ajax's speech Knox does consider in all its real difficulty,
though he does not succeed in explaining it. He writes:

The famous speech . . . has caused a dispute among the
critics which is still alive. . . . Does Ajax intend to de-

ceive his hearers, masking his unchanged purpose, death, with ambiguous words? There can be no doubt that he does deceive Tecmessa and his sailors; Tecmessa later complains bitterly that she was "cast out from his love and deceived." But does Ajax consciously and deliberately deceive her and the chorus? If so, we are faced with a problem as difficult as that raised by the other point of view—a serious inconsistency of character. The character of Ajax is Achillean; it may be all too easily tempted to extremes of violence, but not to deceit. Many learned and subtle critics of the play have tried to skirt this difficulty, to present us with an Ajax who deliberately deceives and yet remains the simple direct outspoken hero of the tradition, but they are attempting the impossible. They succeed at best in finding a more complicated and euphemistic formula for the fact that, according to this view, Ajax consciously and deliberately deceives his hearers. And that, as Bowra forcefully (and rightly) points out, is the last thing we can imagine Ajax doing.

If Knox is unable to answer the question he states so clearly, Kitto tries to dispose of the problem rather than to solve it. He writes: " . . . when at last his [Ajax's] pity is aroused, and he sees what his death will mean to others, he can do nothing for them; only disengage himself from them with words which seem to say one thing but mean another." But this hardly answers our question as to whether Ajax did or did not mean to deceive Tecmessa. As for Knox's solution, it is quite hopeless. He claims that Ajax could hardly be intent on deceiving anyone in making this speech, since for most of it he is talking to himself. But it is the *last* part of Ajax's speech, when clearly he is *not* talking to himself but to Tecmessa, that has to be explained. I quote from Kitto's translation of the text

> Tecmessa, go within;
> Pray to the gods, and pray again, that I
> May win from them all that my heart desires

And you, my friends, pay me this tribute too.
Tell Teucer, when he comes, to care for me
And to be kind to you, for I must make
A certain journey. Do this that I ask,
And though my fortunes now are very low,
Soon you may hear that I am come to safety.

It seems to me evident that the problems that have been raised about Antigone's and Ajax's speeches and about Deianeira's decision made offstage to send her gift of poison to Heracles cannot be resolved by trying to fathom the artistic intention of Sophocles, that is to say, his *poiesis*. Kitto has tried—not too seriously, I should say—and so have Knox and C. M. Bowra and Francis Letters and Jebb, not to speak of the German scholars. And all the efforts I have seen are similar in this respect: they are based on what is taken to be Sophocles' intention. It is time we turned to what may have been hidden from him.

To be sure, we need a new theory of the hidden, a theory that is not just a psychological theory, like Freud's, which assumes that what is hidden in the writer's work is transferred to it from what the writer kept hidden from himself. To find out what he hid from himself we would have to know his life rather well. This is hardly possible with the Greek dramatists, considering how meager are the biographies we have of them. Moreover, the Freudian theory involves a certain monotony and even a mediocrity of the hidden; people tend to repress the very same drives, and it is always a sameness the psychoanalytic critic turns up even when dealing with the most mysterious authors and works. Then, too, is not the range of the hidden wide enough to hold much more than we repress? Gottfried Wilhelm Leibniz once defined music making as "the hidden arithmetical activity of someone who does not know he is counting." Certainly, Leibniz did not mean in offering this definition that the activity of counting is repressed by the music maker or that music making is the sublimation of a drive toward arithmetic.

Just what did Leibniz mean? First, though, I want to call attention to a theory of the hidden available to us that is not psychological and does not require our commitment to a disputable position in philosophy or in any of the sciences. The theory I have in mind is the *phenomenological theory*, which is very simple and almost obvious. It merely asserts that in order to throw light on some particular matter one must actually increase the darkness surrounding other matters. Let me put it somewhat differently: to consider a problem I have to face up to it, concentrate on it, so that it can become the theme of my attention; but then I cannot concentrate on or take as my theme whatever it is in my mind that enables me to make this particular matter thematic. I cannot look two ways at once, let us say, both at some particular object and at the same time at whatever it is in my mind that makes me want to look at that object. The concepts I form about the object are called by the phenomenologist *thematic concepts*; the concepts which are the medium for my thinking about that object are called by the phenomenologist *operative concepts*. The operative concepts of the music maker, according to Leibniz, are arithmetical; his theme, all the same, is music.[3]

So the operative concepts in any act of attention are always hidden, and to say now that his operative concepts were hidden from Sophocles is not to point out something special about him but something held universally, as true of him as of everyone. The something then that was hidden from Sophocles were the operative concepts whereby he made his material thematic, but can we know what these concepts were?

Georg Hegel thought he knew what was hidden from Sophocles, as well as from Aeschylus and Euripides. According to Hegel, Greek tragedy was centered on the conflict between the *polis* and the family, and this conflict was so thoroughgoing that no one who acted drastically was able to escape it. To act meant to sin against either the family or the *polis*. Thus, anyone who acted was necessarily guilty. However, he could be regarded as innocent, since his guilt followed not from a decision to sin

---

3. Paul de Man has superficialized the phenomenological view into his own version of insight plus blindness. He reduces an *idea*, together with the phenomenological explanation of it, to the status of a mere *fact*.

but merely from a decision to act. And does not Aristotle himself tell us that the hero of tragedy is guilty of a deed for which he is in some sense blameless? Here I believe we have the operative concept of Greek tragedy: the hero was necessarily guilty and just as necessarily not guilty. Guilt in innocence and innocence in guilt—this is the only way we can characterize the heroes of tragedy. But we are not to suppose that the Greek tragedians knew that these were their operative concepts.

Let us now take up the question of Deianeira. Why did Sophocles have her decide offstage? Now the answer is simple: the story of Deianeira and Heracles was a purely domestic one and did not involve the issue of family and city; hence the guilt of Deianeira in acting as she did could not be necessary and had to be contingent, just as her innocence, consequently, had to be contingent, too. There was no way in which Sophocles could make her blameless in guilt as Electra, Oedipus, Antigone, and even Creon are. I think Sophocles hid the contingent character of his heroine's guilt and innocence by having her make her decision offstage.

And what about the troubling matter of Antigone's speech? Why does she say that what she has done for her brother she would not have done for a husband or a child? Certainly, we must believe that she would have buried the body of a husband or a child even as she buried the body of her brother. Why then does she say the contrary? My assumption is that Sophocles was no more aware that Antigone represented the family exclusively than he was that Deianeira represented nothing, not even the family. Goethe could know, as could even the Victorian Jebb, something about Antigone which Sophocles could not. Thus, the Greek poet could write a speech for his heroine that is indeed "*ganz schlecht*" (altogether bad)—something that a classical scholar who is not even a playwright would know better than to write.

And, finally, about the speech of Ajax. Was he trying to deceive Tecmessa? What if he was? He had already sinned criminally against the Greek enterprise, having tried to kill the leaders under whom he served; now his aim was to sin criminally against his family: to leave his wife without a husband, his son without a father, and his brother Teucer without a defense against their father, Telamon. One intent on a crime is very likely to conceal what he intends, however distinguished his past outspokenness, especially from those who are bound to suffer from his deed. Knox objects that deceit is not only untypical but contrary to the character of Ajax. To be sure, but Ajax's attempt to kill the Greek leaders while they slept was also untypical of him, and this attempt Knox finds—I don't know why—typical. Knox has not reflected on the fact that one of the miseries of the tragic hero is to be forced on occasion to act out of character. *Éthos anthrópou daímon,* said Heraclitus: character is the daimon of man. To which I would reply: it is not the only daimon, for sometimes the situation, as in the *Ajax* of Sophocles, may impose on the protagonist a daimonism not consonant with his nature.

One may reject the solutions I have advanced, but I think that at least I must be granted this much: my solutions are not forced, nor were they reached by striving after subtleties. Moreover, the hypothesis about Greek tragedy I have advanced may also be helpful in treating Euripides, whose works are on the whole more problematic than are those of Sophocles.

Three general theories have been put forth about Euripides: (1) that his plays are fantasies; (2) that his plays concern not people but symbols; and (3) that each play of his is two plays— an outer play for the general public and within it a play secret to all but the initiated. Now, the very fact that these theories have been presented indicates the difficulties that have been felt in understanding Euripides. Of the three theories, I personally find the third, advanced by A. W. Verrall, the most interesting and the closest to the truth. The trouble with all these theories, including Verrall's, though, is that they all try to explain what Euripides did in terms of his conscious intent. They assume, if I may put the matter in phenomenological terms, that Euripides had no concepts other than thematic ones; they all leave out any consideration of the operative concepts, which I suggest were hidden from Euripides. Some of his plays do seem to be two plays, but did he intend to write one play within another? Could it not be that the themes of some of his works simply did not jibe with the operative notions by which he presented them?

I assume that Euripides wanted to write tragedies; yet it is clear that he did not accept the authority of the *polis* in the same way that his two great predecessors did. To put the matter simply, Euripides, who was something of a pacifist, was for the family and against the *polis*. This stand should be clear not only from the *Trojan Women* but also from the *Suppliant Women*. So, his operative concept could not have been the tragic one that the individual who acts is necessarily guilty and also necessarily innocent—for all his guilt. For this concept of the tragic rested, I submit, on the equality of family and *polis* in the heroes' loyalties. I think Euripides' assumption most often was that an individual's fate was not at all given but flowed from his character. Guilt, I suggest, is given in Aeschylus and Sophocles, but in the plays of Euripides guilt has to be earned. I am thinking here, of course, of the *Medea*. Also, the very opposite movement from tragedy can be found in Euripides, for instance, in such a play as *Iphigeneia in Tauris*. Here, instead of the stripping off of innocence and the revelation of guilt, we have the very contrary movement: guilt is stripped off, and innocence is revealed. First of all, the mere fact that Iphigeneia is alive means Agamemnon was not guilty of her murder. More important, in the action of the play Orestes is cleansed not only of guilt but even of remorse. I grant that Euripides did write one play with a structure like that of old tragedy. When toward the end of his life, turning from humanism to antihumanism, he wrote the *Bacchae*, he presented for the first time in his career a figure guilty in innocence and innocent in guilt; however, this figure is not, like the heroes of Sophocles, a man, but the god Dionysus.

It has been said that the mature Sophocles was influenced by Euripides and that one of the plays exhibiting this influence is his *Philoctetes*, about which many problems have been raised. (Some have been convincingly solved by Kitto in *Form and Meaning in Drama*.) Now, bearing in mind the notion of the hidden I advanced, let us consider the influence of one dramatist on another and ask whether we take as a sign of such influence a change in the conscious themes of the dramatist said to be influenced or a change in his operative concepts. I would suggest that if there were an influence of Euripides on Sophocles, this influence is to be looked for not in the themes of Sophocles' later plays, or in his technique as a dramatist, but in the substitution of different operative concepts for those of the family-*polis* antinomy controlling the *Antigone*, the *Oedipus*, the *Ajax*, and the *Electra*. Let us look at the *Philoctetes* in this light. The play ends happily, and as Kitto notes in the essay he devoted to it (the long and complex analysis in *Form and Meaning in Drama*), it is fundamentally a moral play rather than a tragedy. Does this justify us in looking for operative concepts different from the ones that had led Sophocles to write those of his plays that are unquestionably tragic?

Before looking for the hidden concepts that control the action of the *Philoctetes*, let us look at the play as a whole and consider in what way this play is different from others. What is most striking about the *Philoctetes*? A problem is presented—that of getting the bow of Philoctetes to the Greeks so that Neoptolemus can use it to take Troy. The worst possible way of obtaining the bow is proposed by Odysseus; it is to steal the bow from Philoctetes and leave him alone, sick and defenseless, on the isle of Lemnos. The best possible way of obtaining the bow is proposed by Neoptolemus; it is to let Philoctetes retain possession of the bow (in the action of the play Neoptolemus, having stolen the bow, returns it to Philoctetes) and persuade him to join the expedition to Troy, bringing the bow with him. And so it happens, but only through the intervention of the half-divine Heracles, speaking for the gods and having the power to promise Philoctetes that if he forgives the Greeks for the wrong they did him and joins them in their action against Troy, his sickness will be cured and he can share with Neoptolemus the glory of conquering Troy. It will be seen that the best way of solving the problem—the way envisaged by Neoptolemus and enjoined by Heracles—has no particular appeal to Philoctetes, who does not want the problem solved. And for it to be solved, the divine, represented by Heracles, must put in an appearance. If ever there was a play which required a *deus ex machina*, it is this one. So I, for one, am puzzled by the fact that Kitto thinks it not quite necessary. In any case, what is new about this play and distinguishes it from all others is that the worst and the best ways of solving a human problem are advanced, and the best possible way is adopted. Certainly, for this to happen in life the presence of the divine would be necessary.

I am also struck by a further fact, a certain identity of judgment on the part of Philoctetes and his archenemy Odysseus. The latter wants to take the bow from Philoctetes, sacrificing his need to the Greek enterprise; Philoctetes wants to keep the bow with him on Lemnos, sacrificing the Greek enterprise to his need for vengeance. In a way, both are aiming at tragedy, from which the moral feeling of Neoptolemus and the divine exhortation of Heracles provide a way of escape. As in the plays of Euripides already discussed, what we have in this work is not the insistence on the inescapability of guilt—either the guilt of the Greeks against Philoctetes or the guilt of the latter against them—but rather the indication that guilt may be escaped from. The possibility of a great action in which the main figures are morally innocent is envisaged in this play for the first time by Sophocles.

To be sure, the play does not concern a family-*polis* conflict. Philoctetes is an individual; it is his individual claim that the Greeks have denied, not the claims of an institution, his family. But in some way he must have been thought of as a brother by certain of the Greek warriors; certainly, Neoptolemus' feelings for him are brotherly, and the form of the action is patterned on the family-*polis* antithesis. I think we are entitled to conjecture that by the time Sophocles came to write this play he was somewhat influenced by those plays of Euripides in which the appearance of guilt is stripped from the protagonist and his innocence revealed. In tragedy the opposite takes place. The operative concept of the *Philoctetes,* no doubt hidden from Sophocles and probably derived from Euripides, is an antitragic and a religious one, indicating that escape from tragedy is possible. Even in a military enterprise, guilt may be escaped from if the divine so wishes.

The notion of the hidden I am presenting here should resolve the often debated question as to whether literary works ought to have definite social content or can be enjoyed as purely aesthetic objects, having no other end than to give pleasure. Both positions assume that only one set of concepts is involved in a given work; I have tried to show that there are two such sets, the operative and the thematic, and these are rarely, if ever, identical. The avowed aim of a poem might be to give us pleasure—the poet may even be an aesthete—and the thoughts that are thematic in the poem may be chosen with that end in view; all the same, the poet may be operating unknown to himself with concepts that have more ethical or political than aesthetic meaning. Similarly, the thematic concepts of a writer— a prose writer, let us say—may be as ethical or political as the supporters of commitment in literature could wish, and yet the operative concepts of the writer might be such as to give his work a very different effect from the one which he intended. The assumption of both the defenders of aestheticism and those of ethical or political commitment in literature has to be the identity of the thematic and operative concepts in a given work, something we seldom find and that is not to be desired.

Generally speaking, the operative concepts of a literary work are not the *truth* of what is thematic in it. However, one difficulty with the *Antigone* of Sophocles, if I may return to that play for a moment, may be that the operative concepts of the play lie too close to those Sophocles took for its theme, and the difficulty with Antigone's questionable speech may be that it does not jibe with either what the play makes clear or what it hides. The closeness of its thematic to its operative concepts no doubt gives the play its solidity and force; no doubt, too, this is why it lacks the mysteriousness we find in the *Oedipus*. Hegel, to be sure, preferred the *Antigone*, from which we might infer that he had the soul of a reductionist. We may say fairly that the concepts that are thematic in the *Antigone* can indeed be reduced to its operative concepts, but here, precisely, we may see the flaw of this play.

Once we have recognized what is faulty in the *Antigone*, we are actually enabled to praise Sophocles for something for which he has not yet been praised. Here I must again refer to Hegel.

He tells us that only by acting for the *polis* could the Greek individual achieve the universal recognition he desired; on the other hand, in the *polis,* which he served as a warrior, he was not recognized for the particular traits of character he exhibited in daily life. Within the family his particular traits were recognized indeed, but such recognition was unsatisfyingly less than universal. Thus, his life could take on concrete meaning only in the absence of the universal; it could have universal meaning only in the absence of concreteness. Now Sophocles, of course, could not have known all this; we ourselves only know it from Hegel. Yet surely he must have had some obscure perception of the pattern of life in Athens, always referred to in his plays. And what better way was there for him to make Antigone represent the particularism of family life than to have her assert that only for her brother would she have defied the *polis?* In saying this, she exalts, to be sure, her feeling for a single member of her family rather than her feeling for the family as such. My suggestion is that at the moment when she makes her speech she wants to express only the most absolute concreteness of feeling, at the furthest possible remove from that abstract universality to which the *polis* could, and she could not, make claim. At this point in her story, love for the family as such may even have seemed to her too much like patriotic feeling for the city. Only her very particular love for her brother sufficed her then. Perhaps this was the reason for the sophism Sophocles borrowed for her from Herodotus.

Holding to our view of the hidden we no longer have to distinguish between a literature (unpoetic) that makes statements and a literature (poetic) that does not. This distinction is altogether false anyway, for the difference between the poetic and unpoetic has nothing whatever to do with making or not making statements. If there were any truth in the remark of Northrop Frye that the poet "cannot talk about what he knows," then we would have to call Michel de Montaigne, Voltaire, and Jonathan Swift poets even as we do Wordsworth and Shakespeare. But the poet can indeed talk about what he knows; what he may not be able to talk about is whatever enables him to know it. But this holds equally for the writer of prose.

Kitto realizes that the view of people like Frye is dangerous to his conception of Sophocles, and his tactic is to disagree with this view and yet come to terms with it: he distinguishes poetry from prose very much as Frye does and then claims that the reason dramatists like Sophocles had to make statements is that Greece was lacking in a prose literature. Since someone had to make statements, it was the poet who did. Kitto writes:

> ... we will return to our question of meaning, state-ment. We will put the opposing views in an exaggerated form: a work of art means (a fairly definite) *something;* or, a work of art means *anything.* The status of poetry in Greece being what it was, one to which the last few centuries afford no parallel, it seems probable from the start that we should be ready to move decisively away from anything toward something.... If we speak of "the Aeschylean meaning" of a play (as distinct from Mr. So-and-so's brilliant exposition), or for that matter of "the Shakespearian meaning," we may not be posit-ing something that does not exist.

This is pretty weak, it seems to me. If you are going to say that a play of Aeschylus has some definite meaning, you ought to be able to assert its meaning with more definiteness than merely to suggest you "may not be positing something that does not exist."

Kitto, I think, wants it both ways. He wants to be able to show a definite meaning in each play he analyzes, but he also wants to believe that each play has multiple meanings. At the extreme, this amounts to saying that the plays are mute, si-lent—what Frye asserts. Frye, however, is unable to hold this view consistently and quotes with approval John Stuart Mill's remark that the artist is not heard but overhead. But to be overhead one has to have said something, one cannot have been entirely mute. The concepts I have been trying to point up in the plays of Sophocles are those that, of course, cannot be heard in what is said in the plays but those that we, helped by Hegel, may overhear.

Kitto's *Poiesis* is fundamentally a defense of meaning in Aeschylus and Sophocles, a defense which is witty, learned, inventive, and, in the end, unavailing, since Kitto cannot bring himself to break theoretically with the view held by Frye and others that poetry is silent or says nothing. Kitto wants the Greek plays to be simple but also to be ambiguous. They are both, of course, but their ambiguity arises from the tension produced in them by two simplicities, one of which is hidden, and which the great classicist does not want to bring to light. His tactic is to try to show only those resources that the Greek dramatists knew they were using and that he now knows about. Here, Kitto shows a fundamental modesty that one may admire without accepting. He does not want to teach what men greater than he may be said not to have known. But is not this, finally, a refusal to know them?

METATHEATRE

HAMLET Q.E.D.

I

PEOPLE HAVE GROWN tired, I suspect, of thinking about *Hamlet;* also, of reading further explanations of the play. Will not each new interpretation prove to be a misinterpretation—the moment, that is, it stops being new? This is what has happened again and again, to theory on theory, explanation after explanation, many of which began by provoking our interest—only to disappoint us as wrong.

Yet if *Hamlet* is to be clearer when read and less embarrassing when produced, we do need an interpretation of it. And it is to be feared we need the right one. . . .

Can anyone be right where so many have been wrong, the most ingenious and the most erudite, the most systematic and profound? Yet the many wrong explanations already advanced have surely reduced the possible chances for error now. Moreover, the main error of past critics can finally be generalized. Not a doubt of it—the best critics of *Hamlet*, like Johan Wolfgang von Goethe, Samuel Taylor Coleridge, and A. C. Bradley, were overly psychological in their approach to the play; concentrating on its content, they ignored the problem of its form. And T. S. Eliot has even justified their error as inevitable, asserting, in a now famous essay, that the content of *Hamlet* is so psychologically complicated its form could not but be obscure. Then how could its form be analyzed? Eliot's view, in fact, marks a turning point in the history of *Hamlet* criticism. If Eliot was right, then a purely literary or dramatic analysis of *Hamlet* would have to be barren; the real explanation of the play's difficulties must be left to psychologists.

Since Eliot's essay, of course, other critics have defended the form of the play; they defended the play as tragedy. In so doing, I think, they have ignored or glossed over *Hamlet*'s very real difficulties. So that of the two views, (1) that *Hamlet* is defective as tragedy and (2) that *Hamlet* is a tragedy and great, the first must be preferred.

But a third view is possible. What if our own misunderstanding of the form of *Hamlet* has made its content seem so complicated? What if *Hamlet* is not essentially a tragedy? Then the play might be explained without our having to psychoanalyze either Shakespeare or Hamlet—as if this were even possible, when we have no biography of Shakespeare to guide us!

Surely it is at least theoretically possible that Shakespeare in the process of writing *Hamlet*, finding it difficult to make the story tragic, and personally inclined to treat it differently, turned toward various play-within-a-play devices, but did not indicate his purpose clearly, still calling *Hamlet* a tragedy. My guiding assumption is, to be sure, that it was quite impossible in the age of Elizabeth for any dramatist, including Shakespeare, to make a true tragedy of Hamlet's story.

Could Shakespeare's *Hamlet* have been a tragedy? Now, my aim is not to add still another question to those already raised by the play. Answering this question, I hope to answer all the old questions—once and for all.

II

Would *Hamlet* have been a tragedy if the Ghost had told Hamlet to kill his mother, along with Claudius? Instead of this, as we know, the Ghost expressly forbids Hamlet to harm his mother in any way, urging him to "leave her to heaven," and devote his energies to killing his uncle. But it is not tragic to kill one's uncle or to have been told to do so, even by one's father's ghost. Hamlet, so ready for tragedy in his attitude and character, with such a perfect disposition for the part, is asked by his father's ghost to do something of little tragic consequence.

A great deal has been made of the fact that having been

urged to kill Claudius, Hamlet delays. But what if Hamlet had actually killed the King, his uncle, forthwith? Would the play then have been a tragedy? What if Gertrude had committed suicide? Then Hamlet would have killed his mother, though indirectly, and would have had to sustain the inevitable remorse. Still, even if done in that way, the story of Hamlet would have been a weak one, far weaker than that of Orestes in the *Oresteia* of Aeschylus or of Orestes and Electra in the *Electra* of Sophocles. Moreover there is very little in Shakespeare's play to indicate that Gertrude would have committed suicide had Hamlet killed Claudius. Gertrude, as Shakespeare conceived her, is not of an age or character to feel so intemperately about the loss of any particular husband.

Why did the Ghost not tell Hamlet to kill his mother, as Apollo in the *Oresteia* told Orestes to kill Clytemnestra? It will be said that in *Hamlet* the role of Gertrude in the murder of Hamlet's father was left ambiguous. But Shakespeare could have made Gertrude a participant in the murder, had he wanted to.

III

In his excellent book, *Greek Tragedy*, Professor H. D. F. Kitto has made a number of points which, had he related them to *Hamlet*, would have been invaluable for solving the play's difficulties. Strangely enough, Kitto takes no account of these insights in the essay on *Hamlet* in his *Form and Meaning in Drama*. But in his discussion of Greek tragedy, Kitto compares three plays by the three Greek writers of tragedy, Aeschylus, Sophocles, and Euripides, the plays dealing with the murder of Clytemnestra and Aegisthus by Orestes and Electra. In the play of Aeschylus, Apollo unambiguously orders Orestes to kill his mother. Kitto makes the point that since the command to kill his mother comes from a god, Orestes, in Aeschylus' drama, is able to kill Aegisthus first and then Clytemnestra, without shocking the Greek audience. But in Sophocles' play about the same event, it is less sure—Sophocles was less religious than Aeschylus—that Apollo in fact ordered Orestes to kill his mother. As a result, according to Kitto, Sophocles did not dare end the play with the murder of Clytemnestra by her son, but instead, made Orestes kill Clytemnestra first and then Aegisthus. This is already a great weakening of the tragic climax as compared with the version of Aeschylus.

Next, Kitto takes up Euripides' *Electra*. Euripides was, of course, far more rationalistic than Sophocles; in Euripides' play, Apollo is judged, says Kitto, as " . . . neither the defender of some principle in society nor the embodiment of a universal law; he was simply the god of Delphi, an immoral and reactionary institution. Therefore he [Euripides] brings the god out of the enigmatic background in which Sophocles had placed him, makes him command the act of vengeance, and makes that as repulsive as he can." As a result, the killing of Aegisthus and Clytemnestra by Orestes and Electra is a melodramatic event, showing the avengers as despicable and personally motivated; the victims appear somewhat better than their murderers. The murder committed by Clytemnestra and Aegisthus is in the past; the guilty pair have not just murdered Agamemnon when they are killed by Orestes. From the point of view of Euripides, the present murder becomes worse than the past murder; there is no feeling in his play of either necessity or justice. No cosmic piety is suggested in the motivation of either Electra or Orestes. Their motives are without metaphysics, and we respond to their deed with horror.

The comparison of these three Greek plays with *Hamlet* casts a new light on the difficulties faced by Shakespeare when he set out to make a tragedy of a story so similar to the one Aeschylus had treated greatly, the less religious Sophocles handled subtly, and the skeptical Euripides reduced to violent melodrama. It should be noted, too, that whoever the man was, we have a right to infer that the author of Shakespeare's plays was even less religious than Euripides. Some have questioned this judgment and argued that Shakespeare, if not a believing Christian, had at least a "Christian sensibility." Perhaps. But even if we assume Shakespeare to have had some measure of Christian belief, how could such belief have helped him in making a tragedy of Hamlet's story? The Christian God, with the supernatural realms of hell, purgatory, and heaven at his disposal, could scarcely be imagined as intervening in a human action for a this-world vengeance. The God of the Old Testament, like the Greek gods, had, of course, an interest in this-world solutions.

Shakespeare was, moreover, quite without Euripides' very evident taste for melodrama. Most of Shakespeare's tragedies are defective; they are failures at tragedy, not efforts to write melodrama: *Lear, Othello, Coriolanus, Julius Caesar, Timon of Athens* are inadequate tragedies, if we take that form seriously. But we can assume that Shakespeare did not want these plays to be melodramatic, just as we can assume he did not want them to be imperfect.

The act of revenge, to which Hamlet is commanded, could not be justified religiously by Shakespeare. Would his play, then, have to be a melodrama like Euripides' *Electra*?

IV

Let us assume that Shakespeare has resolved to write his *Hamlet* and does not know how to make the story tragic. If the Prince obeys the injunction of the Ghost and kills his uncle, there is no tragedy; if the Prince kills his mother without a divine order, there is no tragedy either; then how could the play be a tragedy at all? With these questions, which Shakespeare may never have put, we come closer to his intention and to his peculiar resolution of the drama he set himself to write. Since there could be no tragedy in prompt action on Hamlet's part, Shakespeare dignifies Hamlet's inactivity, making it philosophic.

So we have the wonderful soliloquy on being and nonbeing, which quickly becomes a question put by Hamlet: whether or not he should take his own life. But if it is better to be dead than to live, then how could killing Claudius avenge the murder of Hamlet's father? If there is a question whether one should be or not be, then there is surely no answer to why Hamlet should kill Claudius. The great soliloquy is a complete contradiction of the assignment given Hamlet; it is much more than that; it is a contradiction of any assignment, of any action. But since we are speaking of a character in a play we are also speaking of that character's author. Shakespeare, too, had no reason to make Hamlet act, and a very strong reason for making him philosophize at the moment of the famous soliloquy.

Thus it is that Shakespeare, with his unfailing feeling for the common, appealed to a very gross opinion, that thought and action contradict each other. This opinion has helped make Hamlet loved by audiences, who feel him to be a victim, not of his situation, but of his thought.

V

The psychoanalytic critics have said that Hamlet could not kill Claudius because he desired his mother as Claudius desired her; they also suggest that Hamlet wanted his father's death, which Claudius encompassed. According to them, Hamlet could not have avenged his father, since he wanted what Claudius got. The psychoanalytic view thus converts Hamlet into a figure of envy; he envies the resolute action by which a man gets what he wants, no matter what the means. The two objects of Hamlet's envy are Claudius and Fortinbras: Claudius because he has killed Hamlet's father and gotten both Hamlet's mother and Denmark, Fortinbras because he is leading a military action likely to be crowned with success. In this view, Hamlet represents the envy of thought for action, be that action despicable or heroic. I submit that Hamlet, as Shakespeare has presented him in the play, is totally lacking in envy. Even when he expresses admiration for whoever "can find quarrels in a straw," he seems to us like one who has discovered a good where he has not suspected it, and not like one who has a hankering to be somebody else. No, I say, Hamlet's philosophizing about action is a projection into the play of the playwright's difficulty in making his hero tragic.

VI

Shakespeare, to dignify Hamlet's inactivity, gave it, as I have said, a philosophic quality. Those critics who have considered Hamlet the victim of his own irresolution, beguiled by this notion, have lost sight of the dramatic movement of the play as a whole. What is that movement? When this movement is grasped, the new form Shakespeare would turn to, later in his career, may be glimpsed.

Everyone has noticed that there is a play within a play, for Hamlet puts on a show in order to catch, as he says, the "conscience of the King." What has not been noticed, though, but becomes evident once one abandons the notion that the play is a tragedy, or that Shakespeare could make it one, is that there is hardly a scene in the whole work in which some character is not trying to dramatize another. Almost every important character acts at some moment like a playwright, employing a playwright's consciousness of drama to impose a certain posture or attitude on another. Here is Gertrude urging Hamlet to look less melancholy:

> Good Hamlet, cast thy nighted color off,
> And let thine eye look like a friend on Denmark.

The sense of Hamlet's reply is that there is that within him which cannot be dramatized:

> 'Tis not alone my inky cloak, good mother,
> Nor customary suits of solemn black,
> Nor windy suspiration of forc'd breath,
> No, nor the fruitful river in the eye,
> Nor the dejected havior of the visage,
> Together with all forms, moods, shows of grief,
> That can denote me truly. These indeed seem,
> For they are actions that a man might play;
> But I have that within which passeth show,
> These but the trappings and the suits of woe.

The next attempt to dramatize Hamlet and impose on him a particular posture comes from the Ghost, whose revelation is couched in the most theatrical and stagy terms. In fact the Ghost tells Hamlet that he could easily, by revealing the secrets of his prison house, produce an immediate effect upon the Prince:

> I could a tale unfold whose lightest word
> Would harrow up thy soul, freeze thy young blood,
> Make thy two eyes, like stars, start from their spheres,
> Thy knotty and combined locks to part
> And each particular hair to stand on end,
> Like quills upon the fretful porpentine.

This is what the Ghost could do to Hamlet. However, he will not, having been forbidden to tell of his supernatural sufferings. All the same, the Ghost is determined to impose on Hamlet a definite posture. At first, Hamlet seems to accept it:

> Yea, from the table of my memory
> I'll wipe away all trivial fond records,
> All saws of books, all forms, all pressures past,
> That youth and observation copied there,
> And thy commandment all alone shall live
> Within the book and volume of my brain . . .

But immediately afterward Hamlet retaliates against the Ghost by trying to dramatize him in turn, in the wonderful and otherwise inexplicable scene when the Ghost has disappeared under the boards and Hamlet asks the guards and Horatio to swear that they have seen nothing. The remarkable thing about this scene is the fond contempt with which Hamlet addresses the Ghost, who has just sworn him to devote his whole life to revenge. Hamlet calls the Ghost "boy," "truepenny," "old mole," and "worthy pioneer." How are we to understand these contemptuous epithets addressed by Hamlet to the Ghost of his

father? I shall not say that I have a final interpretation of this
scene, which, by the way, will move any audience, however
they understand it. I suggest, though, that the reaction of Hamlet
is that of a man with a playwright's consciousness who has
just been told to be an actor, and is now determined to make
an actor of the very playwright who had cast him for an un-
desired role. What makes the Ghost a serious playwright is
what has happened to him. He has the force of death and hell
behind his stage instructions. Hamlet, however, has the force
of his—that is, Shakespeare's—dramatic imagination. The scene
is one of the most wonderful in all drama. This is not a struggle
between two characters, but between two playwrights. And the
better playwright, Hamlet—in terms of consciousness—happens
to be the lesser playwright in terms of zeal. Hence his dramatic retaliation has to be humorous.

Is not any son forced to be an actor in his parents' script?
They chide him, spank him, dress him, coddle him, order him
around: to be a child means to take direction. (Actors in general are childlike.) Certainly Hamlet, as a child, must have
been through all that. But having been in the play of his parents, almost any individual will want to be in another play,
when grown up. Besides, it was not Hamlet's father who authored
the situation he asks Hamlet to play a part in. The author of
this situation was Hamlet's uncle. Who could want to become
an actor in a bloody show put on by a villainous uncle? Certainly not Hamlet.

Polonius, who dramatizes himself as wise, treats his son Laertes
and his daughter Ophelia as if they were actors in a play
whose meaning he, Polonius, alone understands. In the famous
speech Polonius makes to Laertes, he even tells the young man
the kind of clothes he should wear, the kind of figure he should
cut. With more at stake, Polonius instructs Ophelia on how to
test Hamlet's real intentions toward herself and toward the King.
Ophelia obeys her father's directions, but Hamlet, with his sen-
sitivity to stage technique, sees through her guise of innocence
at once. Polonius, who is able to dramatize both his son and
his daughter, does not try to dramatize Hamlet; this is because Polonius, amateur playwright that he is, thinks Hamlet

is already dramatized, and that he, Polonius, knows exactly the plot of the drama Hamlet is in: Hamlet is infatuated with Ophelia, cannot expect to marry her, and hence is melancholy. Everything Polonius does follows from this fancy, in which he believes as completely as a bad playwright in his crude plot. Finally Polonius goes too far, spies on Hamlet's violent scene with his mother, and is killed by Hamlet, who mistakes him for the King.

Ernest Jones maintains that Hamlet did not mistake Polonius for the King, and would have been incapable of killing the latter. The psychoanalytic critic has not taken into account how useless it would have been to Shakespeare's purpose for Hamlet to kill Claudius at any moment before the end of the fifth act. The "mystery" of Hamlet's incapacity has at least as much to do with dramatic form as with psychology. What is most interesting in the scene, though, is that two playwrights are present in it, Polonius behind the arras, and Hamlet, who gives his mother a playwright's instructions about her future behavior: she is to avoid her husband's bed, and, as Hamlet indicates, by making such avoidance habitual, she may be able to arrive at a truer consciousness of her responsibilities. In this scene Hamlet urges his mother to act without sincerity until that moment when her motives, by force of repeated acting, become sincere. At this point it is necessary for a third playwright to put in an appearance. The Ghost does just that, appearing to Hamlet and reminding him that he, so eloquent in instructing his mother how to act, has forgotten his own role, which is to kill Claudius.

Two vain and very minor playwrights are quickly called upon by Claudius. These are Rosencrantz and Guildenstern, who first try to find out what is in Hamlet's mind and are told by him that they cannot play on him. Nor can they. Their final instructions are to dramatize Hamlet as a corpse when he sails with them for England. They have sealed orders requesting his execution on arrival. Hamlet, of course, rewrites the orders, and when the three arrive in England, Rosencrantz and Guildenstern are executed instead of him.

All of the characters in the play can be distinguished as fol-

lows: some are fundamentally dramatists[1] or would-be dramatists, the others are fundamentally actors. Thus Gertrude and
Ophelia are actors; so is Laertes; but Hamlet, Claudius, Polonius,
and the Ghost are dramatists. There is still another dramatist,
whose dramaturgy in the end Hamlet will consent to.

This dramatist is death. When Hamlet has returned from
England, after having defeated the crude intrigue of Claudius,
Rosencrantz, and Guildenstern, he is ready for death. As he
says, "the readiness is all." He passes with Horatio by the
cemetery, sees the gravedigger at work, and finds the skull of
Yorick, the court clown he had loved. At this moment Hamlet
recognizes the truth of that dramatic script in which no one
can refuse to act: death will make us all theatrical, no matter
what we have done in life. The skull is pure theatre. It is a
perfect mask. I think it is at this moment that Hamlet accepts
death's dramaturgy, not his father's, not his own. He is ready
to die now, no matter what the occasion.

What is the meaning of Hamlet's words to Horatio urging
the latter not to die: "Absent thee from felicity awhile"—if not
that death's dramaturgy is finally the most felicitous? Hamlet
had found the terrible dramatist who could dramatize even him.
And this is why he falls in with the crude, melodramatic scheming
of Claudius; the latter promotes a duel between Hamlet and
Laertes. There could be no cruder plotting. The foil of Laertes
is poisoned, and there is a poisoned wine for Hamlet to drink
if, after exertion, he needs refreshment. Hamlet gives not the
slightest thought to the details of the duel, and acts as if he
suspects nothing. He is ready now to be in the worst play
possible, to act in it, play his part, pretend to believe in it; he

---

1. In calling the important characters of *Hamlet* "playwrights," am I relying on a metaphor? To an extent, yes. On the other hand, I claim that no
other metaphor could throw an equal light on the play's movement. Suppose that we called Hamlet, the Ghost, Claudius, and Polonius "poets" and
compared their rhetoric. This could be done, and might lead to some discovery. But not, I think, to any important discovery about the play as a
whole. When I say that the important characters are "playwrights" what I
want to underscore is that each of them has the consciousness of a dramatist as well as that of a character.

has not accepted the role the Ghost has tried to force on him, but the role from which he cannot escape anyway, the role death will inevitably make him play. The miserable melodrama of Claudius proceeds to its climax. Laertes wounds Hamlet, they exchange foils, Hamlet wounds Laertes and the latter tells him that they will both die from the poison on the foils. It is only then that Hamlet kills Claudius. Dying, he does what he could not do when hoping to live.

VII

I have said that there are four playwrights among the characters of *Hamlet:* Claudius, the Ghost, Polonius, and Hamlet. What kinds of playwrights are they; in other words, what kinds of plays are they capable of?

Claudius is a writer of melodrama from start to finish. He kills his brother horribly, pouring into "the porches of his ear a leprous distillment"; the peculiar detail that the poison was poured into the victim's ear and not given him to drink, as would be more natural, suggests the creator of a sensational story, as well as an assassin.

The Ghost is a typically Elizabethan writer of melodrama; though himself tragically victimized, killed by his brother, and subject to eternal punishment in hell, all he requires of Hamlet is the murder of Claudius. He expressly forbids Hamlet to harm Gertrude in any way. His conception of life, even after death, is extremely gross: he wants what began as tragedy to end as melodrama.

Polonius is the amateur playwright par excellence. Though caught in the bloody intrigue of Denmark's royal family, he looks forward to a happy and practical consummation of events fraught with terror. He thinks that his plotting will resolve the problems of Denmark and of his daughter's relationship with Hamlet. When killed, in the third act, he has not the faintest notion of what will happen in the fourth or the fifth. But his daughter dies a suicide, his son dies a murderer. No playwright could have been more mistaken in his understanding of events than Polonius, striving to control all the other characters by intrigue.

What kind of playwright is Hamlet? This question is more difficult to answer. Like his creator, he has the most excellent sense of theatre, as is shown in his advice to the actors. Certainly Hamlet's melancholy has endowed him greatly for tragic poetry; but he is in a situation in which the Ghost of his own father has forbidden him to define tragically. Now we can assume Hamlet's taste to be quite different from the Ghost's. Hamlet, then, with his gifted playwright's consciousness has the problem of rewriting the melodrama he has been placed in, but with no alternative form in view. For he has been expressly forbidden to convert this melodrama into tragedy. Finally, he yields to the appeal of the one dramatist whose script, like tragedy, involves necessity and places one beyond chance. This dramatist is death. In turning toward death Hamlet is turning toward something outside the play, not fated by the plot as in tragedy, or forced on the plot as in melodrama. He is considering death and accepting it in its universal meaning, not as the fate likely to overtake him because of his particular situation, but as that fate which must overtake anyone, no matter what situation he be in. Death, which I have called somewhat metaphorically the dramatist in whose script all must act, Hamlet appeals to as an ultimate form. To a modern consciousness is not death equal to the immortal gods?

VIII

Let us now see if the questions to which the play has given rise cannot be settled once and for all. If it is borne in mind that Hamlet does not know the form of the play he is in, in other words, that Shakespeare was unable to make a tragedy of *Hamlet*, the major questions about the play can be answered definitively.

(1) Is Hamlet irresolute? Coleridge and Goethe held this view, though they nuanced their judgments differently. Is Hamlet, on the contrary, resolute? That was A. C. Bradley's contention.

These questions become nonsensical when we keep clearly in mind that for a character in a play to be judged either resolute or irresolute, the type or form of play he is in has to be clearly defined. But there is no clear definition for the kind of play Hamlet was placed in by Shakespeare.

(2) Is Hamlet mad? He warns his friends that he may put on an "antic disposition," but we may well wonder whether he does so with any other purpose than to avoid the purposelessness of the plot. No doubt Hamlet enjoys acting as if he were mad. He likes the role no one gave him. In pretended madness there is, of course, a refuge from the seriousness of his task. As a madman, Hamlet can say or do anything he wants to say or do, and at any particular moment. He has been told by his father's Ghost not to express his spontaneous feelings. But pretending to be mad, Hamlet can be himself. Since the structure of the play he is in is so indefinite, and not to his taste, he can only get outside of it by acting as if he were mad.

(3) Is Hamlet in love with Ophelia? He is not. Replying to Laertes' expression of love for Ophelia by her grave, Hamlet does declare:

> . . . Forty thousand brothers
> Could not, with all their quantity of love,
> Make up my sum. . . .

but adds immediately afterward:

> Nay, an thou'lt mouth. I'll rant as well as thou

thus negating his declaration.

Psychoanalysis has established very clearly that no man can love a woman unless he has separated himself from involvement with his own parents. But the psychoanalytic critics obscure the truth of this observation in applying it to Hamlet's feelings for Ophelia. Their claim is that Hamlet *desired* to remain involved with his parents; hence his feelings for Ophelia had to be ambiguous. They forget that it is the plot—a plot Hamlet disliked and did not want to be in—which required him to remain so involved. According to them, the plot corresponds to Hamlet's feeling, and does not contradict it. Here I think they are clearly wrong. Hamlet, in the play he is in, cannot love Ophelia. He would, of course, have preferred to be in another play.

(4) Is Hamlet in love with his mother? There is no evidence for any such assumption, except Hamlet's greater interest in his mother's guilt than in his uncle's, which seems to me perfectly normal.

(5) Does Hamlet believe or not believe in the Ghost? Certainly he believes in the Ghost. The entire action of the play comes from the Ghost's appearing to Hamlet and setting him the most unambiguous of tasks; Hamlet shirks the task, finding excuses for inaction. But the concern and guilt for nondoing which Hamlet expresses throughout imply that he believes in the Ghost's honesty, and ought to obey his command. But what the Ghost has commanded him to do holds no interest for Hamlet.

(6) How is it that the sentinels of Elsinore, as well as Marcellus and Horatio, all see the Ghost, while Gertrude, during the scene in which the Ghost appears to Hamlet in her presence, does not see him? Why should not Gertrude have seen the Ghost too? It has been pointed out that Lady Macbeth does not see the ghost of Banquo, while Macbeth does; but there is no illogic in Shakespeare's one real tragedy: no one but Macbeth sees the ghost of Banquo. There is an illogic in Gertrude's inability to see the Ghost, who is visible to ordinary soldiers. Such illogic would not be possible in a true tragedy.

But this question, raised so many times, suggests a much more interesting one: why did not the Ghost deliberately reveal himself to Gertrude? Why was he not interested in touching *her* conscience? Why was he so exclusively interested in getting Hamlet to kill his murderer? This is in Hamlet's own phrase "a poor ghost." That is to say, one uninterested in tragedy.

(7) When Hamlet in the third act sees Claudius kneeling in prayer and has a chance to kill him, why doesn't he kill him? The explanation Hamlet gives is:

> . . . now he is praying;
> And now I'll do't—And so he goes to heaven,
> And so am I reveng'd. That would be scann'd.
>   . . .
>
> Up, sword, and know thou a more horrid hent.
> When he is drunk asleep, or in his rage,
> Or in th' incestuous pleasure of his bed,
> At gaming, swearing, or about some act
> That has no relish of salvation in't,—
> Then trip him, that his heels may kick at heaven,
> And that his soul may be as damn'd and black
> As hell, whereto it goes.

Is this explanation a rationalization by Hamlet of his inability to act? After all, what likelihood is there that Hamlet will have the opportunity to find Claudius physically defenseless at some moment when he is also morally and metaphysically helpless? Certainly Hamlet is expecting too much of chance for us to consider his explanation reasonable. The explanation is illogical in another sense, too. The Ghost has demanded of Hamlet only that he kill Claudius, not that he decide on the supernatural destiny of Claudius's soul. And if Hamlet believed in the reality of a final destiny for the soul, would he not also have had the piety—unless he were willing to incur damnation—to leave that supernatural destiny to the judgment of God? Certainly he was rationalizing his inaction. But I think there is sincerity in what he says. He can find no satisfaction in a mere physical dispatch of his villainous uncle; Hamlet, once again, has little taste for melodrama. What he wants is something more—a deeper, a more ultimate meaning for his act. The only moral significance killing Claudius could have had for Hamlet would have been to kill him in front of Gertrude and thus quicken her conscience.

(8) When Hamlet killed Polonius, did he know Claudius was not behind the arras? The psychoanalytic critics, who maintain that Hamlet must have known since he had just left the King praying, have to assume two things:

(a) Hamlet went straight from seeing the King to his mother and did not delay, which he might have done, for all we know. If he did delay, then the King would have had time to get to Gertrude's chamber before Hamlet.

(b) Shakespeare did not know what he was doing in writing the two successive scenes, any more than Hamlet knew what he was doing in either of them. For if Shakespeare had wanted us to think that Hamlet was only pretending to kill the King, knowing all the time the King could not be behind the arras, would Shakespeare have made Hamlet say, looking at Polonius's corpse, "I took you for your better"? Shakespeare certainly knew how to indicate insincerity by speech. He could easily have inflected Hamlet's remark to the dead Polonius in this sense, had he wanted to. The psychoanalytic critics thus have to assume that what Hamlet knew—the King was not behind the arras—was clear to him, the character, and not clear to the author, Shakespeare.

It seems far more plausible to me that what Shakespeare intended in the two successive scenes was to contrast Hamlet's lack of interest in killing Claudius and his very great interest in touching his mother's conscience. Hamlet leaves the King whom he has been sworn to kill and goes to his mother to tell her what she must do. In the first scene, the scene with the King praying, Hamlet is supposed to act and does not. In the second scene, with the queen, he does what we know he likes to do—he directs.

(9) What is the dramatic function of the "To be or not to be" soliloquy? I have remarked already that the soliloquy denies the value of action as such; in speaking as he does, Hamlet takes refuge in philosophy, just as he has already taken refuge in pretended madness. So understood, the soliloquy has only psychological meaning. But I think it also has a function in the play's progress. Hamlet's resort to pretended madness takes him out of the plot; so does philosophizing; but, on the other hand, it is through philosophizing that he finally submits willingly to the crudest plotting of all: Claudius' plot with Laertes to kill him. Hamlet's philosophizing is a meditation on death and not very different from the great speech, "Be absolute for

death," in *Measure for Measure*, in which the Duke, disguised as a friar, urges the young and not so serious sinner named, oddly enough, Claudio, to accept death, saying Claudio will thereby find life the sweeter. Hamlet's meditation takes him from the plot into metaphysics, and then, turning him toward death, enables him to feel something metaphysical in the plot.

IX

We are in a position now to dispose of misconceptions of the play, still widely held. The most important of contemporary interpretations, set forth by Francis Fergusson, has been taken up and restated in a somewhat different form by Professor Kitto. Both claim that the play is about the purification of Denmark, that it is a ritualistic play, in which Hamlet is the tragic protagonist whose duty it is to clean up a moral mess for which he is not personally responsible but in which he is personally involved. The notion here is that the problem of Hamlet is to cleanse society, the society of Denmark, befouled by his uncle's crime.

Fergusson, of course, has tried to explain *Hamlet* in terms of Sophocles' tragedy, the *Oedipus the King*. But in Sophocles' play it is stated at the very outset that a plague is afflicting the inhabitants of Thebes. Oedipus understands at once that he must do something to lift the plague, and the oracle has declared that the way to do this is to discover the murderer of Laius. Thus the problem posed at the start in Sophocles' tragedy is one involving the people of Thebes and the gods. Later it will be seen that it involves Oedipus and his family. But at the outset of *Hamlet* there is no problem about the state of Denmark, and there is little indication that the people groan under the rule of Claudius, or suffer from his substitution of himself for Hamlet's father. True, there are some details to indicate that Hamlet is not satisfied with the political and social health of Denmark, but these are not too many, nor are they striking. Oedipus is told first that his city is afflicted, and second that the reason for its affliction is a moral disorder, which he determines to uncover.

Hamlet has first the premonition of a moral disorder; then he is told what the disorder is. But—and this is the essential point— there are no important signs of the effect of Claudius's crime upon the kingdom. While there is certainly something rotten in Denmark, yet Denmark is as certainly not rotting. And the Ghost does not ask Hamlet to save society but to avenge *him*. The Ghost does say:

> Let not the royal bed of Denmark be
> A couch for luxury and damned incest,

but this moral-political statement is obviously secondary, an afterthought. For there is no indication whatsoever that for the royal bed of Denmark to be a couch for luxury and damned incest will have any important effect on the inhabitants of that kingdom. Evil is a problem for Hamlet—not for Denmark.

What I have most against this interpretation of the play is the effort of both Fergusson and Kitto to assimilate it to an older work, when it conspicuously marks a point of division between the Greek world and ours. Kitto and Fergusson interpret the play in the light of Sophocles' *Oedipus*, first, no doubt, because Freud has made the figure of Oedipus so important, but also because they cannot think of *Hamlet* except as a tragedy; and finding it so unlike any classical tragedy, they were perhaps impelled to assimilate it to the most perfect of classical tragedies.

T. S. Eliot judged *Hamlet* a defective tragedy. He was right; as tragedy it is defective. He was wrong, though, in judging the play as tragedy. The interesting point in his essay is his notion that Shakespeare, in writing *Hamlet*, was not able to find the right "objective correlative" for the experience he was trying to express. According to Eliot, Hamlet's feelings are excessive with respect to his situation: he lacks an objective reason for feeling such melancholy and cuts the figure of an adolescent, exaggerating his own anguish and trying to impose on others the norms of an idealism doomed to remain vague.

To be sure, Hamlet is an objective expression of Shakespeare's inability to make of his play a tragedy. But Shakespeare made something else of his play, something quite as extraordinary as tragedy. It is to be noted that Eliot ignores the originality of the character and of the play, too, in which, for the first time in the history of drama, the problem of the protagonist is that he has a playwright's consciousness. Hamlet is not an adolescent; he is the first stage figure with an acute awareness of what it means to be staged. How be dramatized when one has the imagination to be a dramatist? After *Hamlet* it would be difficult for any playwright to make us respect any character lacking dramatic consciousness. In a novel of Miguel de Unamuno, a character actually rejects the fate chosen for him by the author and demands that the latter change it. The problem of author versus character was I think first envisaged in *Hamlet*. From now on—unless there is to be a new culture whose values we can scarcely foresee—no dramatist has the right to set any supposedly self-conscious character on the stage who does not collaborate in his dramatization. In this sense Jean-Paul Sartre was profoundly correct. No one with self-consciousness can ever do anything drastic in life or on the stage, with our respect, that is, unless he has agreed to his commitment.

What Eliot did not take into account is that none of us, no matter what our situation, really knows the form of the plot he is in, and Hamlet was the first theatrical figure who expressed this fact fully. Doubtless, this is why Hamlet was treated so abusively in Bolshevik criticism; to be sure, the Bolsheviks were interested in criticizing the Hamletism of the Russian intelligentsia. And in this they may have been justified. Ivan Turgenev, long before the Bolsheviks appeared, had demanded more Don Quixotes and fewer Hamlets. But I suspect that the Bolsheviks felt a spite against Hamlet that Turgenev could never have known; thinking they knew the real plot of history, the Bolsheviks could not but dislike a theatrical personage who suggests that no one really knows what kind of play he is in. Certainly Hamlet is one of the first characters to be free of his author's contrivances. Some three hundred years later six characters would visit a playwright, who had not invented them, and according to his own testimony, ask him to be their author.

SHAKESPEARE AND CALDERÓN

I

ONLY CERTAIN PLAYS tell us at once that the happenings and characters in them are of the playwright's invention, and that insofar as they were discovered—where there is invention there also has to be discovery—they were found by the playwright's imagining rather than by his observing the world. Such plays have truth in them, not because they convince us of real occurrences or existing persons, but because they show the reality of the dramatic imagination, instanced by the playwright's and also by that of his characters. Of such plays, it may indeed be said: "The play's the thing." Plays of this type, it seems to me, belong to a special genre and deserve a distinctive name.

But is there not already an adequate name for such plays, one which has the advantage of being well known? Are not plays of the kind I mean essentially comedies? We do not believe that what takes place in comedy has really occurred: events in comedy are reduced by humor to examples for reflection and are not irrevocable, as in tragedy. Nor do characters in comedy have to convince us they exist; all they have to do is to make us laugh. Humor, I suppose, consecrates nonexistence. But that which does not exist can scarcely make us sad. So comedies have to end happily.

It is true that the plays I have in mind end happily in the main, but many of them are able to do what comedy never can do, that is, to instill a grave silence—a speculative sadness—at their close. They can do this without being tragedies, which means, without making us believe that the events presented, responsible for our sadness, happened once and for all.

Moreover, such plays make us feel concerned for characters who tell us frankly they were invented to make us feel concerned for them.

Should the plays I am speaking of—if there is any humor in them—be called tragicomedies? I object to this self-contradictory term, which tells us only that humor and pathos may alternate in a play, but does not define that kind of play in which humor and pathos may alternate. Besides, if the events on the stage are not irrevocable, then wherein lies their tragic content? If the events are irrevocable, wherein lies their comedy? The term tragicomedy implies, it seems to me, two different kinds of plays, amalgamated no one knows just how. If it is said: by the "genius" of the playwright—is that not asking the playwright's genius to do the critic's task?

Remember, too, the scorn no less a genius than Shakespeare showed for those satisfied to combine very different dramatic terms, with no clearer concept for joining them than that provided by the hyphen. The false sage, Polonius, whose words, to Hamlet's thinking are "Buzz, Buzz," announces that the actors just arrived at Elsinore are capable of doing all manner of plays: "pastoral-comical, historical-pastoral, tragical-historical, tragical-comical-historical-pastoral."

Surely the plays I am referring to should not be described so variously. Some of them can, of course, be classified as instances of the play-within-a-play, but this term, also well known, suggests only a device, and not a definite form. Moreover, I wish to designate a whole range of plays, some of which do not employ the play-within-a-play, even as a device. Yet the plays I am pointing at do have a common character: all of them are theatre pieces about life seen as already theatricalized. By this I mean that the persons appearing on the stage in these plays are there not simply because they were caught by the playwright in dramatic postures as a camera might catch them, but because they themselves knew they were dramatic before the playwright took note of them. What dramatized them originally? Myth, legend, past literature, they themselves. They represent to the playwright the effect of dramatic imagination before he has begun to exercise his own; on the other hand,

unlike figures in tragedy, they are aware of their ow
cality. Now, from a certain modern point of view, only ...
life which has acknowledged its inherent theatricality can be
made interesting on the stage. From the same modern view,
events, when interesting, will have the quality of having been
thought, rather than of having simply occurred. But then the
playwright has the obligation to acknowledge in the very structure
of his play that it was his imagination which controlled the
event from beginning to end.

Plays of the kind I have in mind exist. I did not invent them.
However, I shall presume to designate them. I call them
metaplays, works of metatheatre.

II

Consider a great seventeenth-century play, Molière's *Tartuffe*.
Molière called it a comedy, and it is generally played as such.
Stendhal, however, noticed that he laughed only twice during
a performance of *Tartuffe*, and that the audience around him
laughed hardly more. The difficulty in laughing when *Tartuffe*
is performed is not because the characterization or the plot
lacks humor, but because Tartuffe, the villain, bulks so much
larger than his victims, and is so much more interesting. As
French critics have pointed out, Tartuffe is no hypocrite in the
ordinary sense of pretending to be spiritual in order to satisfy
carnal desires; he is hypocritical in order to be himself: when
he is most hypocritical, then he is most Tartuffe.

Tartuffe happens to be much bigger than the conventional
comedy in which Molière put him. So, if Molière wrote *Tartuffe*
in order to criticize religious bigotry and moral hypocrisy, his
play is self-defeating: Molière's hypocrite and bigot is not odi-
ous, but interesting to us. No doubt Molière intended a much
different effect. We know from his other plays how he valued
sincerity. Should we think of *Tartuffe*, then, as designed to attack something going on in society, outside the action it presents?
But the villain of that action is not a statement about the world,
but a statement about himself. If we refer Tartuffe to the world,

he will give it more meaning, I think, than it could have without him.[1] I think, too, he was addressed to the imagination of Molière's audience, while the play he is in was addressed to their social reason. In any case, Tartuffe looms up out of Molière's comedy, greater than it, and destroys it.

But in what kind of play should a character of this imaginative size have been placed? In what kind of play should Hamlet have been put? In *Six Characters in Search of an Author*, perhaps the most original play-within-a-play written in the twentieth century, the remark is made that certain dramatic characters— Hamlet is one mentioned—cannot be contained in the works they first appeared in and have had to venture far from their creators into other works by other authors. Now I would say that if Tartuffe and Hamlet seem to break out of the plays and situations they were first placed in, this is not merely because the right dramatic form had not been found for them, but perhaps more important, because these characters are themselves dramatists, capable of making other situations dramatic besides the ones they originally appeared in.

Any play written at a certain depth should have some other aim than to suggest social change or moral reform. The contemplative imagination can and does delight in what moral and practical wisdom urges us to reject. We are all more profound than our purposes seem to indicate. And the playwright who ventures to touch us very deeply ought to know that he is touching a part of us which is irrelevant to the achievement of our most rational goals. Molière was, I think, too profound for the form he relied on in *Tartuffe*.

Take another play, an Elizabethan play—a great play, too, but one in which the events are made unreal by the playwright's inability to decide whether or not they actually happened. When he wrote *Doctor Faustus*, Christopher Marlowe lacked, I think, a definite dramatic horizon. What kind of play is *Doctor Faustus*?

---

1. Tartuffe is a self-referring character: one who has the capacity to dramatize others, and thus put them in whatever situation he is intent on being in. He refers to himself because he has the capacity to make others always refer to him.

Marlowe thought he had written a tragedy, as Molière thought he had written a comedy in *Tartuffe*. But is Marlowe's Doctor Faustus truly tragic? Do we feel that Faustus actually sold his soul to the Devil, signed his transaction with hell in his own blood, and thus was enabled to regain youthfulness, pride, power, and lust at the price of eternal damnation? Do we believe when we watch *Doctor Faustus* that anything of this sort ever happened in the same way we believe when we watch *Macbeth* that Macbeth really talked to the witches, murdered Duncan and Banquo, conversed with Banquo's ghost, massacred Macduff's family, and was finally killed by Macduff?

I am convinced that no one genuinely believes the events in *Doctor Faustus* in any such way. Nor are the events adequately understood by Marlowe. For instance, Marlowe should have made it clear that the transaction between Faustus and the Devil was essentially a theatrical one. Faustus, an old man, is asking the Devil to dramatize him as a youth; here we are on the verge of a new theatrical form. But Marlowe thought of the transaction as one in which Faustus became the tragic protagonist in a play written by the Devil. Therefore Faustus had to be damned. But when we think about the story with a little more sophistication, does it not appear that the Devil was the actor and Faust the dramatist, since it was he, Faust, who called upon the Devil to dramatize him? Such was the interpretation Goethe made when he took up the story, and he was able to give it such clarity and lightness—not simply because he was more philosophical than Marlowe, but because the form for a play like his *Faust* had already been invented. Goethe found that form in Shakespeare and in Pedro Calderón.[2]

---

2. Goethe saves Faust, perhaps, by applying the logic of appearance. Faust looks serious, well intentioned, and seems to have dignity. I will not go so far as to say that he is saved because he is better looking than Mephistopheles (any actor playing the part, of course, should be), but I will assert that he is saved because he looks better dramatically than the Devil. Mephistopheles, who exhibits so many likable qualities, lacks dignity. In Goethe's play he never convinces us by his appearance that he is entitled to possess Faust's soul. Of the two, it is clear that Faust is the true dramatist, Mephistopheles, yearning to dramatize, a true actor.

III

Why is it that neither Marlowe nor Molière was able to invent the dramatic form both needed, Molière for a proper presentation of his character Tartuffe,[3] Marlowe for fantasizing adequately the dealings of Doctor Faustus with the Devil? But then how is it that neither Lope de Vega, Calderón's predecessor, nor Pierre Corneille, with whom the great period of French theatre began, nor any of the English dramatists before Shakespeare had been able to lift the play-within-a-play—which many of them used as a device—to a truly philosophic height?

Of all the European dramatists, Shakespeare was the only one possessed by a complete confidence in the power of imagination, not simply in its power to make speech splendid—Marlowe had that, too—but in its power to arrange, order, and judge all manners of persons and every single type of action; in other words, to put the whole world on stage. Generalizing that power of imagination, which guided his best inventions, Shakespeare could make his philosopher, Jaques, say, "the world's a stage."

Calderón achieved his great invention not solely from his trust in the imagination but through the influence of two predecessors who anticipated the theatrical form he perfected in *Life Is a Dream*. These were Miguel de Cervantes and Tirso de Molina.

Cervantes was of course a playwright for a period and has some excellent works to his credit, including a fine tragedy,

---

3. I do not mean to imply the Molière was lacking in invention. He lifted comedy to a level of artistry and refinement it had never had before nor has had since. Was he perhaps a "victim of his own invention," to use the phrase Nicola Chiaromonte employed about Pirandello? In any case, *The Misanthrope*, which most critics agree is Molière's masterpiece, has difficulties similar to those presented by *Tartuffe*. If you laugh at Alceste, you have to think he is wrong, and then the play is a comedy; but since you tend to think Alceste is right, you do not want to laugh at him, and then what kind of play is it? Ramon Fernandez, in his fine book on Molière, says that in this work Molière subjected his own chosen art of comedy to a certain skepticism. Is there something immoral about a play that is funny? And is this thought in *The Misanthrope*? If so, is not the play close to theatre about theatre? I must confess I cannot answer this last question to my own satisfaction.

Numantia. But he had little success on the stage and could not compete with the extraordinarily prolific and inventive master of the period, Lope de Vega, whom Cervantes called a monstrosity of nature, meaning by this that Lope de Vega was able to write splendid works without ever pausing to reflect. Reflection was something natural to Cervantes. *Don Quixote* was published just one year after the production of *Hamlet*, and the two works, equally admired, have always been associated by critics. Ivan Turgenev said that a true intellectual has to be a Hamlet or a Don Quixote; Herman Melville said these are the only two real characters in literature.

In any case, Don Quixote, though he appears in a novel — the novel of a former playwright — projects in the most complete and perfect way the dramatic horizon of all plays about self-referring characters. Don Quixote is, of course, his own dramatist, and, if we can use modern terms, his own director, his own set man, his own stage manager. He seeks out those situations he wants to play a part in; he will not wait for life to provide them in a natural way. He calls upon his imagination to substitute itself for reality wherever the real is lacking in quality, bravura, excitement, delicacy. His imagination obliges; most often, as in the case of the windmills, to his discomfiture. But Don Quixote is not discouraged. In fact he even learns — for Cervantes's work is in some ways a *Bildungsroman* — how to develop and refine his own taste for illusion. He grows wiser before our eyes in his lust for great adventure.

Then, of course, Calderón had seen the *Don Juan* of Tirso de Molina (from which Molière took his own masterpiece). Tirso's play was no comedy, but it was certainly not a tragedy. Molina had invented not only a new theatrical type in the figure of Don Juan, but also a new kind of event which certainly does not convince us by its plausibility. The event in fact is utterly implausible, yet one of the greatest imaginative creations in dramatic art. The statue of the dead commander — Don Juan had killed the commander in a duel — invites Don Juan to dinner, dines with him, and then carries him off to hell. It is hard to think of any event less believable — or which affects us more powerfully.

Calderón, who had been trained as a theologian, was more logical than Shakespeare and had behind him the great creations of Cervantes and Tirso de Molina. He had himself experimented with almost every known dramatic form: cloak-and-dagger plays, romantic comedy, tragedy, and farce. Finally, he wrote a number of plays addressed purely to the metaphysical imagination. These are *Devotion to the Cross, The Great Magician*, and perhaps the most perfect play-within-a-play, *Life Is a Dream*. So profound is the appeal of these plays by Calderón, addressed to the metaphysical imagination mainly, that they cannot fail to touch the imagination on every level. Shakespeare, on the other hand, in writing *The Tempest*, was appealing to every level of the imagination, thus including the metaphysical.

IV

Shakespeare experimented throughout his whole career with the play-within-a-play, sometimes introducing play-within-a-play sequences in his tragedies, almost always introducing such sequences in his comedies. *As You Like It, A Midsummer Night's Dream, Twelfth Night, All's Well That Ends Well* are not really comedies, for we cannot account for the pleasure we take in them in terms of their humor, which is often labored, sometimes gross. These are all works of the imagination; but saying this does not define their character or indicate the perfection of form they prefigure. Again, in his chronicles, Shakespeare introduced play-within-a-play sequences, notably in *Henry IV;* by doing so, he was able to set on the stage one of his greatest characters, Falstaff. Falstaff is nothing if not a dramatist,[4] for not only is he witty himself, but he is the cause of wit in others. Acting, he causes those

---

4. Falstaff is a self-referring character par excellence, being a dramatist. A witty eighteenth-century writer, Morgann, was led to speculate on Falstaff's birth, parentage, childhood, early associates, and adventures *before* Falstaff's appearance in Shakespeare's play. True, Morgann's essay on Falstaff, defending his character, led to a new, misleading kind of criticism. On the other hand, one cannot think Morgann completely wrong in his observations and judgments. It was objected that Morgann's mistake was to take Falstaff for

near him to act in their turn and sets the stage for his own super-lative performances. Dramatizing not only his cronies but even his Prince, Falstaff elicits in them the desire to dramatize him. Our pleasure in those episodes of *Henry IV* involving Falstaff springs from his spontaneous dramaturgy. He makes the tavern wonderful as he makes the battlefield livable—for him.

At the heart of the play there is a question—who will plot the career of Prince Hal? Will it be Prince Hal's father, Henry IV, or will it be Jack Falstaff? If Jack Falstaff, then Prince Hal is almost certain to be defeated or eclipsed by Hotspur. But if Henry IV, less interesting than Falstaff, is able to plot his son's career, then the young man has at least a chance of becoming Henry V. Great issues are at stake here, between the lively, fat knight and the dying King.

We should not understand merely as comedy the fantastic scene in the tavern when Falstaff, acting the part of Henry IV, urges Prince Hal to do the very contrary of what his father desires: "Peremptorily," says Falstaff, playing the King, "I speak it, there is virtue in that Falstaff. Him keep with, the rest ban-ish." Prince Hal and Falstaff then change roles, the Prince playing Henry IV and stating his father's objections to the knight; the latter this time defending himself: "But for sweet Jack Falstaff, kind Jack Falstaff, true Jack Falstaff, valiant Jack Falstaff, and therefore more valiant, being, as he is, old Jack Falstaff, ban-ish not him thy Harry's company, banish not him thy Harry's company. Banish plump Jack, and you banish all the world!" But when Prince Hal is crowned Henry V, he does banish Falstaff, and in words hot with hate.

The scenes involving Falstaff and Prince Hal are pure theatre, of the most imaginative kind. But they are set, after all, in a historical play, where the actual fortunes of the King and the Prince must be dominant. Falstaff is too large for a purely historical drama; he is greater and more interesting than Henry

---

a real person, instead of as a character in a play. But this character, being essentially a dramatist, can be said to have the capacity and impulse to exist apart from the playwright who created him. Falstaff, the creation of Shakespeare, is himself a creator. Morgann must have felt this.

IV, greater and more interesting than Prince Hal. And so we are dissatisfied by Henry V's harshness to him. We cannot help but feel that the king of the tavern was greater than the King of England. This is not the right feeling to have in a work celebrating one of the better rulers of Britain.

Thus *Henry V*, in which Falstaff does not appear at all—we merely hear of his death—is more unified and playable than *Henry IV*, which Falstaff dominates imaginatively, but cannot dominate in fact. The play cannot contain him.

The feeling that characters can be superior to their situations may have suggested to Shakespeare the idea for his treatment of Hamlet. Why not for once justify the great character stuck with a bad plot? I think Shakespeare did just that in *Hamlet*, and created his most popular figure—for who, unhappy, will not be consoled by thinking that the plot he is in is at fault, and his soul greater than his fate? "Nature," says Hamlet, "cannot choose its origins." He, Hamlet, could not choose his own mother. This is what disturbs him, not lust for her, as the psychoanalytic critics have insisted.[5]

Yet Shakespeare must have desired to produce a work of a formal structure not incompatible with the presence in it of a greatly conceived character. He achieved this in one tragedy: *Macbeth*. That kind of absolute success he never achieved with the play-within-the-play until he wrote *The Tempest*. *Measure for Measure* is wonderfully structured, a new kind of philosophical drama; but there is no great character in it. *Cymbeline* and *A Winter's Tale* are fascinating works, but finally must be judged as exercises which made *The Tempest* possible. In *The Tempest*, Shakespeare presented two of his greatest figures, and in a work as great as they are.

The Tempest tells not of a utopia, but of a utopian event, a perfect revolution, which restores the true ruler of Milan after he has been deposed by the treachery of his brother. Events in life are generally so imperfect that to think of a revolution

---

5. Hamlet is possessed of a dramatist's imagination to the highest degree. And, of course, he has appeared again and again in literature and drama, bearing his own name or a pseudonym like Stavrogin or Lorenzaccio.

accomplished without bloodshed and to music seems like dreaming. Some dreams are antithetical to thought; the particular dream actualized in *The Tempest* is not. For a perfect revolution is not theoretically impossible. Such a revolution, of course, has never occurred.

The hero of *The Tempest* is the deposed duke, Prospero. He has acquired a power not precisely political: magic. His power is, I think, the magic of thought. This power he uses like a dramatist, creating a false tempest which causes the shipwreck (on the island Prospero rules) of his brother and of his brother's chief supporters. Thrown on Prospero's island, the false Duke of Milan, his counselors, and his son Ferdinand become actors who have lost their cues and do not know how to perform. Ignorant of where they are and misunderstanding their roles, they are easily dominated by Prospero.

Prospero has two servants: the spirit Ariel, who carries out his imaginative orders, and the very body of all bodies, Caliban, who performs certain physical labors, albeit unwillingly. Never was a playwright better served: his theatre an island, his villain the brother who has wronged him and is now at his mercy, his choreographer a spirit, his stagehand the monstrous Caliban.

(I must interpolate here that neither Ariel nor Caliban is properly represented in productions of the play. Ariel should not be seen at all, being too delicate for visual representation. Caliban, on the other hand, is too gross for us to look at. There is something sublime about his grossness; and what is sublime, as Immanuel Kant noted, lacks form. We should never see more than some part of Caliban's body—a tremendous foot, a huge hand. perhaps for one moment a masklike head covering the whole stage. His voice should not be unlike the tempest which caused the shipwreck of the treacherous Duke. Certainly Caliban should never be represented naturalistically, and the attempt to do just that has spoiled productions of *The Tempest* to this date. I must add that Caliban is in the purest sense a self-referring character, that is to say, a dramatist. One does not need the play to understand him, although unlike Hamlet and Falstaff he is at home in the play he was put in. But a character of this sort can visit other minds, as Caliban did when he visited the mind of Browning, who was then able to write "Caliban upon Setebos," in which Caliban is seen dramatizing the universe and even its creator.)

What of Prospero himself? Some have said that he is none other than Shakespeare, and that Prospero, drowning his book and breaking his staff, is Shakespeare deciding to quit the stage and retire as a country gentleman. I shall not venture to correlate Prospero's action with any so-called fact of Shakespeare's life. But some correlation between Shakespeare and Prospero is justified.

Certainly the events of *The Tempest* were put on by a dramatist. Prospero controls these events throughout, and at the end, attains what he desires through his art. It is then that he gives up his art.

It must be admitted that there is something unpleasant about Prospero: he lacks the naïveté to appear in any drama not produced by him. Shakespeare makes this quite clear. When at ease, in a form congenial to him, Shakespeare was capable of judging with utter impartiality. (Thus he is able to judge jealousy and infidelity without prejudice in a nonrealistic work like *A Winter's Tale*, as he is unable to do in *Othello*, which he conceived as tragedy.)

Prospero has the values and disvalues of consciousness to the highest degree. Such a man will strive never to be the actor is someone else's play. Will he try to make others actors in his own story? The temptation is there for anyone with that much power of thought. Perhaps this is why, finally, Prospero breaks his staff and drowns his book "deeper than any plummet ever sounded." His final act implies acceptance of the role life gave him originally, and which he did not invent, and which he will no longer be able to control by thought. Prospero will perhaps not be so unpleasant when he no longer is in charge of events.

But having ventured to use theatrical means to their magical limit, Prospero understands that in some sense all of life is a pageant or show, and he carries this thought to its ultimate consequence, foreseeing that the earth. "the great globe itself," will dissolve, leaving not a rack behind.

Wonder, including metaphysical wonder, is, in *The Tempest*, part of the motivation of the principal figures Caliban, Ariel, and Prospero. Wonder, even metaphysical wonder, has set the stage with the simple direction for the first scene: "a ship at sea." It is expressed in the personality of Prospero's daughter, Miranda, when she first sees Ferdinand, and in Ferdinand himself when he dreams not only of his own father's death but of his father's father's death before him. We wonder at Caliban, Ariel, and Prospero. We watch every character in the play being forced to wonder. The play, in its characters, story, setting—except for some jarring moments of low comedy—is all of a piece.

There is a thesis by a German writer attempting to prove that Calderón must have read *The Tempest* and, influenced by Shakespeare's play, wrote *Life Is a Dream*. As I have already indicated, it is not necessary to account for Calderón's great play by any such hypothesis. If we look for influences on Calderón, they exist in the Spanish theatre and literature. Calderón did not have to read Shakespeare to think the world a stage or that life can best be represented when felt to be a dream. All this the Spanish playwright could glean from Cervantes's great novel.

There is still further reason for not associating *Life Is a Dream* with any work by Shakespeare. The latter, as I have tried to show, felt the need to rationalize and purify the play-within-a-play form in order to accommodate to it characters of a certain imaginative size who would not be at home in tragedy or comedy, in chronicle or farce. Calderón needed the theatrical form he perfected in *Life Is a Dream* for quite a different purpose. Calderón had never been a great creator of character; he could never have felt that a personage he set in a play was independent of that play. Yet even in his less significant theatre pieces he always aims to give the dramatic event the maximum meaning it can have, to give dramatic action the quality of thought. In *The Great Magician*, not a successful play, the event is what is interesting, not the characters. It seems to me that the model or paradigm for Calderón of a real event was a true thought.

Life Is a Dream is a play-within-a-play, and of the most subtle design. The Prince of Poland, Sigismund, has been imprisoned by his own father since birth. He has been educated in all those matters which a prince should know, but he has been kept chained in a cave until his twenty-first birthday. The reason he has been so treated by his father, King Basilio, is that just before the Prince was born, the King, an astrologer, had read in the stars that the child about to be born would kill both his mother and father. In partial confirmation of this prediction, Sigismund's mother had died in giving birth to him. Basilio at once sentenced the infant to imprisonment. On his twenty-first birthday, still chained in a cave, Sigismund cries out: "What crime did I commit except that I was born?"

Basilio's drastic treatment of his son is an attempt to prevent the predicted tragedy in which he, Basilio, has been cast as victim. To prevent the play which he has been told is going to terminate with his death, Basilio determines to take responsibility for the drama's conclusion, rewriting it. His play is to be an antitragedy.

On his twenty-first birthday, Sigismund is given a drug, and when he returns to consciousness finds himself in his father's palace and is told that he had merely dreamed he had been in chains. The young Prince, suddenly freed, at once expresses the violence stored up in him. He threatens everyone, hurls a courtier who contradicts him out a window, and menaces the King, his father. The Prince is overpowered, again drugged, and when he recovers consciousness, is told that he had only dreamed he was a prince, that in fact he had never left the cave, never been freed of his chains. As a result of this second extraordinary revelation, which he cannot refute by any facts he knows to be true, Sigismund concludes that all life is a dream, in which our dreaming is of dreams.

But the people have seen the Prince; they know he lives, there is a revolution, and Sigismund is released. He now has his father, Basilio, at his mercy. Will the prophecy of the stars prove correct? Will the Prince kill his own father? But the Prince spares his father's life, for he has learned that life is a dream. Only virtue is real. (At one point in the play the Prince has dreamed of doing a good deed and is told that goodness, even dreamed, is praiseworthy.)

What has happened in this play? A tragedy was predicted, but did not occur. And if it did not, this was because of the dramatic invention of King Basilio, who substituted for the play intended by fate one of his own invention. The tragedy fails. Basilio's play succeeds. Metatheatre has replaced tragedy.

THE MYTH OF METATHEATRE

I HAVE IMAGINED that Aeschylus, leaving the theatre after a performance of his *Oresteia,* is kidnaped and taken to a chi-chi Athenian home. He is treated with courtesy, forbidden to leave, and then introduced to his kidnaper, a young Athenian named Orestes.

"Why have you brought me here?" the Greek playwright asks. Orestes replies, "I am your greatest admirer, Aeschylus." The dramatist: "Is that supposed to excuse your treatment of me? Release me at once." "No, Aeschylus, you'll have to stay," responds Orestes. "Besides, I grant you, I would have no right to do what I did if I had no other feeling for you than admiration. So I must now tell you frankly that though I admire you greatly, I am critical of you, too, very critical. Your *Oresteia* begins wonderfully, gets better as it goes on, rises to the very greatest height of drama, and then ends miserably. I brought you here to get you to change the ending of your trilogy. Perhaps you will when I explain how important this is to me. You took note of my name, didn't you? Whatever concerns Orestes must concern Aeschylus as much."

At this point Aeschylus becomes interested. He has never before heard this criticism of his great work. "I love the end of my play," says Aeschylus. "And if I am to listen to any criticism of it, I must have a glass of wine." He makes himself comfortable and accepts a glass of wine from his host, who then tells him the following story:

"I happen to have the same name as the hero of your play. But my mother was not named Clytemnestra nor my father Agamemnon. Nor was my mother's lover's name Aegisthus. But what Clytemnestra and Aegisthus did to Agamemnon, my mother and her lover did to my father, who fought, Aeschylus, with

you at Marathon, and who, like you, killed many a longhaired
Mede. When my father returned, my mother and her lover
chopped him to death with an ax. I felt that it was my duty,
in turn, to do something terrible to them. I did not. No oracle
urged me to. Besides, if an oracle had, I would not have believed it. Being enlightened, I was opposed to oracles. Instead
of killing the murderers of my father, I became their friend. I
looked kindly on my mother's guilty partner in lechery and
murder. He likes me, too, and always wants to go to the theatre
with me. We both love the theatre. What else is there in life?
But most of all I love your play, which is about me, not as I
am, but as I should have been. For the truth is I should have
killed my mother and her lover, and since I have not done so,
my life has become an empty dream. A dream in which the
only bit of reality is your play, which I see as often as I can.
Now perhaps you can understand why I am so critical as well
as so admiring of it. I, Orestes, go to your *Oresteia*. The beginning, as I told you, is wonderful. I see my father murdered,
I watch my mother affirming her guilt; then I appear in the
second part of the trilogy, and naturally I like that part of the
play best. I have been told unequivocally by Apollo himself to
kill my mother and her lover. I am going to do so, no matter
what my suffering afterward will be, though I do not myself
realize to the full how dreadful it will actually be. I kill the
murderer, then the murderess. The Furies appear and follow
me offstage. I am the object of their divine sadism, which means
that my own masochism becomes divine. Then comes the final
part of your trilogy. It is made clear that I have undergone
much suffering from the vengeful Furies. I take refuge in the
Temple of Athene. Apollo and the Furies appear, he for me,
they against me. The gods sit in judgment. Their verdict finally
is that I am no longer to be punished for killing my own mother!
A vulgar arrangement is made between Athene and the Furies;
it is a political deal: the Furies are to get some recognition in
the State and, in return, are to be less implacable. As for myself, I am cleared of all further guilt, declared free henceforth
to do as I please. But, Aeschylus, having killed my mother,
what could there be for me to do?

"Aeschylus, you must change the ending of your play. Since I did not kill my mother and can do so now only in imagination, since my real life now consists only in your work, you must make the end of your play as terrible as the beginning. I want to see myself die by torture. Do this for me, and you will have given meaning and worth, on certain occasions— when the *Oresteia* is shown—to an otherwise empty life."

GENET AND METATHEATRE

I

JEAN GENET'S EXTRAORDINARY play, *The Balcony*, is most certainly *not* a piece of avant-garde theatre; it is not eccentric or odd; modern, to be sure, it makes no claim to being especially modernistic. The play is neither peculiar nor perverse; yes, *The Balcony* is a new play, but it is not unlike some rather old ones; it is original, but it belongs in a tradition, and that tradition is none other than the great tradition of Western dramaturgy. *The Balcony* is a metaplay; and the metaplay has occupied the dramatic imagination of the West to the same degree that the Greek dramatic imagination was occupied with tragedy.

As I have already said: Shakespeare and Pedro Calderón did not write tragedies; at least, they did not write good tragedies. (Shakespeare wrote one great one, *Macbeth*; Calderón, not even one.) What these playwrights did create was a new type of drama, one with very different assumptions from those of Greek tragedy, and with very different effects. Often they produced this characteristic and new form while intent on writing tragedy.

I have asked myself: Can I be the first one to think of designating a form which has been in existence for so long a time, about three hundred years? It is a strange and not undramatic fact of life that something shiningly individual will continue to be seen darkly until it has been given a name.

Let us see why tragedy was not the characteristic form of the Elizabethan or Spanish theatre. Why have most Western dramatists, bent on writing tragedy, been unable to do so successfully? Much of their difficulty can be summed up in a single word: *self-consciousness*. First, the self-consciousness of the

151

dramatist himself, and then that of his protagonists. For consider: If Antigone were self-conscious enough to suspect her own motives in burying her brother Polyneices, would her story be a tragic one? Now the Western playwright is unable to believe in the reality of a character who is lacking in self-consciousness. Lack of self-consciousness is as characteristic of Antigone, Oedipus, and Orestes, as self-consciousness is characteristic of Hamlet, that towering figure of Western metatheatre.

Another insurmountable difficulty: one cannot create tragedy without accepting some implacable values as true. Now the Western imagination has, on the whole, been liberal and skeptical; it has tended to regard *all* implacable values as false.

Let us look for a moment at a typical Western drama which was meant to be a tragedy, seems to be a tragedy, and has, in fact, been so designated. I am referring to Herman Melville's *Billy Budd*. Now in this short novel—it was made into a play by an adapter, and with all its defects, is still the best dramatic work by an American—the young sailor, Budd, accused of mutinous action, but whom the officers of the drumhead court-martial want to exonerate, is finally sentenced and executed on the insistence of Captain Vere; this is a man who we have been led to believe appreciates Budd, loves him, and is more convinced of his innocence than any of the other officers. Did Melville then accept as true at least one implacable value: ship discipline on a man-of-war? I do not think so. For why is Melville unable to make Captain Vere's action in demanding Budd's conviction convincing to us, at least to me? I never believed, in reading *Billy Budd*, that it was necessary for the sailor to hang for discipline on the *Indomitable* to be preserved. Moreover, the consciousness of Captain Vere is not expressed in his action, which is simply a mirror reflecting the regulations of the Mutiny Act. Melville was only able to get to the externally tragic ending of his story by depriving Captain Vere, at a crucial moment, of the very kind of self-consciousness he has throughout his work led us to believe Captain Vere possessed. Now for a character not to have self-consciousness is one thing; for a character to be deprived of self-consciousness by the author in order to be capable of representing some implacable value is quite another.

Melville, if Captain of the *Indomitable,* would *not* have sentenced Billy Budd to hang. Of course, one can only speculate, but I think Sophocles would have buried his brother in defiance of the State. The Greek playwright's heroine is of the same culture as her creator. So, of course, is Creon, but Captain Vere, at the moment of his dramatic decision, belongs to a world not Melville's. This is one of the superiorities of *Antigone* (it has others) over *Billy Budd.*

But to come back to the metaplay. It is the necessary form for dramatizing characters who, having full self-consciousness, cannot but participate in their own dramatization. Hence the famous lines of Jaques, Shakespeare's philosopher of metatheatre, "All the world's a stage, and all the men and women merely players." The same notion is expressed by Calderón, who titled one of his works *The Great Stage of the World.* For both the Spanish and the English poets there could not but be an essential illusoriness in reality. We cannot have it both ways: a gain for consciousness means a loss for the reality of its objects, certainly for the reality of its main object, namely the world. Obviously it takes a high degree of consciousness to become aware that the world cannot be proved to exist. However, I shall not insist on this point, for I think the objectivity of the world is maintained not by logic, but, like some fabled treasure that dragons guard, by those monsters to the sensitive and skeptical mind: implacable values. Thus it is that if, in Greek tragedy, the hero is defeated, on the other hand the reality of the world is underscored; in the metaplay, the hero, however unfortunate, can never be decisively defeated, perhaps he can never even be heroic (as Henrich von Kleist's wonderful *Prince of Homburg* suggests); but on the other hand, the reality of the world is mortally affected, illusion becomes inseparable from reality. *Life Is a Dream* is the title of Calderón's greatest play, and Shakespeare's theatre terminates with the famous: "We are such stuff as dreams are made on." The point I am making here is that these phrases are not chance expressions by Calderón and Shakespeare, but fundamental concepts of the dramatic form which they initiated.

In the metaplay there will always be a fantastic element.

For in this kind of play fantasy is essential, it is what one finds at the heart of reality. In fact, one could say that the metaplay is to ordinary fantasy as tragedy is to melodrama. As in tragedy the misfortunes of the hero must be necessary and not accidental, so in the metaplay life *must* be a dream and the *world* must be a stage.

All this would have by now been much clearer if it had not been for the appearance in the nineteenth century of a very great dramatist, Henrik Ibsen, who tried to give to the realistic play a necessitarian structure like that found in Greek tragedy, and this without sharing the premises of either Sophocles or Aeschylus, Ibsen's own view of the world being actually closer to Shakespeare's and Calderón's. As a result, a wrong belief was propagated—it dominated the stage for more than fifty years—that without the Greek metaphysic the form of tragedy was possible and valid. Now if this view was never formally challenged, its inadequacy was felt by the best playwrights of the present century. Their plays, in the main, are metaplays. Among these playwrights is Jean Genet.

II

The Balcony is a brothel whose clients arrive equipped, in Madame Irma's phrase, "each with his own scenario." Surely this identifies the drama as a metaplay. Among the clients are three more or less nondescript persons, one of whom wants to dramatize himself as a bishop, one as a judge, one as a general. The prostitutes assigned to these men play up their illusions of greatness, degrading them in certain instances, just to make the act seem more real. The Grand Balcony is, indeed, "a palace of illusions." For the clients are fitted out with costumes appropriate to their dreams. We watch them don these costumes as they prepare for peculiar satisfactions. It is to be noted that in watching them change before our eyes from their uncostumed reality to the bravura figures they become when arrayed to act, we get an altogether new feeling of the reality—not of character but of costume. Seldom does it happen in

any play, modern or classical, that costume means much to
the audience. In most revivals of Elizabethan dramas, costume
is actually an impediment to our acceptance of the situation or
the scene. Hence directors have experimented with doing the
old plays in modern dress. But there is something poetical in
costume as such, and the theatre would be disadvantaged by a
complete loss of it. In *The Balcony*, Genet has done nothing
less than restore the poetical value of costume to the stage.
For the fact is that when we see costumes being put on, we
can accept them as the necessary garb for the characters, whereas
if the characters come on the stage fully costumed, we think at
once of the work of the director and the costume designer. The
effect Genet achieves here by the metatheatrical device of having us present at the dressing up of his personages is akin to
certain characteristic effects of Luigi Pirandello. I am thinking,
for example, of the scene in *Tonight We Improvise*, in which
an old man rehearses his death-scene; here Pirandello is able
to touch us with the feeling of the real imminence of death in
a way he never would have been able to do by showing us a
man really dying. We tend to think of real blood on the stage
as a fake; now the magic of metatheatre can make stage blood
seem real; at least we can think of it as real for a moment
and without feeling that we have been taken in.

Outside the brothel a revolution is taking place. In a remarkable scene, the revolutionaries discuss a bit of theatre designed
to impose their aims on the populace. Should they not make of
Chantal, a prostitute from Madame Irma's "Palace of Illusions,"
a saint of their revolution? If they were to kill her and claim
that she fell as a martyr to their cause, would not her image
impel the people to victory? But what good is our victory if
come by that way, protests one of the revolutionaries, "it already has a dose of clap." The point is made that the
revolutionaries must make a determined effort to do without
illusion. Perhaps they can. "Have they jumped into reality?"
asks the Police Chief from his headquarters in Madame Irma's
brothel. Evidently the real adversary of the revolution is none
other than Madame Irma. Moreover, she has already conquered.
The revolutionaries will not be able to remain real; what is

more, they do not want to. They may conquer the palace, the legislature, the army, the courts; they will not be able to control the old whorehouses.

It is the revolutionaries in Genet's play who represent implacable values. Actually, in the modern world, only revolutionaries have been able to represent such values. Hence, the prestige of revolutionaries. But Genet has taken their measure, too, and finally renders them ridiculous. We have the impression that they will all come finally to Madame Irma's Balcony. They are would-be tragedians in the world of metatheatre.

Yet in a way Genet shares the weakness of his revolutionaries in *The Balcony*; he, too, would like to create something other than the kind of play he can make so magnificently; this master of the metaplay would like to create tragedy. And the sentimental inclination toward something impossible for him is responsible, I believe, for the one bad scene in *The Balcony*, a scene almost fatal to the second half of the play, lasting for almost an hour and boring from beginning to end. Having absorbed the revolution with its insistence on reality into the illusionist world of The Grand Balcony, Genet suddenly reverses himself and tries to see illusion itself as inexorable. But this is an impossible idea, contrary to all dramatic judgment or good sense: it may be our fate to have illusions; this does not mean that illusion can have the same force as fate. Or to put the matter better, fate might free us from illusions, but is probably itself illusory. This is more or less what Genet has said throughout his play, but at the very end he seems to want to say the contrary. I noted this weakness in another play of his, *The Maids*. It was not necessary for one of the two girls actually to take poison in that work, since when she did I felt that she was acting. There is something similar in *The Balcony* at the very close. The Chief of Police wants to be apotheosized and as a phallus. He achieves this grandiose aim when a client (none other than the very revolutionary who had wanted to keep the revolution real), pretending to be the Chief of Police, castrates himself. The episode is brutal, vulgar, and utterly undramatic. Should illusion also have sacrifices, martyrs? I explain the weak thinking here as not peculiar to Genet but present in modern intellectuals. They are afraid of the implications of their own ideas, which have rendered the world less real than they would like it to be. They do not want to think of life as a dream, but as serious, valid, overwhelming maybe. They would like nothing better than to come upon some implacable value they could regard as true. So the one real fault in Genet's play is not just his. We all have some share in it. Yet, in the main, the point of view of Genet is that the destruction of illusion, as represented by *The Balcony*, would be the destruction of life as such. Is this thought shocking? Some of the reviewers evidently thought so. But is the French dramatist's view really so different from that expressed by Prospero at the conclusion of *The Tempest*? If anything, I should say that Genet's play ends less cynically than Shakespeare's. For Genet the revels have not ended. The action will continue. The more or less humble characters will again mount on stilts and costume themselves to be again extravagant in sex. Illusion and reality cannot be segregated; they will continually change places, and be the Same to the Other, the Other to the Same.

My contention is that the dramatic philosophy of *The Balcony*, as of Genet's *The Maids*, and of his play *The Blacks*, while certainly his own, is yet, when we think of it formally, the same dramatic philosophy present in *Twelfth Night, Measure for Measure, Hamlet, The Tempest, Life Is a Dream*. Let none then reproach Jean Genet for his ideas. His thought proceeds on a level where one can only think what has to be thought. Without tragedy, of which we may be incapable, there is no philosophic alternative to the two concepts by which I have defined the metaplay: the world is a stage, life is a dream.

BECKETT AND METATHEATRE

I LINK SAMUEL BECKETT with Jean Genet because the plays of both are modern works of metatheatre. Beckett's metatheatre is very special. His plays almost never present a play-within-a-play sequence. And his characters, although imaginative creations, have a kind of sad naturalness. Their physical oddities, inflictions, and illnesses are exhibited; they wheeze, they whine, they groan or sigh unguardedly, as people do in real life. James Joyce, who in his writings never overlooked human infirmities, no doubt influenced Beckett to describe people naturalistically. All the same, Beckett's plays are very far from realism. How does he get his strange effects?

Every one of Beckett's plays suggests that some decisive action has gone on before the characters have come into our view. Take Beckett's two principal works, *Waiting for Godot* and *Endgame*. The characters in these plays, Estragon and Vladimir, Pozzo and Lucky, Hamm and Clov, Nagg and Nell, are made dramatic, not so much by what they do as by what has already happened to them. They show us the results of dramatic action, but not that action itself. Their drama consists in having been capable of drama at some time, and in their remembrance of that time. On the stage, they remember that once they had a stage for their thoughts, feelings, and better bodies.

All of Beckett's plays are epilogues and hence contracted. His people are people who have dwindled, as a result of what they did or what was done to them. Moreover, all that is left for them to do, as we catch sight of them, is to play. And the action, insofar as there is action in any play of Beckett, consists precisely in playing. Estragon's life with Vladimir is a series of scenes they put on to while away the time. Certainly

158

Pozzo and Lucky have nothing particular to do; Pozzo's only possible action is to exhibit Lucky's tricks as a theatre manager might put on those of an acrobat or a freak. In *Endgame*, all that is left for Hamm and Clov is to play, but without joy. Here is one of Beckett's strongest dramatic effects. In *Krapp's Last Tape*, the protagonist, who is also the only person on the stage, plays with himself. If this sounds masturbatory, then I have not been misunderstood. As a matter of fact, Krapp's eating of a banana is done in such a way—and Beckett's stage directions are very precise—as to give just this suggestion. Moreover, Krapp plays with his tapes, on which his memories are transcribed. He plays with his memories, too—all writers do that—but Krapp does it without any aim or purpose. What has happened to him? This we are not told. Perhaps nothing much more than that time has passed. But the passage of time, however slow it may seem, however gently said our farewells to each particular moment, is drastic in the extreme. Time brings infirmity and death closer; it effaces the thrill of past enjoyment. As an individual's past time increases, the future time left him dwindles. It is at this moment that an individual becomes interesting to Beckett, and worth setting on the stage.

In *All That Fall* there is a definite and simple action. An infirm, old woman, weary and wheezing, struggles to the station to meet her blind husband and take him home with her. But the real event is not in the action presented; rather, through this action the real event is indicated: what time has done to both the woman and her husband. We see their different infirmities, caused by the same enemy of both—time. Weakness, tiredness, blindness, lameness, deafness, oldness—these are its effects.

In Beckett's play *Happy Days*, he presents a woman buried in the ground to her waist. Just as much of her is gone as is present when the curtain rises. The action of the play consists in her sinking deeper into the ground, so that when the curtain falls, only her head is visible. In the meantime, there is nothing for her to do but to recall what is absent from the stage and to play with her husband, who circles about her on all fours. Is he like a dog on the scent, trying to find the trail of all that is gone?

Why are time and its effects so important to Beckett? Because,

I suspect, of his nostalgia for eternity. Should we not be, at the very least, the playthings of eternity and not merely the playthings of the time? Such is the question Beckett poses in his plays, thus suggesting that the actual characters are themselves the scenes of an invisible action: the action of time, which might be eternal itself, or the surrogate, although we cannot be sure of this, for eternity.

But these plays cannot be understood or appreciated fully unless we recognize that for all their special content, oddity, and purely personal lyricism, they conform to the kind of dramatic work I have designated as metatheatre: what makes them so special is that life in these plays has been theatricalized, not by any attitudes taken by the characters, not by any tricks of dramaturgy, and not by the author's intent to demonstrate any propositions about the world, but by the mere passage of time, that drastic fact of ordinary life.

But we should expect in metatheatrical works some element of metaphysical wonder; and there is that in Beckett's plays. Who is the real enemy of Vladimir, Estragon, Lucky, Pozzo? Of the characters of *Endgame, All That Fall, Krapp's Last Tape*, and *Happy Days*? Who is their enemy? If the author knew for sure, he would have told us in works of didactic character; he would not have played with his doubts and fancies, nor would he have presented characters who do little other than play. He would have written works with a thesis, not pieces of metatheatre.

BRECHT AND METATHEATRE

I

HOW DID BRECHT come to metatheatre?

From the very start of his career as a playwright Brecht rejected the individual and moral experience, so important in the realistic European drama as it was shaped by Henrik Ibsen, and in Germany continued by Gerhart Hauptmann and Hermann Sudermann. For Brecht, these playwrights, and Ibsen, too, represented the bourgeois drama which he was interested in subverting and in replacing with some other dramatic form. Now, of course, to one who rejected the individual, the realistic or naturalistic play could not but become an impossible mode. Curiously enough, the Communist theoreticians of the theatre strongly supported realistic and naturalistic techniques in playwriting, acting, and even stage design. (One must except Vsevolod Meyerhold, but he was liquidated by Stalin.) The Communists were for the Stanislavsky type of theatre, with its concentration on close analysis of individual motivation in a realistic setting. But Brecht, even when he became converted to Communism as a political doctrine, never yielded to the Communist theory of what theatre should be. The Communists of course did not believe in the individual or in moral experience any more than Brecht did, but they did not want to admit this publicly since they were interested in appealing to individuals and in justifying Communism morally. For them the theatre had value insofar as it could make propaganda for their policies; for Brecht the theatre could have value only insofar as it expressed the convictions he felt deeply. He could not write realistic plays about individuals, treating their moral conflicts seriously, since he thought the individual a phantom, and hence the dramatization of moral sufferings would have to be comical rather than serious. Certainly the Ibsen type of drama was an impossibility for him, and he knew this from the start.

It is very interesting, too, that he felt strongly opposed to any form of tragedy. Much of what he has written on this topic is uninteresting, since his objections to tragedy are generally framed in the context of an attack on what he terms the Aristotelian play, and by way of defending a kind of rambling, loose-knit, reviewlike type of play, favored early in the thirties by Erwin Piscator and which both Brecht and Piscator designated by the term "epic theatre." It is to be noted, though, that at the time Brecht opposed his own epic theatre to Aristotelian theatre, he was much more interested in the propaganda content of his plays than later on in his most creative period, when he admitted that the fundamental purpose of theatre had to be art and diversion rather than propaganda or edification. In any case, the term "epic theatre" is not a very clear one and has little value in the way of explaining the great plays Brecht came to write finally.

But obviously one could not write tragedy if one did not believe in the importance of moral suffering. Thus Brecht was opposed both to the mode of psychological realism, a mode still fashionable in this country, and to the violent fillip given that mode by Ibsen, who had imposed a necessitarian structure on his realistic plays, a structure taken from Greek tragedy.

Actually, Brecht was not spontaneously opposed to implacable values, and in fact, had a kind of yearning for them. His play *The Measures Taken* may even be described as an experiment in submitting to implacable values. It is the one play of his, too, which comes close to tragedy. What prevents it from being deeply tragic, though, is that the victim in the play, destroyed because he is an individual, is only that abstractly, by definition. We never feel his individuality, and the recital of his death is not moving. But, in any case, the Communist Party, in its disapproval of *The Measures Taken*, indicated that it did not want Communist values to be expressed in absolute terms.

II

I have defined metatheatre as resting on two basic postulates: (1) the world is a stage and (2) life is a dream. Now I am not going to assert that Brecht entertained either of these postulates as truths to be demonstrated by his works. What I do claim is that Brecht, by having rejected the significance of the individual and of moral experience, had to rely on these concepts to give his plays form.

Let us look first at the proposition "the world is a stage." If one does not believe that individuals are real or their sufferings of any great moment, then do not all human actions, reactions, and expressions of feeling immediately seem theatrical? Now what was Brecht's most characteristic theatrical device? It was his deliberate insistence that feelings be played by his actors as if they were acted and not directly felt. One of his favorite devices was to ask his actors to act out a feeling as if they were telling of how some other person felt. Surely this is the furthest possible extreme from the kind of psychological realism we get regularly on the American stage, based very often on the notion that the most infantile and absurd expressions of feeling of so-called individuals are of the very greatest importance. Whether, then, Brecht believed the world to be a stage or not, his plays, his concepts of acting and stage design, were all calculated to produce that effect. The reality in his plays is that of theatre and not that of life, except as the latter happens to become theatrical. Ronald Gray says that Brecht's technical innovations were almost always in the direction of making the action on the stage not believable but "strange."

The other proposition of metatheatre is more difficult to ascribe to Brecht than the first. Could this hardheaded, practical-minded man have believed that life is a dream? Again I do not think he would have consciously asserted any such thing. But if one does not see any inner necessity in the lives of people, will not their lives appear dreamlike? Brecht was so far from finding inner necessity in the lives of persons that in *A Man's a Man* he even dramatized the foisting by others of a new identity on his main character. I think in the main it is by the fact that they are capable of feeling pain that others proclaim they are real to us. And by sympathizing with their feelings we in fact maintain their reality. Cool, dispassionate thinking of the sort Brecht always advocated, and claimed he wanted to induce in his spectators, is precisely the kind of thinking that can never assert the reality of any person not oneself. Life, in a way, had to be a dream for Brecht, given his extreme devaluation of individual feelings.

Now the type of play Brecht wrote—it is the same type of play that Shaw and Pirandello developed and was continued by Beckett and Genet—implies the notion that life is a dream, and that the spectator will either form this notion or feel its suggestiveness as a result of the play's effect. Perhaps Brecht did not want this to happen, and I think it correct to say he did not want this to happen because of his political views. Hence his idea of interfering with, interrupting, restraining the response of the spectator. Note that no writer of tragedy ever did or could be conceived as doing what Brecht set himself to do. For the effect of tragedy is to induce in the spectator an almost overwhelming sense of reality. You cannot call a spectator back to reality from a tragic moment, for that moment, if truly realized by the dramatist, is a concentrate of reality beyond anything that might be felt in life, and certainly beyond any sense of things that one might feel when stimulated to exercise one's "critical" powers. Certainly Brecht's idea of recalling the spectator from involvement would be a contradictory one had Brecht been trying to write tragedy or realism; it is not contradictory, considering that what he actually wrote was metatheatre.

Here we may compare Brecht with Shaw, whose political and social views were not dissimilar to those of the German dramatist. Unquestionably Shaw used the theatre as a platform for criticizing society, and he would have furiously protested against our ascribing to him any such notion as that life is a dream. But when we look at some of his finest works this is what they say. Take such a masterpiece as *Pygmalion*, for example. Here we have the complete transformation of a vulgar, dirty, and illiterate girl into a dazzling lady, brought about by cleansing her, dressing her, and altering her diction. The play is incidentally a Cinderella story. And let us consider *Don Juan in Hell*. This is a thoroughgoing metaplay. Each character in it comes directly from the stage and the opera. Each one of them has behind him Tirso de Molina, Molière, and Mozart. The place is hell, which, according to Shaw, is a place of illusion. Heaven is for serious-minded people like Rembrandt or Friedrich Nietzsche, whom we never see and know of only through their admirer Don Juan, who finally decides at the play's close to be as serious as his heroes and to join them in heaven. This decision may be taken to stand for Shaw's personal feeling that life ought not be regarded as a dream and that one should not take it as such. But the play he wrote, the place he was interested in describing, was hell, namely, according to his own view, the place of illusion. Comparing Shaw's *Don Juan* with Brecht, one might say that the German dramatist went one step further. Don Juan merely announces he will go to heaven; Brecht assumed he was already there, that is, in the heaven of the Communist movement. However, his plays, since capitalism still existed, could take place only in hell and hence would have to share hell's characteristics. But from his strategic seat in the Communist heaven, the German playwright could call out from time to time, interrupt and divert attention from the action of his own productions. Such, I think, might be the explanation of Brecht's famous theory of "alienating" the spectator.

THE HERO OF METATHEATRE

WE SPEAK OF the "hero of tragedy" as if we had at hand some notion—clear or unclear—of the kind of individual who becomes known to us in an action we can call "tragic"; in a work based essentially on the plays of Sophocles, Bernard Knox has even characterized such individuals as being of "heroic temper." I like Knox's term; it correctly describes those figures who satisfy us with the attitude they take when resolved to act at the cost of suffering. If they do not altogether satisfy us in this respect—certain characters of plays known to us as tragedies do not—by this fact alone they cast doubt on the nature of the drama which shows them forth.[1] It has been alleged that the dramas they appear in—however catastrophic, however designated by the author—are not "true" tragedies.

Now it has been my claim that there is a form of drama distinctive enough to be characterized as "metatheatre." Can it also be said that a particular type of individual may be singled out as the likely or even paradigmatic protagonist in such a dramatic work?

But let me first of all ask this: Can the heroes of metatheatre— assuming there to be such—be said to have the same *temper* as heroes of tragedy? My answer: they may or may not have the qualities claimed for the heroes of tragedy, which brings me to the question I have been leading up to all along: What are the qualities which a character *has* to possess to be a hero of metatheatre?

I have chosen as my paradigmatic metatheatrical figure not a character from some work written for the stage, but one taken from a novel, the first of its kind, and written by a

---

1. Hamlet, for example.

novelist who had previously failed as a playwright. I have chosen Don Quixote to represent the character traits especially *appropriate* to the metatheatrical hero, as well as those which are *essential* to him.

What is essential for the hero of metatheatre is that he be conscious of the part he himself plays in constructing the drama that unfolds around him. He may, like Don Quixote, have foisted on the scene the action in which he is caught, and in which he can no more hope to be successful than if he had been thrust into it against his will. Hamlet, it will be remembered, was so thrust by his father's ghost. Hamlet, of course, did not himself invent the circumstance in which he was entangled, though at times he suspects himself of having done so. Swinging counterweight, Don Quixote has actually chosen to be caught in the circumstance he imagines he is in. He wants to fight a giant, the windmill promptly becomes one, and he spurs Rosinante to charge the giant he has postulated to be there. Is he mad? To be sure. But his madness, like Hamlet's, has method to it. . . .

The value to a playwright of such a character is that he is capable of inserting himself into a plot without ever consulting his author. The six characters of Pirandello's masterpiece tell the stage manager they accost that they are in search of an author, but once onstage and given a chance to enact their roles, show that they do not need an author at all. Released on the stage they commence to live—at the risk of life itself. Their belief is that "the play is the thing," whatever its outcome for them.

The individual of heroic temper is, as Bernard Knox has indicated, *undaunted*. Now the hero of metatheatre is not necessarily that firm. He would not say like "the undaunted daughter of desire" that "it kills me not to die for thee." The hero of one remarkable work of metatheatre, Prince Frederick of Homburg, is so dominated by fear that at one point he rejects the woman he loves and even suggests that she marry another of her suitors if in this way he may escape death. He is certainly unqualified to be the hero of a tragedy, as the Prussian militarists were quick to point out. After a single exhibition of cowardice, they said, one can no more be a hero than a woman once seduced can be called "pure." Let me add that even the quite fearless Cyrano yields, if not to the force, position, or skill of another, yet to the shame he feels for part of his own body, his too prominent nose. Thus he volunteers to help his rival Christian, instead of boldly speaking to Roxanne of his love for her. Is Hamlet undaunted? How could he be, weakened by doubt as to his mother's role in his father's murder and by his loss of faith in womanly virtue? There are all sorts of critics who have labored to transform Shakespeare's hero into one more appropriate to tragedy, but such efforts fail to convince. It is time to see them for what they are: obstinate refusals to desist from the shallow reading of an ever enigmatic and ever revealing play. . . .

But is not Don Quixote undaunted in his persevering effort to be a knight errant in a world which rejects his efforts as mad? My answer is that he has moments when he recognizes his efforts for what they are, as in the wonderful scene which Vladimir Nabokov in his splendid book on the knight has singled out for praise. Sancho Panza has gone off to administer the island procured for him, and over which he expects to rule, and Don Quixote now has a countenance especially mournful, recognizing that he is old, alone, poor, and out of his mind. . . . Undaunted, nevertheless. . . .

Another Russian writer, the literary theorist Mikhail Bakhtin, has stressed the importance of Cervantes's novel, which he has assimilated—I myself would not—to the Rabelaisian novel. I am struck by the fact that the two great Russians, the novelist and the theorist of the novel, have given such importance to the book of Cervantes, Nabokov emphasizing in the work he devoted to it the aesthetic strengths and weaknesses of the book, while recognizing that its greatness is based on the quality of its main character. Bakhtin, for his part, saw something of equal importance which Nabokov characteristically missed, by which I mean he *set out to miss it;* for he was interested exclusively in aesthetic qualities, and against giving, or recognizing any necessity to give, any credit for insight that might be called *moral.* And Bakhtin? He took the very opposite view. In an early essay on form and content, he made it clear that we can get something important from novels which we can no longer get, or even expect to get, from moral philosophy, namely, a moral explanation and judgment of experience. For philosophers no longer feel able to defend the moral views they happen to hold. Can the novelist? Not cognitively, but aesthetically. Feodor Dostoevsky does not have to supply an argument to prove Prince Myshkin's goodness to us; we know this as simply as we know gold from lead, as we know the goodness of Don Quixote, which in fact inspired Dostoevsky to create Prince Myshkin, and Miguel de Unamuno to write a book titled *Our Lord Don Quixote*. That vindication of the morally good which Bakhtin points out can no longer be made in the language of philosophy indeed can be made in literature, and to the handful of writers who are able to do this, readers and critics have spontaneously accorded the respect formerly reserved for moral philosophers.

It is still the case that we cannot defend cognitively what we support morally. Surely our relationship to the good is fantastic, being inextricably connected—as Karl Jaspers pointed out—with our inability to demonstrate its rightness. Who then could better represent our relationship to the good than one who can represent the Ought which is not discoverable in all that it can be said Is? Cervantes's hero has the quality of a goodness as evident as it is unprovable, and of a goodness that is not confined to the aid which may be offered one person by another. This knight errant has also set himself to address wrongs in the social order to which he belongs, and in the natural world as well. He is not only for right actions, those he is ready to perform against all reason (which is to say when they are not required); he is also for an order of things in which chivalrous action is demanded, and not only for damsels in distress. Don Quixote is also thinking of the earth, which men persist in torturing with blunt-edged instruments. (What would he have said about the disfigurement of nature we tolerate to-day? Martin Heidegger, perhaps speaking for him, has remarked that we put a gun to nature and take its wealth, to our own future impoverishment.) Let it be noted that Don Quixote has notions about the morally good, the socially good, and of what is good for the natural world.

Having chosen the Hidalgo as the paradigmatic figure of metatheatre, I realize that I must explain why I preferred him to any character of Pirandello, although the latter wrote most of the great plays of our own or any time that can be called metatheatrical, and it is to him we owe whatever understanding we have of the form. My reason for not selecting a character from one of his plays is this: great as a playwright, Pirandello was not a great creator of character. Of all the characters who come onstage in *Six Characters in Search of an Author*, there is not one who is convincing as more than a stage type. And in his other plays, many of them masterpieces of construction, fulfilling Aristotle's requirement that plot be plausible even if the characters are less so, there is no individual we can find who is deeply touching or deeply true. To be sure, the protagonist of *Henry IV* has been compared to Hamlet. But the comparison should not have been made; it will not help us understand either figure. Granted that the hero of *Henry IV* has endured a tragic loss—twenty of what might have been the best years of his life—yet his calculated revenge, made possible by society's notion that he is mad, is surely an unworthy deed. We cannot admire him for it, or pity him for having as a consequence to remain in the asylum which has become his home. And it is to be noted that the Father in *Six Characters*, while philosophically keen and eloquent in his contention that characters of fiction like Sancho Panza are immortal, is hardly more memorable than the other stage types composing his family. These are certainly not immortal figures; they hardly survive in our memory the curtain's fall.[2]

Pirandello's limitations in character creation may be laid up to his skepticism about moral values and his disinclination to make moral judgments. It is only by showing moral differences,

---

2. It is interesting, too, that in arguing for the immortality of the great characters of fiction, the Father, advised by Pirandello, chooses Sancho Panza, and not Don Quixote, as an example. I would suggest that the Knight of the Mournful Countenance seemed too great a figure for the Father (or his creator) to put on the same scale with any of the Six Characters. This tells us that Pirandello was much wiser than the dramatic critics who compared the protagonist of his *Henry IV* to Hamlet.

as Aristotle noted, that characters can be differentiated on the stage. But for Pirandello, a moral crisis is always resolved into an intellectual crisis, terminating in some paradox. Action in his plays is stripped of all value terms and treated as a fact among facts. He seems not to have noticed that the very reality of a deed is in some important sense related to our judgment of its worth. In the saying "Murder will out," the word *murder* stands for something other than the fact that one person has been deprived of life by another. For surely we do not mean that every deed of this kind will necessarily become known. By "Murder will out," we mean that every deed we judge ethically (and emotionally) as "murder" *should* out, that we are not willing to allow an evil intent bringing death with it to remain hidden forever. Now I am not saying that this conviction of ours is justified. It shows only that a moral judgment is embedded in the very word *murder*, which is conveyed by Hamlet when he says:

> Murder
> Though it have no tongue will speak
> With most miraculous organ.

An act of killing, not judged ethically or emotionally, may have no such miraculous organ and may not speak at all. The killing of Belcredi in Pirandello's *Henry IV* is not "murder" in this ethical sense, and we are quite unmoved by the deed. We do not care about Belcredi and think the less of the false Henry IV for having killed him. The contradiction between Pirandello's skeptical positivism and what is morally required for serious drama is very evident here. Though he does not believe in truth, he subjects feelings and values to truth tests they are simply unable to pass. Pirandello's limitations here are, of course, not just those of a thinker. They also define his failings as a dramatist.

It is my contention that the term "tragicomedy" is confusing; it implies that one can go at will from tragic to comic effects. But one has to care about a character if his mishaps are to affect one seriously, and one cannot care in the same way about a character if one is to enjoy seeing him ridiculed. If you care for M. Orgon, you will not laugh at his credulity vis-à-vis Tartuffe. This problem bedeviled Anton Chekhov. He loved his characters, but he wanted the plays he set them in to be comedies, and they seldom make us laugh. He has created exquisite moments, to which we often do not know how to respond. We do not know whether to laugh or cry when Vanya, who is bringing a rose to Elena, finds her in Dr. Astrov's arms. But a whole play can hardly be constructed around such moments. Here I think the notion of metatheatrical form has its real use. Metatheatre can convey both the comic and the tragic, since it can keep them separate. And here, too, the novels of Cervantes provide a model. We do care about Don Quixote, and yet all the same we laugh at his mistakes, failings, and misadventures. Now how is this possible?

First of all, the fact that his actions are inspired by what we take to be a kind of madness lightens the gravity of his serious collapses; the comic effects of the novel are not quite grotesque, and such pains as the knight suffers do not seem lasting as they might seem if realistically described. Events do not lead to or call finally for tragedy. Now it may be that "metatheatre" is simply a clearer term than "tragicomedy": it suggests a re-strained comicality, together with a serious painfulness, one not pushed to the point of tragedy. Such effects are characteris-tic of Cervantes's novel.

But I should like to be clearer about the difficulty of joining the comic to the tragic in a unified dramatic work. Here I shall rely on a distinction made by Bakhtin in the essay on form and content which I have already cited. He distinguishes the *architec-tonic* from the *compositional* form in a literary work. The architectonic is the aesthetic object provided us by a work; let us say of a play: in that case, its architectonic would tell us whether the play is a romance, a tragedy, a melodrama, a comedy, or a farce. The compositional form describes the work convention-ally; it distinguishes a play from a novel, but it cannot distinguish a comedy from a tragedy or the picaresque from an educational novel. Let us ask now: is there an architectonic form or only a compositional form for what is called "tragicomedy"? Tragedy results from seeing an action from the viewpoint of perfection, comedy from the viewpoint of common sense. Can these viewpoints be easily substituted one for the other, and in a unified work? But something very different follows from seeing an action from the one viewpoint than from seeing that same action from the other. The fact is that the Greeks and the dramatists of the French classical theatre were, I think, quite right in separating tragedy from comedy. If the values of the comic and the tragic can be brought together in a unified work—and it is my claim that they can—it is certainly not by making a mix of the two, for we can see in Chekhov's plays that when mixed they destroy each other. Yet the comic and the tragic may appear harmoniously in a single work if, conforming to the metatheatrical canon, it is a play-within-a-play. In this case, one of the plays can have a form stipulating tragedy, the other a form stipulating comedy, so that once again there will be a separation, though in a single work, of the comic and the tragic. *But there is no form, no nonconventional, architectonic form for tragicomedy.* There is just one other possibility, realized most perfectly by Pirandello, of bringing the tragic and the comic together under one architectonic: this can be achieved when the effects of comedy and tragedy are *both* subordinate to the theatrical, and this becomes possible in a *play about theater*, as in *Tonight We Improvise*, by no means Pirandello's masterpiece, but yet a work in which the comic and the tragic are brought together under a single architectonic form.

In *Tonight We Improvise,* the play of that title is in the process of being rehearsed, and one character in it, the actor, Penny-Whistle, is onstage. He is doing a death scene, but then, too, he is actually dying. To be sure, there is much more of the sophistry of feeling in his playacting than of the true feeling of a man facing death, but this sophistry of feeling takes on the accents of truth because we know the actor is really dying. We also know that he wants to be affecting and are touched by the fact that a man who is dying can have such thoughts. On the stage with Penny-Whistle is Dr. Hinkfuss, the stage manager, also a Customer, and a Chanteuse. Here is just a fragment of this wonderful scene, too long to quote in full:

PENNY-WHISTLE: I am saying that I have not been able to die, Mr. Manager; I have not been able to pull it off; and I can't help laughing when I see all these people have it over me, and me not able to die. The maid . . . (*He looks around.*) . . . where is she? She was supposed to come in crying: "O my God! . . . they're bringing him home wounded!"

DOCTOR HINKFUSS: But what difference does that make now? Did I tell you we could take your homecoming for granted?

PENNY-WHISTLE: Well, then, it seems to me you ought to take it for granted that I am dead, and not expect me to say anything more.

DOCTOR HINKFUSS: Nothing of the sort! You must speak. Go on with the scene. Die!

PENNY-WHISTLE: Very well. Here's the scene for you: (*He lies back on the divan.*): I'm dead.

DOCTOR HINKFUSS: But not like that!

PENNY-WHISTLE (*Leaping to his feet and coming forward*): My dear Mr. Manager, why don't you come up here and finish me off? . . . For me my entrance was everything. You've seen fit to skip that . . . I needed that maid's scream to get properly worked up. And Death was supposed to come in with me . . . And I was supposed to speak . . . as I leaned on this lady here. (*He draws the* CHANTEUSE *to him and leans against her, an arm around her neck.*) . . . I was supposed to make you weep—really weep—with the last bit of breath in my body, bringing my lips together like this (*He tries to whistle, but is unable to.*) . . . it was to be my last little whistle; and now . . . (*He calls the* CUSTOMER *to his side.*) . . . come here . . . (*He puts one arm around the* CUSTOMER's *neck*) like this— between you two—but closer to you, my dear—dropping my head—as little birds do—when they die. (*He drops his head on the breast of the* CHANTEUSE; *a moment later, his arms relax and he drops to the floor dead.*)[3]

---

3. Excerpt from *Tonight We Improvise* by Luigi Pirandello, trans. Samuel Putnam (New York: E.P. Dutton & Co., Inc., 1932)

I cite this scene to make my point, but also in tribute to Pirandello, who has helped us understand one of the essential forms of narrative drama, the kind of drama in which Don Quixote appears.

And now I can ask this question: How does Don Quixote *differ* from heroes of tragedy?

Nabokov describes the knight as possessed of a "whimsical nobility." I find the phrase capital, for Don Quixote's "nobility" is never required by the facts. He actually arraigns the facts insofar as they do not require it of him. The hero of tragedy, Bernard Knox has told us, replies to argument with arguments and to force with force. Don Quixote initiates argument, and against those he sees as villainous—like the windmills—he resorts to the test of strength. But we best understand his character in the way he responds to efforts to free him from the illusions he holds. These are not petty, but grandiose. Which is why he cannot do without them. He cannot be cured of his beliefs by any evidence that they are false, like the petit bourgeois Hjalmar Ekdal in Ibsen's *The Wild Duck*, or the trivial bums in O'Neill's *The Iceman Cometh*. When Sancho Panza presents a snub-nosed farm girl without delicacy or beauty to the knight as the Dulcinea of his dreams, saying that she has been transformed by an evil enchanter, Don Quixote sees nothing false in the explanation and is simply saddened by Dulcinea's fate. As for Sancho Panza, he permits himself to laugh at the knight's credulity and then strives on some other occasion to be as credulous.

Now no hero of tragedy would cling to the illusions to which Don Quixote holds fast. But then Don Quixote is an artist, which a hero of tragedy may be by chance, but is certainly never obliged to be. What is the knight's art? It is the art of playing with life. The notion that there is such an art was formulated by Max Scheler—"The Artist in the Art of Playing with Life" was the title for an essay he planned but never actually wrote. A similar idea was envisaged by Charles Baudelaire in his essay, "The Painter and Modern Life." And I think the notion of such an art is implicit in the behavior of certain

exceptional personalities, fictional and historical. Is it not implicit in the tales of Lord Genji's many affairs? Closer to us in
time and culture there is Jean François Cardinal Retz, who
opened the gates of the palace to revolutionary mobs. Then
there are Stendhal and his hero, Count Mosca. And we might
add to the list Lord Byron and Oscar Wilde. The art of playing with life is a literary art, requiring that one turn a chance
event into an advantage, as a writer must do at all times. We
admire Cyrano as he does this when anyone dares to affront
him. We have to admire the way he is able to find an artistic
outcome in what at first looks like an insult to him.

And Don Quixote? He has given himself the role of looking
for adversaries; it is not his duty to do this. For whatever
befalls him, he has no one to blame but himself, and, in fact,
he is uncomplaining. And as Nabokov points out against Joseph
Wood Krutch, he is often victorious. The number of his victories is equal to the number of his defeats. So Rosa Luxemburg's
gibe against the Knight recoils against her. She ridiculed those
who ride off on "that old nag Rosinante, named Justice, only
to come back with their eyes blackened." It is indeed odd that
she should have launched this *boutade* against Don Quixote,
being herself in worldly terms much the greater failure.

Here I must enter into conflict with Unamuno, the remarkable
Spanish thinker for whom I have the greatest admiration: he has
claimed Don Quixote as a hero of tragedy, while I have to
claim him for another dramatic form. That Don Quixote suffers
is true, but he does not suffer tragically; he dies of old age, even
denying the value of his deeds. What we have here is not the
death of a tragic hero. He has admitted that he was his own
playwright, and that the plots in which he was embedded were
of his own devising. His adventures did not always turn out
well—but he could no more be in control of everything he
contrived to happen than a good writer of narrative can be—
there are hazards in dramatic writing where chance, too, has a
role. Now, Unamuno claiming his hero for tragedy also says
that he made himself ridiculous (which no hero of tragedy does).
He notes that Don Quixote is very like a "brother" to Sigismund,
the hero of Calderón's *Life Is a Dream*, the greatest of metatheatrical

plays.[4] But I shall belabor the point no further. I like Unamuno too much to enjoy being on the other side from him, even in a matter of pedantry.

What about the fact that Don Quixote repents of his illusions on his deathbed and admits that his deeds were mad? Much has been made of this scene by critics, but I believe it has been misinterpreted. All Don Quixote is saying as death approaches is that the curtain of the stage he acted on is coming down. To act, as he did, on the stage of life, one must be possessed, as indeed he had been. Don Quixote's last words, in repenting his follies are certainly not his best. They hardly belong to the great figure who formerly held center stage and seem to me more appropriate coming from someone sitting in the audience, possibly a critic, perfectly sensible and inescapably mediocre, as are all of us in death, which, as Shakespeare says, "makes the odds all even."

---

4. Robert Ter Horst in his book, *Calderón: The Secular Plays*, suggests that Calderón made a dramatic science of the insights first explored by Cervantes. He writes: " . . . despite this greater and more symmetrical elaboration in Calderón, Cervantes made the initial discovery. . . . In transferring his major creative activity from the public stage to the privacies of prose fiction, Cervantes creates and discovers . . . a whole new universe. . . . With elaborations and adaptations of genius, Calderón integrates Cervantes's new theatre into his own stage. . . . In this fresh field of knowledge, Calderón is a great scientist. He fashions its corresponding principle." I think this could hardly be better said.

TRAGEDY—OR METATHEATRE?

THE GREATEST PLAYWRIGHT in the nineteenth century was, no doubt, influenced by Goethe's *Faust* in writing his own piece of metatheatre, *Peer Gynt*. Here again we have a drama of philosophical depth expressed in fantasy, mixing comedy and satire. And again we have a self-referring character, Peer Gynt, a kind of milder, more mediocre, and more bourgeois Faust. Shaw thought Ibsen's play the greatest comedy ever written; Shaw, however, was wrong in calling it a comedy; Ibsen's gift for comedy was not marked. But in *Peer Gynt* the seriousness of the great Norwegian, shining through all of his plays, becomes exceptionally subtle, evocative, and delicate.

Ibsen did not later continue to work with the form he handled so masterfully in *Peer Gynt*. He was attracted on the one hand by the new realistic vision of life already expressed in the European novel, and on the other by the necessitarian structure of fated events which he found in Greek tragedy. And he devoted his genius, for much of his life, to unifying his critical and highly realistic observations of middle-class life in Norway with a dramatic form derived from Sophocles.

There was a great perception in this effort of Ibsen. He must have realized that no form of drama gives such a compelling effect of the real as does the form of tragedy. Why not utilize that form along with direct observation of people and places? Why not combine the realist's critical attitude of mind with the tragic poet's feeling for the ultimately real in action, and thus produce the most overpowering illusion of reality ever achieved by any dramatist? Such must have been Ibsen's hope in writing *Ghosts, Hedda Gabler, The Wild Duck, Rosmersholm,* and *The Master Builder.*

So stated, Ibsen's objective seems a valid one. It always seems a valid hope to combine widely separate modes of thinking into a new pattern. Yet the strength of the human mind is not expressed in marriages of convenience, but, I think, as Ibsen might have learned from Sören Kierkegaard, in the resolute confrontation of a real "either, or." I believe that it is in the light provided by the burning of its own bridges that the mind can best see. When Francisco Pizarro burned his own ships, he had all Peru at his mercy.

What did Ibsen achieve in the realistic "tragedies" of his most productive period? He never convinces us of the necessity for the fate of Oswald in *Ghosts*, of Hedda Gabler in his play about her, of Hedvig in *The Wild Duck*, of Solness in *The Master Builder*, of Rosmer and Rebecca West in *Rosmersholm*. His critically observed characters are alive, and today his plays still live. But the "fatality" suggested in his dramas remains suggested, and does not convince us finally. Take *Ghosts*. The play would be just as moving and much truer to its real subject, the rigidity of Norwegian middle-class society, if Oswald did not have hereditary syphilis and were simply "disturbed"— he is that anyway—as a result of his separation from parents whose marriage was unsatisfactory.

There is an artificial imposition of fate on his characters, which today makes us feel some of Ibsen's greatest works are clumsy and contrived—often unreal. In a certain sense, the truth of Ibsen is in Chekhov, who, powerfully influenced by Tolstoy's insistence on utter truthfulness, deliberately softened the oppositions in his plays, toned down their climaxes, broke up the structure of the "well-made play," of which Ibsen was so proud, and eliminated altogether any suggestion that what happened to his characters happened because of fate. Interestingly enough, Chekhov was able to do all this and yet produce plays which have some dynamism because of an accidental fact of history: the characters he presents are derived from the Russian intelligentsia, which European history, long before Chekhov became a dramatist, had already placed on the stage.

Thus Chekhov could produce a kind of metatheatre while remaining genuinely realistic. The characters he described were already theatrical. Social forces had doomed the Russian intelligentsia to extinction; their consciousness of this, though, was what interested Chekhov, not the fatefulness of their situation. And insofar as Chekhov ever yields to the sense of fatality—as he does in *The Cherry Orchard*—instead of magnifying it or making it more drastic, his whole effort is to render it delicately. He understood, no doubt, that there was no such thing as fate, even in the historical sense of that term, without the willing collaboration of men.

There is another point I want to make about Ibsen's peculiar effort and the results of that effort on subsequent dramatists. There is something else about tragedy which is interesting besides the fact that it thrusts one against the ultimately real: in a true tragedy one is beyond thought. Thus the writer of a tragedy does not have to express ideas. He only has to have, as the phrase goes—I do not think it a good one—"a tragic view of life." Actually, Ibsen, supposedly an intellectual playwright, was strikingly lacking in ideas. When in *Rosmersholm* Rosmer speaks of carrying out "the new ideas" one never knows what he has in mind. *The Wild Duck* becomes absurd insofar as Gregers Werle has no genuinely intellectual motive for making the revelation he makes to Hjalmar Ekdal, which results in the painful suicide of Hedvig. In *Ghosts*, Ibsen makes Mrs. Alving too easily superior to Pastor Manders for any real criticism of the Protestant clergy to emerge in that play. When Kierkegaard attacked the Protestant church, he attacked the greatest Protestant pastors of Denmark; Ibsen's Pastor Manders is a plain fool. How could the Protestant church be made ridiculous by the exhibition of Manders's mainly personal folly?

If the truth of Ibsen is in Chekhov, Ibsen's false tragedy is to be found particularly in the American theatre, whose outstanding playwrights so far, Eugene O'Neill, Tennessee Williams, and Arthur Miller, are all continuers and imitators of Ibsen. Here (for once) I agree with Mary McCarthy, who has pointed up the dependence of the realistic school of American playwrights on the work of the great Norwegian. Miss McCarthy is quite wrong, however, in saying that all realistic plays are badly written. O'Neill and Tennessee Williams, at least, are excellent writers; Ibsen was a great writer and, as T. S. Eliot said, actually made prose do what before him only the verse form could.

What *is* true of O'Neill, Tennessee Williams, and Arthur Miller, though, is that all of them were attracted to Ibsen's form because it suggests the possibility of a serious play without the dramatist's having any need to think—except dramatically. Like Ibsen, and thanks to him, these playwrights have accomplished what they have without the need for ideas.

If Shaw, who admired Ibsen so greatly, was never an imitator of Ibsen, this was because Shaw had a gift for comedy, which Ibsen lacked, and also because Shaw had an interest in expressing ideas. There is an intellectual structure in most of Shaw's important plays which we do not find in Ibsen at all. Moreover, in addition to his irrepressible and beneficent humor, the Irish playwright had a feeling for philosophical drama. Thus I account for his having written works of metatheatre without having thought seriously of going beyond the form of comedy. The *Don Juan in Hell* episode (a complete play in itself), *Pygmalion*, and *Saint Joan* are not comedies, but metaplays.

When Shaw saw a performance of Pirandello's *Six Characters in Search of an Author*, he is said to have remarked: "This playwright is greater than I am." If true, the story would indicate that Shaw was sensitive to a dramatic form irrelevant to his own social and moral purposes. For the effect of Pirandello's *Six Characters in Search of an Author* is not at all upon the critical reason, but almost entirely on the metaphysical imagination. In fact, the Italian dramatist is lacking in moral interest: his dramaturgy counts only when he is excited by the metaphysical side of a conflict.

One might say that Pirandello was the epistemologist of metatheatre, not its ontologist. Pirandello is always interesting when he explores dramatically our inability to distinguish between illusion and reality; he was not prepared to assert, though, that the unreal *is*. Illusion, for Pirandello, was that which defines the limits of human subjectivity. But for the contemporary playwright Jean Genet illusion is something objective, something splendid, too, not an error. Thus in *The Balcony*, the characters are most real when dressed up for their peculiar roles. In *The Blacks*, the Negroes are presented not as perhaps Negroes feel themselves to be, but as they see themselves reflected in the mirror of the white race.

The logician of metatheatre was Bertolt Brecht. He took care to order not only his plays but also their décor and the style of acting he needed for them. He introduced an antinaturalistic logic into acting and stage design as well as into his own dramatic construction. His characters are his puppets, to be sure, but he insists on the fact that they are puppets, does not try to pass them off as real people, and delights in exhibiting their mechanisms. The cynicism which modern dictators have shown toward real people was in Brecht; he showed it toward his own characters. Never could he have succeeded in doing so had he relied on a realistic or naturalistic form of drama. What led him to metatheatre? Certainly it was not reflection on past art, nor was it some deep intuition of the importance of consciousness. But he did come to metatheatre; and having come to it, he was more thorough about it than any other playwright of his time.

So there are two trends in contemporary drama, one going back to Shaw of *Don Juan in Hell* and *Saint Joan*, to Ibsen's *Peer Gynt*, and still further back to Shakespeare and Calderón; the other springing from the realistic period of Ibsen's so-called tragedies. This second trend does not go, and cannot go, further back than Ibsen's works, for authentic tragedy, which can give a stronger feeling of reality than "realism," implies an acceptance of values which contemporary writers are unlikely to hold. I shall not say that tragedy is impossible, or, as George Steiner has suggested, dead. If Shakespeare, with his skepticism, could write even one tragedy, there is no reason at all to assert that the form is impossible to any modern dramatist, whatever his cast of mind. A dramatist may appear to whom the Furies are real—and I do not mean just symbolically real—and still uncompromising in their demands for blood vengeance, as they were before Aeschylus pacified them in the third part of his *Oresteia*.[1] Georg Hegel thought that after *Hamlet*,

---

1. Are not the witches in *Macbeth* something like the Furies of the *Oresteia*, but more morally ambiguous, more symbolical, more literary, if you please,

all modern tragedies would be tragedies of the inte
think he should have said tragedy would be repla~
metatheatre.

To summarize the values and disvalues of tragedy and metatheatre:

Tragedy gives by far the stronger sense of the reality of the
world. Metatheatre gives by far the stronger sense that the world
is a projection of human consciousness.

Tragedy glorifies the structure of the world, which it supposedly reflects in its own form. Metatheatre glorifies the unwillingness
of the imagination to regard any image of the world as ultimate.

Tragedy makes human existence more vivid by showing its
vulnerability to fate. Metatheatre makes human existence more
dreamlike by showing that fate can be overcome.

Tragedy tries to mediate between the world and man. Tragedy wants to be on both sides. Metatheatre assumes there is no
world except that created by human striving, human imagination.

Tragedy cannot operate without the assumption of an ultimate order. For metatheatre, order is something continually
improvised by men.

There is no such thing as humanistic tragedy. There is no
such thing as religious metatheatre. George Lukacs has said
that the principal spectator of tragedy is God. I cannot imagine God present at a play of Shaw, Pirandello, or Genet. I
cannot imagine Godot enjoying *Waiting for Godot*.

Tragedy, from the point of view of metatheatre, is our dream
of the real. Metatheatre, from the point of view of tragedy, is
as real as are our dreams.

---

than the terrible figures in Aeschylus' work? Also, did not Shakespeare, to
find them, have to plunge into a darker and more superstitious past, whereas
Aeschylus was able to go with his Furies into the clear light of Athenian
society? Certainly, the pacification of the Furies in the *Oresteia* made problematic the future of tragedy as an art form. Modern dramatists, trying to
restore that form, have been forced to seek it among the primitives: the Irish
peasantry (J. M. Synge), the Spanish peasants (Federico Lorca), half-mad sin-
ners of the sixteenth century (Michel de Ghelderode), and, in America,
culturally deprived characters like the protagonists of *Death of a Salesman*
and *A View from the Bridge*.

Nicolai Hartmann distinguishes the "depth of succession" from the "breadth of simultaneity." The first is the province of tragedy. The second belongs to metatheatre.

Tragedy transcends optimism and pessimism, taking us beyond both these attitudes. Metatheatre makes us forget the opposition between optimism and pessimism by forcing us to wonder.

Shall we not stop lamenting the "death" of tragedy and value justly the dramatic form which Western civilization—and that civilization only—has been able to create and to refine?

RELEVANCIES

BAD BY NORTH AND SOUTH

NORTH: I've been   sent a verse play to review—O, I'll review
it. But don't people know that I'm opposed to plays in verse?
I've said it often enough. From Djuna Barnes's *The Antiphon*
I've gotten further arguments to back up my prejudice. I'm
more against the whole enterprise of so-called poetic drama
than ever.

SOUTH: I have a bad verse play to review, too, Archibald Mac
Leish's *J. B.* But I'm not opposed to verse plays in general,
as you are. After all, even if both of these works are as bad
as we think, that doesn't mean the form as such is to be
condemned. What if someone writes a good verse play?

NORTH: Most unlikely.

SOUTH: What about *Murder in the Cathedral?*

NORTH: That was not bad, to be sure. Very good, in fact. It's
about the best thing we have in the genre. Nevertheless, I
don't consider it an important play, and as Edmund Wilson
noted, the one really good dramatic scene in it, is in prose. . . .

SOUTH: You told me you're against verse drama, but not why.

NORTH: *The Antiphon* is a perfect example of what is wrong
with this kind of play. You get the impression that each character is trying to make a poem of his or her feelings; no one
is swept into speech by action or emotion. Now who wants
to go to the theatre to watch people writing poetry? In this
activity, there is indeed labor and pain, but not the kind of
labor or pain we can enjoy—unless the result is a poem we
ourselves produce.

SOUTH: But do not even Shakespeare's characters sometimes
give the impression that they are writing poems?

NORTH: They do, at times, and at such times, the less
Shakespearean they.

187

SOUTH: I was thinking of Othello's

> It is the cause, it is the cause, my soul:
> Let me not name it to you, O chaste stars!
> It is the cause. Yet I'll not shed her blood ...

NORTH: Let's take these lines. There is, of course, an element of "poetry writing" in them, at least in the first two lines, but in the third Othello quickly comes to the point when he says

> Yet I'll not shed her blood ...

which directly relates him to the act before him. However, all references to the verse plays of the Elizabethans—and of Shakespeare in particular—when applied to the problem of the modern verse play, are very misleading. Poetical expression, I take it, was more spontaneous under the Elizabeth of those days, than of ours. It was, if you like, prereflective; nowadays, it is postreflective. The last person you would expect to express himself—nowadays, that is—with poetic eloquence, would be a simple person involved in a serious action. The person most likely to express himself in life with poetic eloquence would be someone who had given thought to the problems of poetry. Nowadays, it takes *time* to write a poem, a lot of time to write a *modern* poem, and what we want on the stage is the direct, immediate expression of feeling. You know something? I mean I want to tell you something you may not know: I would be interested in reading a verse play that was written overnight, as it is claimed that some of Lope de Vega's plays were. But I think the thing is impossible. I am sure the play I just read by Djuna Barnes must have taken years to compose. One result is that the characters scarcely talk to each other. Each one is intent on subtilizing and distilling his own thought and feeling into a verse expression adequate to the author's norms of rhetoric, and these are not at all dramatic norms. The result: there is no dialogue in any proper sense of the term in this play, and the words spoken by any one character have scarcely any effect on the others. It is as if the real action lay in the production of words, poetic words, and as if each character was too exhausted by this effort to listen to what the others have to say.

SOUTH: Your judgment of Djuna Barnes's *The Antiphon* may be correct, but I think the play I have to review, MacLeish's *J. B.*, is worse, though in exactly the opposite way. Take the title, for instance, *J. B.* is, of course, short for Job. Now Job is short, and wonderfully so, as short as a cry, or a lifetime. Why abbreviate the name that sums up all abridgments and abbreviations? To bring Job up to date. But why bring Job up to date when there is nothing antiquated about him? Just as the name, which is so wonderful, is diminished poetically by the initials J. B., even so the story is banalized by being consciously placed in a modern setting. What makes MacLeish's play so objectionable is the author's effort to make it a real theatrical work with gags, punch lines, fast dialogue. We get all the dramaturgical tricks that are required by Broadway audiences; but every once in a while, the author sneaks in here and there a great line from the old book. Now I am not against MacLeish's trying to write a verse play, since no matter what you say, I remain unconvinced that the form, as such, is impossible. What I find obnoxious is MacLeish's utter lack of poetic inspiration, and his acceptance of cheap dramatic standards in retelling one of the greatest stories of our literature.

NORTH: I think I'm against cheap dramatic standards as much as you are.

SOUTH: What I am driving at is that the great affliction of drama is not, as you seem to think, that people are trying to write plays in verse. I'm inclined to think that type of effort a very commendable one, no matter how great the difficulty is. What I can't stand about MacLeish is his utter thoughtlessness. He has no point of view toward the story of Job that could justify his retelling it. Here is what I mean: a famous modern philosopher has said that the greatest tribute to being is for someone to desire not to be. The greatest tributes to being in literature, then, would be Job's curse of the day on which he was born, the choruses in Oedipus, and Hamlet's famous soliloquy. These would be the moments when being really *was;* they happen to be the greatest moments in our dramatic literature. Now from this point of view, we could understand why God preferred Job's curse of his own birth to the practical advice of Job's friends; also, why in response to Job's curse, God asserts the mere fact that He *is*. Now I'm not saying that a good drama about Job could be written from such a point of view, interesting though the view is. I'm trying to suggest something else; all the modern mind can add to the old story is reflection; now reflection is not the basis for a dramatic work. On the other hand, why take up a story of this kind if one has no significant thoughts about it? I do think drama is only possible where the dramatist's thought is involved, and where that thought is a direct, immediate, intuitively perceived sense of the meaning of some action.

NORTH: Now you're coming around to my point of view, that poetry is impossible in drama when it is postreflective. You're going even further, saying that the dramatist's thought should be prereflective; and I'm inclined to agree with you about that, too. Unless the dramatist relied on some form which could reconcile the dramatic and the reflective.... But let me give you an example of the kind of speeches we get in Djuna Barnes's *The Antiphon:*

> That was the day that story-book Augusta
> Feather-headed, fairy-tale Augusta
> In her mind's wild latitude laid out
> And armed such battlefield, tilt patch and list
> As out-geared Mars. My maximed mind
> Out-maximed Circus Maximus.
> I hung the bright shields up, I spun the drill,
> Clubbed the spears and standards, ax and mace.
> I teased the olive, and all budding things
> Into the loop that wheels a victor's head
> And for his blood their own bright berries drop

Now I won't make the obvious point that no human being would ever talk like that. What I will say is that it would be impossible for even the most intelligent audience to decipher the meaning of these lines when hearing them spoken on the stage. But I want to make a still further point, and thus bring out the difference between a stage work and a piece of writing which looks like a play yet really isn't one. Now then, suppose the audience for Barnes's *The Antiphon* could be cajoled into studying her play before seeing it: what would be their reward? They could not have an immediate contact with the play until after they had studied it—which means they could never have an immediate contact with it. They would have to know the play by heart to hear it—that is, to see it—for the first time! Let me put the matter differently. A really good dramatic work should reveal itself most essentially when produced. I never really understood the Antigone, not of Jean Anouilh, but of Sophocles, until I saw it done on the stage by the Comédie Française. But it is quite clear that no light could be thrown on Barnes's play by any production of it. I have read it through twice, and I am still not sure I have gotten the story in its dramatic details. . . .

SOUTH: Can you be so sure it's bad if you don't know what it's about?

NORTH: Oh, I know what it's about. Or, to be precise, I know what it means, rather than exactly what happens in it. And this, I think, is the play's fault, not mine. . . . *The Antiphon* is an Electra play. The action takes place in a contemporary setting—the time is 1939—and there is no supernatural machinery, which, from my point of view, would be all to the good, if there were only some other kind of machinery—that is, plot—to get the action going. But there is scarcely any action, the play being the end and term of what happened before offstage. Here, too, we have a modernization of an old myth, but with much more justification, apparently, than in the case of MacLeish's handling of the Job story. Barnes *does* have a reason for modernizing, personalizing her Electra figure, for in *The Antiphon*, the daughter represents to the mother the full horror of what has happened to her at the hands of the father, as well as representing all the humiliations women have suffered at the hands of men. Barnes's Electra, parodying the Ghost's "Hamlet, remember me!" in *Hamlet*, says to her mother, "Woman, remember you." But the mother does not have the strength for this, and the play ends with her murder of her daughter. I should add that there are several male characters, including an Orestes and a Pedagogue, all with good English names, of course. And the general theme of the play is rather strong: the horror of what men do to women in making them mothers, and women to men in giving birth to them.

SOUTH: Now that sounds interesting!

NORTH: I don't deny a certain distinction in the writing. But I am judging *The Antiphon* as a play—I don't know if there are any categories for judging a closet-drama. A play has to be capable of being presented on the stage, as even Thomas Beddoes's *Death's-Jest Book* could be, I believe. Now *The Antiphon* is simply unplayable. I note that on the book jacket Edwin Muir is quoted as saying it would be a "disaster" if this work were not known. The disaster of this work, I should say, is that it cannot be known. For it *cannot make itself known on the stage as its form requires it to do.* And how hard it is to read! I sat up all night over it, and would never have kept on reading if I didn't have my review to write.

SOUTH: I'm going to suggest that nobody read MacLeish's *J. B.* or go to see it either, yet I read it quickly enough, in about half an hour to be exact, and from it turned to the Book of Job, which took me all night.

NORTH: In any case, you see what modern verse plays are like.

SOUTH: I still don't see why it should be impossible to write a good one.

NORTH: I would not say that a good verse play is impossible to achieve. What I think is that such an accomplishment is unlikely, and that what is unlikely is hardly a proper object of a sensible man's activity. Now a good dramatist must be fundamentally sensible.

SOUTH: Don't you think T. S. Eliot is?

NORTH: Unquestionably. But just look at his plays. He has been writing prose plays disguised as verse ever since *Family Reunion.*

Since that work, which he himself admits was a failure, he has devoted himself to writing a kind of *nonpoetic* verse play. The results, if we are to judge by *The Confidential Clerk* and *The Cocktail Party,* are works which are fundamentally prosaic— much more so than Anton Chekhov's plays in prose, for instance. Perhaps Eliot has to write plays in the way he does since his whole sensibility had already been formed on the basis of verse when he turned to the theatre. In that case he is a sport, an accident, a chance event in the theatre. . . .

SOUTH: But *The Confidential Clerk* and *The Cocktail Party* are in verse of a sort and they are good plays.

NORTH: Oh, I don't deny that. What I deny is that Eliot has succeeded in what is the *main* task of a dramatist, which is to produce a new dramatic system. Ibsen did that, and Strindberg, and Shaw, Pirandello, and even Giraudoux. Eliot did not, though he did create a poetic system before he turned his hand to writing plays. Now my contention is that no play can be truly poetic if it does not express the discovery of a new dramatic system. Thus we get the paradox that all the play-wrights I mentioned wrote dramas fundamentally more poetic than Eliot's, though none of them, except for Ibsen in his early phrase, wrote plays in verse. Perhaps I can now formu-late more clearly what seems to me the almost insuperable difficulty of the verse play in our time. In the past, the cre-ators of new dramatic systems made their discoveries *in verse,* since verse was the accepted medium. It is almost inconceiv-able that this type of discovery could be made today in verse, for the creation of an adequate verse for stage purposes would exhaust the invention of even the most gifted poet. Eliot's career in the theatre should be a warning that what we are going to get from the effort to bring poetry to the theatre will probably not be a revitalization of the theatrical art, but a compromised, flat, and diluted poetry, which can scarcely uplift us either on or off the stage. Have I convinced you?

SOUTH: My problem is to convince my readers that I am right about MacLeish's *J. B.*

NORTH: And I must convince mine that Djuna Barnes's *The Antiphon* is no worse than they should have expected.

NOT EVERYONE IS IN THE FIX

YOU ARE NOT where you wanted to be, nor will you get what you expected. But do you want to go somewhere else? Where? Not easy to say, but it's not easy to say where you are, either. You will stay, too, unless you are like the reviewers for the dailies, who damned this play[1] almost to a man. Why will you stay? Not in any great hope of pleasure, but as you stay in a dentist's office, motivated by an aching tooth. If you had come to be relieved of your boredom, then you will not be satisfied. You will not be relieved. You will be even more bored than you were when you first came in. More bored and more amenable to further boredom, a state in which there is a certain fascination. You are bored stiff by the junkies on the stage; they are bored stiff, too, with each other and with themselves. They are waiting for a "flash." What are you waiting for? They know what they want. You might decide of course that you know you don't want to wait with them. But for some reason you do wait, until their chance for a "flash" comes. And while you wait as they wait, certainly not for God and not even for Godot, you lose your perspective, that is, assuming you had one; in this there is a definite pleasure. The fact of the matter is you don't know what you are doing or why you go anywhere. Probably that is why you have to come to see *The Connection*. And on the stage there are people, recognizably real, who are as disoriented as you are, but know that they want something, or at least need something. They are waiting for "horse," that is to say, heroin; it will be brought to them by a Negro appropriately named Cowboy. Shall "horse"

---

1. *The Connection*, by Jack Gelber, first presented at the Living Theatre in New York City in 1959.

take them somewhere, and you along with them? Can you jump on after them and gallop out of your dull time into some undrugged eternity? This is not to happen. They get their dose of heroin but I think you will get no charge out of their "flash." After the waiting there is little release, the same dissatisfaction. These people certainly take no special attitudes; they're immersed in ordinary life, just as you are. No one is particularly bad, nobody notably good. Anyway, moral postures are hardly taken, and clearly do not count. If there is any hero, it is Cowboy, who gets the stuff, takes the risks involved in getting it, administers it to the others, and behaves generally like the doctor, which his white uniform makes us feel he is. Does he take the stuff himself? Probably. But certainly there must be a greater thrill for him in getting hold of it. Also, he is master of the situation; he alone determines the quantity of each dose, how much each junkie can take, what amount might be fatal. Is there anyone who can ride "horse"? If anyone, that one is Cowboy. Yet we never see him take the stuff, and in this fact I see the only concession to conventional morality made by the talented young playwright, Jack Gelber.

Dull the place is, dismal the prospects, cretins the people, and yet you don't have a desire to go home. Certainly the music keeps you. The musicians, stacked up like instruments for most of the time, come alive once or twice or maybe three times, and improvise brilliantly, beautifully; this is music such as one seldom hears. However, the music is merely an interruption of the waiting; it serves better, I will grant, than a movie would between the time you get to a station and the time your train is supposed to leave. After all, the musicians are also in the fix. They, too, are waiting for "horse." And when they get "horse," they, at least, do something: they play, and marvelously. "Horse" really takes them somewhere, and us also. But not for long and not far enough. We come back.

And now a question is forced on us—it was insinuated all along—but we only come to recognize it after a while. The question is: What do we want, we who are not junkies, if we are not? Don't we, too, want a "flash" of one kind or other? A "horse" of some sort, a charge, if you please, a sharp sensation, a quick connection? Does any of us want something more than that? The "flash" may be a new girl, a new thought, a new job, a new compliment; what is the difference between these and the connection the people we watch are waiting for? And you will wonder: Am I different from these junkies? Do I aim at more than a few sensations, and if I think I do, isn't this because I have shored up my pride and health against ruin with a number of platitudes? Can you answer these questions? If you can, you'll be able to get up and leave the play at its most exciting moment, which, by the way, is not terribly exciting. But if you cannot answer these questions (and how many can?), then you will have to stay to the very end, which is long in coming, and scarcely distinguishable from the beginning. *The Connection* is a moral trap; but nowadays people like to get caught. Why not?

What adds to the play's power is that the characters are so like other people, though in such a different situation from most people. The junkies of *The Connection* are no "invalids of happiness." They are not people who have paid a great price for a great joy; if they were, they would be on a higher level than their audience; they would have a right to be on the stage. They don't have that right, in fact, except that Jack Gelber was cunning enough to put them there. There ensconced, they dominate, mainly by being so similar to the people watching them, which means also to you.

How many plays ask a real question as this one does? The answer is evident, and makes of *The Connection* something outstanding. I must add, too, that it is brilliantly directed and admirably played. It lacks incident, but why should there be any in such a work? I must add, too, that there are some Pirandellian details—I mean the playwright, producer, and cameramen who intrude on the junkies to harass and photograph them—which are not in keeping with the general spirit of the work, and are, if the author will forgive me, plain dumb. Certainly a better way to involve the audience with happenings on the stage would have been for Cowboy to announce that anyone seated in the theatre had a right to a shot of "horse." Actors could have been stationed in the audience who would respond, and we would have been fascinated by the possibility of being in the fix, too.

Heroin, I understand, does not induce beautiful dreams as opium and hashish do; this is not a drug for aesthetes; Charles Baudelaire would not have favored it. Heroin is the drug of hijackers and band players; a Faustian drug, then, one which adds risk to risk, danger to danger, exhilaration to action. Certainly this particular drug seems consonant with the character of the times; it is not eccentric to take it while taking hashish or opium would be. Curiously enough, if we are normal people, not too odd, we have already opted for heroin even if we never take it. For if we were to become addicts, this would be our drug. Our lives turn toward it, and away from the more "aesthetic" drugs. So still another question is asked by the play: Why don't we, too, take heroin? We are, in fact, connected with it.

Not that there is any propaganda in this work in favor of addiction, for there is none of that. And thank God, there is no moral cant either; no moralizing à la Broadway. Nobody is shown on the stage in a state of torment because he would like to give up taking heroin. The torment of these people, and ours, too, insofar as we identify ourselves with them, is that for the space of more than two hours there is absolutely nothing else to take but heroin. Only that.

As the effect of heroin relates to action rather than to contemplation, so the play's focus is on moral rather than aesthetic values. Certainly there is little beauty on the Living Theatre stage; no pleasure at all to the eye, little in the language spoken. There is the thrilling music at times, to be sure, but even this is disturbing. It, too, suggests the drug which is to be or has been taken. Why go to see such a play? Why expose oneself to the nagging question: what's better than "horse"? Speak up.

I think it is the moral difficulty one feels in answering that gives this play its fascination. But to be fascinated is to admit to being without goal or purpose, to be unable to justify one's undrugged and apparently directed actions. Fascination or pride, we prefer fascination.

So the play judges its spectators, and the latter's judgment of it scarcely counts, be it favorable or unfavorable. What does aesthetic judgment matter? What is really of import is surely not one's judgment of dramatic merits or demerits. What matters is what matters most: life itself, how you and I live it, with what aim, what resolve, what enjoyment. What but prudence would keep us from getting on the stage ourselves if Cowboy did indeed offer to minister to us, too? There is the thing forbidden; but what is so bad about it? No effort has been made to make it seem alluring; the whole business of waiting for it, getting it, taking it, and getting that all-meaningful "flash" from it has been shown in as grim a way as the most conventional moralist could wish. No, there is nothing wonderful about taking heroin, not according to what I saw in *The Connection*. The disturbing thing, though, is the insinuation of the question: what else is wonderful?

For how many people, I wonder, is anything wonderful? If there are as many in that fix as I think, and if the play's effect is as salutary as I assume it to be, people everywhere should be urged to see it. I promise faithfully that whenever I see anyone in a state of moral disarray, spiritual collapse, worry about his goals, I shall send him to see *The Connection*. A play, of course, cannot provide one with a new spiritual state, but only sustain whatever spiritual state you have brought with you into the theatre. Anyone who finds his life boring will find *The Connection* less so. But this is not for people who know what to do with their time.

There are what have been called "high" experiences. These are limited in number, we can count them: love, friendship, heroic adventure, martyrdom (this is ambiguous, it is probably the lowest—not meaning by "lowest" basest—as well as the highest of experiences), the act of creation. Not much has been left out of this list, but it will be noted that for very few people are many of these so-called high experiences possible, particularly today, and they are becoming increasingly less so. In fact the widespread yearning for artistic creation on the part of so many people not gifted in that special way reflects something negative, not something positive. Namely, the absence of "high" experiences of another sort. But to come back to *The Connection*, is getting "high" a high experience? My judgment would be that it is not. But what is the view of the author? At one point in the play we have the following absurd and yet revealing incident: when the junkies are finally getting their shots of heroin and are being photographed by the cameramen, who are presumably to make a film about dope addiction, the writer of the script rushes onto the stage and begs for a shot, too. He, who can create something, needs the "flash" like the others. Who that cannot create doesn't need it?

A play is essentially a game but a game played with something sacred. A play is seldom made badly simply because the playwright doesn't know the game—dramaturgy is not as difficult an art as is generally thought, and most playwrights, even hacks, are able to pick up at least the elementary rules, occasionally even some of the finer points. What makes most plays bad is the fact that the playwright does not genuinely feel as sacred the particular value or experience which he pretends to so regard for the sake of his play's structure. For actually, the question of the sacredness of something is intimately linked to the very form of any play. I always notice in bad dramatic works the moment when the dramatist begins to pretend to have an enthusiasm for some value which his whole work belies. The falsely sacred—that is the bane of theatre. Whatever be the faults of *The Connection*, it does not give us that. In this play something really is at stake: our estimation of our pleasures, their occasionalness and their worth, our estimate of our health, too, for what good is it unless we can be enthusiastic about something else than merely retaining it? There is nothing delightful in *The Connection*, little poetry, and a degree of pain; but from the fact that we are shaken up, disturbed, and self-questioning when we leave the theatre, we know that we have seen a good show.

WRONG AND RIGHT: THE ART
OF COMEDY

I DO NOT think anyone has yet tried to describe the proce-
dures of comedy, taken as an art, by contrasting them with
those found in our chief instances of the art of tragedy—though
an approach to such an approach may be seen in Aristotle's
Poetics, where the philosopher tells us that tragedy deals with
men as better and comedy with men as worse than they are in
fact. Evidently, in Aristotle's view, there is a logically sharp
opposition between comedy and tragedy, insofar as for him the
two forms involve, and are dependent on, opposite movements
of the impulse to exaggerate morally. In fact, Aristotle's pro-
nouncement tells us a great deal: among other things, why it
is so difficult to unify the tragic and the comic in a single
work. Suppose we ask: Why is it so hard to present both, what
is morally high and morally low, in one dramatic work, when
it is not at all uncommon to find good and bad men in the
same room? But a room can be the same without having any
decisive unity of meaning; a dramatic work cannot.[1] Then, too,
such a work can hardly preexist the characters who appear in
it, being born along with them and of the very same moral
enlargement of the real which will make them, if it be a tragedy,
better and, if it be a comedy, worse than men are in fact.

---

1. But novels are in a sense dramatic works. And do they not mingle moments of the comic and the tragic? Are they not unified? I think these
questions have to be answered affirmatively. All the same, there is something
peculiar about the unity of a novel somewhere between that of a room and
of a play. That is why Paul Valéry could say of the novel that its deviations
from its form are integral to it.

This essay first appeared in *Salmagundi*, Winter 1975, pp. 3–19.

But let me go back to my original remark that somehow or other writers on tragedy and comedy have usually refrained from making an explicit comparison of the two genres. Is there any reason for this? To be sure, it would not be easy to find anything directly opposite to that emptying (or refining) of pity and terror which Aristotle made the identifying feature of our response to tragedy. And if we accept the Aristotelian view of tragedy, then we ought to see at once how impossible it would be to derive from it a view of the opposing form of comedy. For it is to be noted that the Aristotelian view does not really uncover a form, but rather what happens to us when that form is experienced. Tragedy stimulates us to feel pity and terror, and we are no doubt right to identify as tragedy any dramatic work affecting us in this way. But what about the work itself? That, taken objectively, is hardly uncovered by the uncovering of its effects on us.

Perhaps the reason that Aristotle did not give us as definitive an insight into comedy as into tragedy is that his understanding of tragedy—indispensable to our thinking since—was fundamentally psychological.[2] And if we want an objective description of tragedy (from which we might infer some description of its opposite, comedy), then we shall have to turn to another philosopher who has indeed described tragedy objectively, though he agrees with Aristotle about its effects on us. I am here referring to Georg Hegel, who told us that tragedy is a conflict between the right and the right or, as the idea has been stated since, between the "good and the good," or the "good and the right."[3] It will be seen at once that there is little that is psy-

---

2. It is to be noted that Freud and the Freudians, who have written so extensively on tragedy and on comedy, seldom think of situating the two genres in opposition to each other; their approach has led them to go further with psychology than Aristotle but further away, too, from the forms in question here. Freud tells us himself that he is less interested in the form of *Oedipus* than in why we like it. And why we like it—assuming Freud is right about this, though I do not think this to be the case—cannot be in opposition to why we like *The Miser* or *Tartuffe*. On the other hand, the form of *Oedipus* may very well be sharply opposed to that of *The Miser* or *Tartuffe*. In any case, this is what we are trying to find out in this essay.

3. See Sidney Hook's essay "Pragmatism and the Tragic Sense of Life" in *Contemporary American Philosophy* (1970). I must add that by now even

chological or subjective here. If tragedy induces us to feel pity and terror, that is *because* pity and terror are induced in us by conflicts between the right and the right, the good and the good, or the good and the right, and *not* by conflicts between the good or the right and any of the contraries. I suggest that here Hegel has provided us with an objective description and definition, too, of the form of tragedy, as well as, by inference at least, with an objective description and definition of its opposite, comedy,[4] which according to my theory consistently presents us with the very opposite kind of conflict, pitting the wrong against the wrong, the bad against the wrong, or even the bad against the bad. Formulating these terms into a single logical model, I shall say that comedy presents us with what is essentially a fallacious argument against some false position. What is right or good in comedy? Not the positions strongly taken but rather, as Suzanne Langer says, "The pure sense of life ... developed in countless different ways."

Would this model hold without exception for all plays that cause our laughter? But let us first confront the difficulties raised by my notion. For one thing, does it not follow from the view held here that comedy can have no message, that is, no moral message? If every position asserted in a comedy is fallacious

---

philosophers who are opposed to definition accept at least conditionally the definition of tragedy as a conflict of right with right. Thus, Renford Bambrough, in his essay "Literature and Philosophy," relies on Hegel's definition of tragedy, writing: "Tragedy is often concerned with moral conflict, and that to some extent explains and to nearly the same extent justifies the belief that tragedy is the conflict of right with right. ..." (See *Wisdom: Twelve Essays*.) In the same essay, however, he does not scruple to attack the idea of defining tragedy, writing: "The definition of tragedy has by this time turned into the tragedy of definition. ..."

4. It may be asked: How is it that Hegel was *not* able to give us an objective view of comedy? This question I cannot answer. Possibly, Hegel was influenced by the example of Aristotle, whose attention had been focused almost exclusively on tragedy. In any case, Hegel, while his remarks on comedy are always full of depth and understanding, never formalized them into a clear logical model. Certainly, he could have done so, as can be seen from the following judgment of his in a passage centered on tragedy: "What ... is inseparable from the comic is an infinite geniality and confidence capable of rising superior to its own contradiction."

or wrong, then what are we to say about the pacifist plays of Aristophanes, for example, *Lysistrata?* And what are we to say of the playwright's denunciations of Athenian democracy, of his attacks on Euripides and Socrates, of his defense of Aeschylus and Alcibiades? Can we say that there is no moral message in Aristophanes and that the first great master of the art of comedy argued always and only from fallacious or false positions?

These questions, of course, can be best answered by the Greek scholars. One of our modern classicists, the late A. W. Gomme, has given us in an essay, "Aristophanes and Politics," his consideration of the political opinions of the comic poet. Gomme's argument is addressed against two propositions that have been put forward: "First, that Aristophanes was convinced that the theatre had a moral and didactic purpose, in the strictest, narrowest sense, that it was its business to improve its hearers, and especially that it was the business of comedy to give good political advice; and that he himself had always given such advice.... Secondly, that he was conservative in his attitude both to politics and to cultural movements." These propositions Gomme disposes of in his subtly argued piece.

Was Aristophanes at the very least "a lover of the old ways" and of "the older generation, the men of the country, the small farmer who tills his own land, of simple thought, of little speech, who had fought hard and loved the old songs of Phrynicus"? This, writes Gomme, is the general view, and he adds that it may even be true. Then comes his argument:

> But it is a view which, combined with the other that Aristophanes had a policy to urge upon his hearers ... leads at once to contradictions and so to self-deception. It will not hold water for a moment. For a politician there is a right and a wrong; for a dramatist, though he represents a conflict, there is no right or wrong side (whatever his private opinions may be).

I must interpolate here my own conviction that for the dramatist there is seldom a right side if his heart is for comedy. But to continue with Gomme's argument:

If Aristophanes was a politician, then a single reading of the play makes one thing clear: the older generation, whenever they appear expressly as such, when they are described as brave old men of Marathon, are invariably on the wrong side or *are* the wrong side, the side which Aristophanes is attacking. In the *Acharnians* it is the old men, the farmers, who are most fiercely patriotic, militant, pro-war; it is for them treason for anyone to suggest a parley with the faithless enemy.... In *The Wasps* the chorus enter singing one of the most attractive of Aristophanes' songs—the old men helping each other along in the mud and dark, regretting the days of their youth—what a time we had, you and I (do you remember?), on guard duty at Byzantium, when we stole the mortar from that old baker woman?—but still capable of doing their duty today.... What more sympathetic picture could you have of the older generation? Aristophanes must surely be going to contrast them with the younger lot of men, smart, clever, but without grace of manner, honesty, or character. Not at all: they are the dicasts, the life and soul of the system it is the purpose of the play to attack and overthrow. It is younger generation which exposes their folly.

Let us test Gomme's general view of Aristophanes against one of the playwright's masterpieces, the *Frogs*. In this work Aristophanes presumes to judge between the tragedies of Aeschylus and those of Euripides; on the judgment of their tragedies depends the decision of Dionysus as to which poet will be returned to Athens from Hades. The two poets recite their verses into a scale, and Dionysus has to decide whose verses are the weightier. Finally, he decides in favor of Aeschylus. But on what grounds? On purely aesthetic grounds? And what about the scale? Does it weigh only the aesthetic worth of the verses cast on it, or is their moral worth also weighed? Certainly their moral worth is not discounted. But what finally determines Dionysus to judge Aeschylus the better poet than Euripides is the answer the former gives to a purely *political* question: What should Athens do about the talented political adventurer, Alcibiades, at that moment in exile? Euripides' answer is very simple and is immediately intelligible to us. If it is at all proper to translate it into contemporary terms, it might be expressed in this way: "Have nothing to do with him. He's a plain fascist." The answer of Aeschylus, more portentous and certainly less intelligible, goes like this: "It is better not to whelp a lion, but the city that does will have to serve it." Of course, one must admit that this answer is more brilliant than that of Euripides, and it has been remarked, too, that the political ideas of Alcibiades had an audacity not unlike that shown by Aeschylus himself in his imagery. All the same, the answer does not really say what the Athenians *at that time* should have done about Alcibiades. In fact, when we compare the two answers to the question put to the two poets, we cannot really think that Dionysus (or Aristophanes) preferred the answer given by Aeschylus, politically that is, for we do not really know what the politics of Aeschylus' answer would have been. All we know is that it was more interesting. So finally, even in this instance, it would appear that the Greek comic poet was judging aesthetically and was not delivering a moral message to his audience. One further point: the logical model I proposed for comedy *does* hold for the answers of Euripides and of Aeschylus, for if the answer of the former is too simpleminded, the answer of the latter is too complicated for us to find it politically sound. What we have here is a fallacious argument pitted against a false position. The fact that Aeschylus was preferred proves nothing. Sometimes, especially in a democracy, our preference has to go to one of two false positions.

Gomme rounds out his argument against the conception of Aristophanes as a political moralist by making a similar judgment of the modern George Bernard Shaw:

> Shaw has himself said that art ought to be didactic. . . . Moreover he has been, quite definitely, an active politician—a vigorous member of political societies, a speaker at street corners, a member of a borough council. And he is nothing if not autobiographical: he writes a long

preface to every play, in which he tells us his opinions on its main theme. We are in possession in fact of the materials for a very full biography of Shaw in his public capacity—both as politician and as playwright. But take them all away, burn his prefaces and the record of his political activities: would it make much difference to our understanding of his plays? I think not. We should still know the most important thing about him, his general attitude to life; we should know his critical and satiric view of existing institutions—that he was, as artist, neither indifferent to them nor quietly content, that is, that he was neither anarchist nor conservative.

Edmund Wilson viewed the playwright similarly in his essay, "Bernard Shaw at 80":

> And I am inclined to believe that the future will exactly reverse the opinion which his contemporaries have usually had of him. It used to be said of Shaw that he was primarily not an artist, but a promulgator of certain ideas. The truth is, I think, that he is a considerable artist, but that his ideas—that is, his social philosophy proper—have always been confused and uncertain . . . The political writing of Shaw does not drive you into taking up a position as the greatest socialist writing does: indeed, before he has finished . . . he has often seemed to compromise the points which you had imagined he was trying to make. . . . Both his intelligence and his sense of justice have prevented him from assailing the capitalist system with such intolerant resentment and unscrupulous methods as Voltaire trained on the church. With Voltaire, it is the crusader that counts, with Shaw, it is the dramatic poet.

This view, however, has been powerfully contradicted by Louis Crompton. I quote from his essay, "Shaw's Challenge to Liberalism":

> It is . . . the unique dramatic form which has first of all confused, puzzled, and exasperated critics. What Shaw

does is to mix together a Molièresque comedy and a Socratic dialogue. Each play begins by presenting us with a high-minded idealist who takes himself with earnest seriousness and looks upon himself as an enlightened reformer. He is then made the subject of a comedy in the style of Molière, not with the idea of unmasking his hypocrisy, but of exposing the comic contradictions within his ideals and temperament. The problems raised by this character, which appear originally in a farcical-satirical light, are treated more and more seriously until they are shown to be bound up in what Shaw calls "the destiny of nations," and the audience, which has settled down to a night of fun, finds it must either transform itself from an audience of pleasure seekers into a "pit of philosophers" or flounder hopelessly in the dream sequence of *Man and Superman* or the last acts of *John Bull's Other Island* and *Major Barbara*, an impossible procedure, you will complain. But not, Shaw would answer, to someone who believed that "every joke is an earnest in the womb of time" and that the prophet who did not make his audience laugh would suffer "at worst, the fate of Socrates and Christ, and at best that of Rousseau and Tom Paine."

It seems clear to me that Crompton's judgment of Shaw's comedies cannot be set aside as Gomme set aside the judgment of Aristophanes as a moralist. This is a real difficulty about Shaw's comedies; moreover, it is one which cannot be inconsiderable, seeing that a masterpiece like *Major Barbara* has occasioned such puzzlement, even to a critic like Francis Fergusson.

I said that there is hardly a *right* side for the author of comedy, but there is often a right side for Shaw, and he happens to be the greatest master of comedy in the English language. So here we have a paradox. It is this paradox, I believe, that caused the puzzlement of Fergusson and was ignored by Gomme; it is this paradox that Wilson has tried to get around by calling Shaw a dramatic poet rather than a consistent thinker.

Crompton described Shaw's plays as combining a Molièresque

comedy with a Socratic dialogue. They do. But those dialogues of Plato in which Socrates appears do not always end with the victory of the true over the false, the right over the wrong, and even in the *Protagoras*, where Socrates seems to have the better of the discussion, he often relies on arguments we do not always find fair or to the point. In any case, what cannot be denied is that Shaw in many of his comedies has presented characters who seem to speak for him on important matters; they seem to state what Shaw himself thinks to be the case. It looks very much as if Shaw in his plays has indeed tried to present the true against the false, the right against the wrong. Has he not then complicated, perhaps even defeated, the form of comedy in which I have asserted it is wrong that asserts itself against the wrong?

Here we might look at French classical comedy, especially as instanced by Molière. Now, it is simply not the case that in Molière's comedies the right or the true is never expressed, though in the most dramatic moments of his plays Molière invariably pits the wrong against the wrong. Take *The Misanthrope*, for example, generally regarded as a masterpiece. Here we see the wrong pitted against the wrong in the conflict between the spontaneous flattery for those present and the scorn for the same persons when absent as expressed by Célimène, as well as in the unflattering frankness of Alceste in all his face-to-face encounters. If Célimène is wrong insofar as she deceives, Alceste is certainly not right in telling—without respect for other's feelings—what he takes to be the truth. But is there anyone in *The Misanthrope* who may be said to be right? Yes, to be sure, there are Philinte and Eliante, who moderate truth with politeness and finally can marry, whereas Célimène and Alceste cannot. Yet, though Philinte and Eliante are right, they are not active in Molière's comedy; they are its *raisonneurs*.[5] And the *raisonneurs* in a comedy by Molière, representing the right and true position, are always less active than those characters who, representing the wrong positions, bear the burden of comi-

---

5. In French comedy the *raisonneur's* role is to be right, or reasonable. I shall use the French term simply because no equivalent term in English is as good.

cality. Now the characteristic and peculiar feature of Shaw's comedies is that his *raisonneurs* tend to be active and have the task of carrying both the burden of being comical and the very opposite burden—that of representing what is presumably the right (the Shavian) position. It is to this, I think, that the difficulty in comprehending his art is due.

To be sure, Shaw is more various than I have implied in what I said about his *raisonneurs*. In fact, they are not always active. In *Candida*, the remarkable woman from whom that comedy takes its title plays the role of *raisonneur;* as in Molière's comedies, however, the *raisonneur* here does not act at all. There is one peculiarity, nonetheless, that is strikingly Shavian: Candida is also the play's heroine, being the one who is right, the one whose opinions and judgments Shaw backs, even while it seems proper for her to be the *raisonneur*, since she does nothing. Incidentally, I would suggest this purely formal reason for her rejection of Marchbanks and her remaining with her husband. Had she left with Marchbanks, she could still have been the heroine, but could she also have been the *raisonneur?* The play required her to be both.

While a wonderful comedy, *Candida* is probably less original than *Major Barbara*. Here again, Shaw's protagonist, Andrew Undershaft, is also the *raisonneur* but, unlike Candida, he is an active figure, powerfully influencing the other characters, especially his daughter Barbara. This comedy is both one of Shaw's finest and also one of his most problematic; Fergusson has dismissed it as an unresolved series of paradoxes. The paradoxes are undeniable. Undershaft is a maker of munitions, but does he represent self-interest, business intrigue, social chaos? On the contrary, Shaw takes him to represent self-respect, hard work, and earning power. Undershaft has even set aside for his workers places of leisure that could be described as "parks of culture and rest," like those found in the Soviet Union (where, by the way, the munitions industry has long enjoyed top governmental priority. It should be noted, too, that Shaw's play was written two decades before the Russian Revolution.). Undershaft is for Shaw a positive figure representing positive values, though in a paradoxical form. A capitalist, he represents socialism; a munitions maker, he represents peace; disinheriting his son, he represents paternal wisdom and justice; and giving his daughter Barbara a serious lesson in cynicism, he sets her on the right way to a proper spiritual life. All this Shaw asks us to believe about the hero of his play, and we do not really believe it—at least we do not believe it when the play is over. This is why the play is puzzling.

In *Misalliance*, Shaw allows each of his major characters and some of the minor ones, too, moments in which to play the *raisonneur*, so that in a way all of the characters are *raisonneurs* for a time, but there is no character who is the *raisonneur* for the play taken as a whole. To be sure, this is not one of Shaw's more serious plays. What is interesting about *Misalliance*, though, is the inventiveness and unconventionality with which Shaw has *pluralized* the role of speaking for the right and the reasonable. Of this play it may be said—as of his theatre generally—that he always seems to be doing something new and unexpected with his *raisonneurs*.

Man and Superman I take to be one of Shaw's greatest comedies, and one of the finest of the century. It is also one of Shaw's most serious plays. What is its message? That we ought to free ourselves from every kind of romanticism in every sphere of life—in manners, in morals, in religion, in politics, in marriage. This message is expressed verbally by the principal figure, John Tanner, and since the ideas he expresses are surely those of Shaw, we can take him to be the play's *raisonneur*. Moreover, he is not especially comical, except for one rare moment at the play's climax. It is the other characters in the play who provide the moments of humor. All the same, it would be wrong to think of Tanner simply as the play's *raisonneur*, for if the ideas he expresses are adequate to that role, the same cannot be said of his actions. On the other hand, the actions of Ann Whitfield are in support of and realize the ideas expressed by Tanner, though the ideas she puts into words are a continual denial of everything for which Tanner says he stands. Who is the *raisonneur* of the play? John Tanner for what he says; Ann Whitfield for what she does. Together they make one *raisonneur* and, in fact, at the end of the play they marry, not as a result of Tanner's thinking but as a result of one of Ann's comic stratagems.

What about the dream sequence? I shall have to say here that I agree with the judgment of those directors who refuse to include it—despite its undeniable virtues—in productions of the play. There is certainly fine talk in the dream sequence, even as it must also be said that the ideas in it have not worn too well, though this is not the real reason for my objection to including it in production. Fundamentally, it is the conflict between two *raisonneurs*, the Devil and Don Juan, each of whom seems to be in the right when he is doing the talking and whom we only begin to suspect may be wrong when his opponent takes the floor. And when we consider the extraordinary subtlety with which Shaw has already managed to integrate the words of one of his characters with the actions of still another in the play proper, we become all the more critical of the dramatic obviousness in pitting two *raisonneurs* against each other.

But to justify more thoroughly Shaw's way combining the roles of *raisonneur* and of comic protagonist in a single character, I shall have to note the difference between *l'esprit faux* and *l'esprit juste*—the two kinds of wit we find in comedy, most especially in the comedy of manners. I have used the French terms for these two kinds of wit even though the distinction between true and false wit exists in English, having been made by Joseph Addison in the *Spectator* (No. 62). He writes: " . . . *true Wit* consists in the Resemblance of Ideas, and *false Wit* in the Resemblance of Words. . . ." For one thing, the distinction as he makes it is inadequate, and, for another, it is artificial and much too intellectual; I have never heard true or false wit referred to in English conversation. On the other hand, *l'esprit faux* and *l'esprit juste* are regularly used in nontechnical French talk. Moreover, the distinction between them as it is made in French is a clear one: *l'esprit faux* is simply wit through error, wit through missing the mark; and *l'esprit juste* is wit through truth, through hitting the mark dead center.

Why is it witty to be in error, to miss the mark? Isn't it much harder to hit it? Very often this is not the case. No doubt it would be difficult to speak the perfected English Eliza Doolittle delights those around her with at the end of Shaw's *Pygmalion*. Such speech may occasion our appreciative wonder, but it hardly makes us laugh. On the other hand, the Cockney spoken by Eliza Doolittle does cause us to laugh, to be sure, at her. So her speech at the beginning of the play is not intended as wit. Yet skillful comedians are able to make us laugh by imitating the kind of speech errors she makes, as well as those common to certain localities or ethnic groups. Now I do not regard this as a high form of *l'esprit faux*. I merely wish to establish that such errors may belong in that category.

Much wittier and much more interesting is *l'esprit faux* that results from missing the mark logically as, for example, the statement in *Alice* that butter applied to the watch's mechanism may repair it because it happens to be the best butter. Still wittier and even more complex is *l'esprit faux* that is involved in saying positively what anyone with less aplomb would prefer not to say or to say negatively. Take the remarks of Lady Brancaster in her exchange with Algernon in Oscar Wilde's *The Importance of Being Earnest* (original version):

LADY BRANCASTER: It is very strange. This Mr. Bunbury seems to suffer from curiously bad health.
ALGERNON: Yes; poor Bunbury is a sad invalid.
LADY BRANCASTER: I must say, Algernon, that I think it is high time that this Mr. Bunbury made up his mind whether he was going to live or not. This shilly-shallying with the question is absurd. It shows a very ill-balanced intellect and a lack of decision that is quite lamentable.

And in this remark:

GWENDOLEN: Algy, kindly turn your back. I have something very particular to say to Mr. Worthing. As it is of a private character, you will of course listen.

I have chosen to illustrate *l'esprit faux* by instances of it from *The Importance of Being Earnest*, for in that comedy—a masterpiece of masterpieces—there is hardly a single instance of *l'esprit juste.*[6] The sparkle of wit is continuous, and it is a true sparkle, though provided by a wit which we are obliged to say is false (though perhaps we are best advised to say that of it in French). The play's power, coherence, unity, and dramatic firmness can be best seen when we note that the author is at one with both the wrong positions pitted against each other in the actions: Bunburyism, or leading a double life deliberately, as against hypocrisy, or leading a double life because you can't help it. Furthermore, I think he is at one with Lady Brancaster in opposing Gwendolen's marriage to Jack Worthing, should it turn out that the prospective bridegroom is without a proper family; Wilde also supports Gwendolen's desire to marry Jack Worthing simply because his name is Ernest (it is). Thus, Wilde is at one with the conflicting and wrong positions, arguing for each of them with a like wit, the wit one achieves by missing the mark—*l'esprit faux.* This wit, the wit of error, enfolds all of the characters, enters into the actions, and is part of the atmosphere, even as it forms the dialogue. At the very end of the play, Jack Worthing, who has called himself Ernest, finds out that this is his real name and that in giving himself the name Ernest he has not lied at all. He apologizes:

JACK: Gwendolen, it is a terrible thing for a man to find out suddenly that all his life he has been speaking nothing but the truth. Can you forgive me?

Probably there are few persons who ever enjoyed being in the wrong as much as Wilde. Shaw, however, wanted not only to amuse but to be right, and for him this meant to produce a kind of comedy not entirely dominated by *l'esprit faux.* There

---

6. Except perhaps for this remark of Algernon, rendered, Wilde tells us, "drawlingly and sententiously": "All women become like their mothers. That is their tragedy. No man does. That is his." I make an exception of these lines, for I do not know whether the wit in them expresses *l'esprit faux* or *l'esprit juste* or, as I suspect, some very profound mingling of the two. It is the closest Wilde comes in the whole comedy to a witticism arrived at by simply saying what one thinks is true.

had to be in his plays some occasions for expressing right reason through wit, some occasions for *l'esprit juste*.

The two forms of wit, of course, can be expressed within a single work. The Spanish master of comedy, Miguel de Cervantes, who as a matter of fact began his literary career as a playwright, actually opposed them in his two great characters, Don Quixote and Sancho Panza. But it is evident, too, that it is *l'esprit faux* of Don Quixote that provides the dynamic element in Cervantes's novel; reading it we see at once that Sancho Panza is far more interested in Don Quixote's misses than in his own hits. Don Quixote is a knight, Sancho Panza his squire. Are we to conclude that the difference in social station between them also represents the difference in value of the kinds of wit they represent? It all depends on what value one has in mind. *L'esprit juste* may be the more morally elevated; *l'esprit faux* is more important to and certainly less eliminable from comedy.

L'esprit faux has entered into the very character of Don Quixote, even as it appears in his observations. He has taken the wrong route, but for reasons we inevitably find right. The Knight of the Sorrowful Countenance has made up his mind to come upon the same kind of adventures, situations, and persons he has responded to in books. He is determined to have a reality that is like the books he has enjoyed, even if this requires him to imaginatively alter whatever situation he happens to be in. Now then, are we not determined like him to find in the real world some of the characteristics it seemed to have in books? I submit we are so determined and would probably not accept a reality utterly unlike the world described in the literature on which we have been brought up. All the same, for the sake of our sanity, we make distinctions that Cervantes's hero refuses to make. As Wilde's proponent of Bunburyism is in favor of deliberately opting for a double life, so Cervantes's hero opts for a single one, one from which everything that is not romantic, however dubiously, has been expunged. Was it wrong for Don Quixote to decide as he did? Not a doubt of it. He admits his error before he dies, but it is an error we often feel we should be glad to have the courage to make. If it is wrong to make this error constantly, it is in some curious way not right if one never makes it. In his hero, Cervantes created not one but a whole gallery of comical figures; Don Quixote has become the model from which every comic character who also carries with him some positive message has been drawn. He is the model for Shaw's *raisonneurs*, certainly for Andrew Undershaft, who expresses views that Lady Britomart describes as the "religion of wrongness."

Now *l'esprit faux* that has entered into the creation of a character such as Don Quixote is of a polemical sort, ordered to rebut any assertion made by *l'esprit juste*. Why does the wit of Don Quixote have to be polemical? He sees the world upside down, if I may use Hegel's term for the vision of the philosopher, and seeing the world thus he cannot but address himself to refuting any and all assertions of whoever sees the world right side up. As we read Cervantes's novel, our ability to see the world upside down, an ability we do not often have, lasts only so long as the arguments of Don Quixote against his adversaries appeal to us as wit.

Let us look at another heroic character modeled on Don Quixote: Saint Joan. In Shaw's *Saint Joan,* she is a young woman from the French countryside, full of sensible ideas and observations except on two matters: first, without military experience, she expects to lead the French armies in battle; second, she claims to have been told to take this task on herself by two heavenly messengers, Margaret and Michael. Now, the notion that someone as sensible as Shaw claims Saint Joan to have been could also have been as mystical as the record seems to show is simply not convincing as an idea, nor is Shaw's Joan an altogether convincing character. I would say that she embodies Shaw's polemic against whoever thinks the real Maid of Orleans lacked either common sense or mystical vision. Andrew Undershaft in *Major Barbara* similarly incarnates a polemical point. His career and wit are arguments against all those who think a socialist has to be long-suffering, modest, and poor rather than dynamic, self-assertive, and rich. That one is not quite convinced by the polemic governing the wit often expressed by these characters does not, however, prevent us from yielding to their charm. In fact, they embody the very great charm of a quite strong argument that yet does not quite convince. Incidentally, it is such characters as Joan and Undershaft, into whose creation *l'esprit faux* has entered, that Shaw seems to have entrusted all the striking comments in his plays that can be said to fall under the rubric of *l'esprit juste*. The characters who express right reason, and so carry the political or moral message the playwright wants to leave us with, are themselves in some important sense wrongheaded or in error, and thus they are appropriate, true figures of comedy.

What we have to realized here is that in literary art assertions are converted into "quasi-assertions," to use the excellent term suggested by Roman Ingarden. The assertions that Shaw, socialist and iconoclast, eugenist and feminist, wanted to make and made in life and politics are converted in his comedies into quasi-assertions by the fact that those who put these assertions forward in the plays are themselves constructions of the author's *l'esprit faux*. What is involved here, of course, is not any lack of seriousness in Shaw the man, but the seriousness of the transforming power of the art of comedy. Turning aside for the moment from Shaw himself, and even from the theatre, another Irish genius comes into view—the pamphleteer, satirist, and moralist, Jonathan Swift. In *A Modest Proposal*, Swift recommended that the people of Ireland suffering famine be encouraged to eat their own children, and he argued that the result would be an improvement over the state of affairs in Ireland at the time, when infants and nurslings, along with their parents, died of famine. Now, Swift's attack on the British administration of Ireland was serious; but his means of attack were literary, and this is one reason why his satire could be a comic masterpiece. For if what was asserted in *A Modest Proposal* were taken to be other than a quasi-assertion, one could hardly respond with laughter. To be sure, Shaw has insisted that the assertions he has made in his plays are not literary but altogether serious. To Arthur Bingham Walkley, he writes (as a preface to *Man and Superman*): "... for art's sake alone I would not face the toil of writing a single sentence." But I think we can regard this remark, too, as a quasi-assertion, as forming part of Shaw's dramatic presentation of himself before the public.

Shaw's main inventions as a writer of comedy have been in his wholly original use of the *raisonneur*, and it is because of his *raisonneurs* that his comedies have been misunderstood. I should say, too, that Shaw by his prefaces has helped us misunderstand them. Shaw's *raisonneurs* are intriguingly, charmingly, wittily in error and often surprise us as they make judgments we think are right. But no assertion made by a character in a comedy, no matter how just, need be taken as a full assertion if it is made by a character into whose constitution *l'esprit faux* has entered.

I think Jean Giraudoux followed Shaw in making his heroes and heroines his *raisonneurs*, as for instance, in his masterpiece, *The Madwoman of Chaillot*. Here the heroine's proposition is a very clear and simple one: bring the people who have ruined the quality of life down into this basement and we will drown them in the sewer one after the other. If only this could be done! Who would be against it? A true Christian would perhaps oppose it, and his objection would be: "Are you going to do to others what you would not want done to you?" To which I can easily imagine the madwoman answering. "Do this to me too, as long as you get rid of them." And what would the Christian answer to that assent? Here we may see the depth at which *The Madwoman of Chaillot* was conceived. We all want to do as she did, and our only criticism of what she does is in fact that we shall not do the same.

Bertolt Brecht also followed Shaw's trick of dividing the *raisonneur* in *Man and Superman* by dividing some of his own characters morally, like Puntilla, the rich Finn, who is generous and democratic when drunk versus a calculating member of the landowning class when sober; also like the prostitute in *The Good Woman of Setzuan* who is good on certain days of the week and allows herself some days to be the contrary. I think, too, that the message Brecht wants to remain with us and thinks right is most often expressed musically—the form a rational message originally had in the earliest Greek comedies. The right that is sung is somehow less right than if it were merely said. One other thing Brecht does with the *raisonneur* which Shaw did not do: in some of his plays the dramatist's aim is not to set a *raisonneur* before us but to make us, the audience, the *raisonneur* of the action. Surely, this was the sense of the famous *alienation* from the action which Brecht was interested in creating in the audience. And here we may see why Brecht's plays never had a revolutionary impact and only became popular when the period of political action was over. *Raisonneurs* traditionally reason, and reason inhibits action.

If the *raisonneur* is so important in comedy, then I should say something about this role in *The Importance of Being Earnest*, the *raisonneur* here being Lady Brancaster. To be sure, practically everything she says is an almost perfect instance of *l'esprit faux*. But these remarks do not express the influence she exerts in the play, an influence directed toward preserving the society to which she and the other characters belong and which none of them thinks of challenging. This society is hardly a reasonable one. It is the world of leisure, in which smoking can be considered a way of being active; it is hardly a world to be justified by reason as normally understood. Though no character challenges the validity of this world, Lady Brancaster may be considered the one character in this play who has completely recognized it for what it is, and in this sense she is the play's *raisonneur*—the *raisonneur*, of course, of an artificial world, a false world that can only be justified by *l'esprit faux* and that would be destroyed by *l'esprit juste*.

Wilde's *raisonneur* is a conservative; Shaw's *raisonneurs* are reformists, revolutionaries, or mystics. Here in political terms we can see one of the chief differences between these two great masters of the art of comedy, although in a conventional sense they both had the same politics, for both were socialists.

Going backward in time from these two modern masters, we find the true genius of the art of comedy, Molière, who is not only the finest writer of comedy we have had but the one whose aesthetic taste was most perfect. In his comedy, right reason is represented by the *raisonneurs* who do nothing. His protagonists express themselves in terms of *l'esprit faux*. But *l'esprit juste* of Molière is not confined to those of his characters to whom he apportions it. It is fundamentally in the aptness with which *l'esprit faux* of his main characters is understood and dramatized. We feel Molière's rationality in the unerring way he presents his characters wittily missing the mark. It is in this sense that his comedies can be called syntheses of *l'esprit faux* with its opposite, *l'esprit juste*.

We are a long way, of course, from the world of contemporary comedy—the world of Samuel Beckett, Harold Pinter, and Eugène Ionesco—which Martin Esslin has called the Theatre of the Absurd. I once denied the usefulness of the term and the novelty of the theatre it purports to describe. Despite my protests, the term has remained with us, and there are times now when I myself feel the need to use it. Is it possible to give this term a definitive meaning? Might it not be said that "Theatre of the Absurd" describes a kind of comedy in which reason can never be expressed, in which a *raisonneur* cannot appear? Or, if admitted, the *raisonneur* has to be mad or incoherent like Lucky, who puts on a dunce's cap in order to think in *Waiting for Godot*, or like the messenger who, bringing the host's message to humanity, brays like an ass in *The Chairs*. Oddly enough, these mad *raisonneurs* of the Theatre of the Absurd may be said to have been anticipated by the rationalist Shaw, who along with his active and even revolutionary *raisonneurs* gave us Father Keegan in *John Bull's Other Island*, a *raisonneur* who it is suggested may be mad. The humor of plays in which no *raisonneur* appears or in which the role of reason is taken over by the incoherent or the mad is bound to be disquieting and frightening, and such indeed are the characteristics of the comedies so far produced by Beckett, Ionesco, and Pinter.

SAMUEL BECKETT AND JAMES JOYCE IN *ENDGAME*

AFTER THAT MARVELOUS wondering at the world which the performance of Samuel Beckett's *Waiting for Godot* occasioned, came a wondering at certain characteristics of the play itself, which, not being clear in their purpose or meaning, puzzled without astonishing. When the curtain was rung down on *Godot*, a certain number of questions remained. Who was Godot? Why were Vladimir and Estragon waiting for him? Why were Pozzo and Lucky in the play at all, since they seemed to have no definite relation to the tramps? Why was Lucky's famous "thinking speech" a parody of James Joyce? Finally, was the mood of the play one of despair or of hope?

Some of these questions can now be answered. Samuel Beckett's subsequent play, *Endgame*, treating the same experience dealt with in *Godot*, illuminates, at least speculatively, much that remained obscure in the latter, and most surprisingly. *Endgame*, though less effective on the stage, is superior in many respects to *Waiting for Godot;* it is purer in form, denser in meaning, a deeper expression of Samuel Beckett's ultimate purposes. *Endgame* is one long act whereas *Godot* was somewhat repetitious in two. Those who felt that Beckett's talent does not lie in dramatic construction, contrivance of plot, or development of character—at least, as customarily understood—and would be best expressed in the simpler rhythm of a single act are justified by the proportions of the more recent play.

So much for the question of form. My question, though, was: Who is Pozzo? And the answer to this question, which *Endgame* makes possible, provides a key to other questions which *Godot* provoked. Pozzo, it will be remembered, was the man with a whip driving the slave, Lucky, before him, who burst onto the scene to terrify, entertain, and in a way console the two tramps, Estragon and Vladimir. It will be remembered, too, that when he reappears, he has gone blind and he speaks poetically (in a manner which seems out of keeping with the ferocious character he has shown) of the nonexistence of time, and the all-encompassing power of eternity. Hearing that speech in the theatre, I had a distinct impulse to believe that Pozzo himself was Godot, the Mysterious Personage the two tramps were waiting to see, and who both felt could possibly justify their sad and trivial existences. In the end, however, this did not seem to be the case. From *Endgame* I think I have learned that Pozzo is none other that Beckett's former literary master and friend, James Joyce.

This play is directly and undeviatingly about Joyce and Beckett's relationship to him. It is abundantly clear now why Lucky, in his monologue, parodied the Joycean manner. There are any number of such parodies in *Endgame*, and by the central character, Hamm. (In this very name there is a suggestion that Shem and Shaun were just masks, that the real personality was Hamm-Joyce.) Whereas in *Godot* it was Lucky—that is, Beckett—who parodied Joyce, in *Endgame*, it is Hamm—that is, Joyce himself—who does the parodying.

Hamm is, among other things, the ham actor of the story of his life. He is blind, like Joyce, and tyrannical, yet human; he is cruel and yet with great dignity. His associate in *Endgame* is a younger man, Clov, who is apparently his adopted son. Clov (Beckett) is the less human of the two. He is the younger, the less ailing, and he has at least one hope; Hamm has none. Clov's hope is that he may some day leave Hamm. On this topic Hamm is humorous: "Without Hamm no home." In fact, in *Endgame* there is no home without Hamm, for the attic, which he shares with Clov, is all that remains of the world, everything else having been destroyed. "Why don't you kill me?" he asks Clov. "Because I don't have the key," Clov answers. This is the key to their cupboard. I think it is also the key to literary preeminence. A strange ménage, certainly, as Arthur Rimbaud remarked of his relationship with Paul Verlaine, and like that relationship, literary in essence.

For Hamm is a writer; he is apparently occupied with a

Work in Progress, and surely with this detail Beckett wants us to identify him as Joyce. This work is also the story of his own life. Perhaps it is even the story of how Clov-Beckett became Hamm-Joyce's son.

As in *Godot*, there are two other characters. But in *Endgame* the two extra characters are definitely related to the principals. The subordinate characters are Hamm's parents—his father, Nagg, and his mother, Nell, both of whom have lost their feet in an accident. Hamm keeps them in ashcans, sometimes getting Clov to lift the lids of the cans to inspect or feed or annoy them, as in this wonderful instance:

HAMM: It's time for my story. Do you want to listen to my story?
CLOV: No.
HAMM: Ask my father if he wants to listen to my story. (CLOV goes to the bins, raises the lid of NAGG's, stoops, looks into it. Pause. He straightens up.)
CLOV: He's asleep.
HAMM: Wake him. (CLOV stoops, wakes NAGG with the alarm. Unintelligible words. CLOV straightens up.)
CLOV: He doesn't want to listen to your story.
HAMM: I'll give him a bonbon. (CLOV stoops. As before.)
CLOV: He wants a sugarplum.
HAMM: He'll get a sugarplum. (CLOV stoops. As before.)
CLOV: It's a deal. . . .

Hamm, in this scene, wants to tell his father, Nagg, the story of his life, and the father can only be persuaded to listen to it by pitiful bribe. All of Joyce's megalomania and cruelty are in the episode. Beckett has not spared his master any more than Clov would have spared Hamm, or than Lucky would spare Pozzo if he were able overpower him finally. And from this comes the suggestion that like Hamm, Pozzo was Beckett's image of Joyce, only more caricatured in the first than in the second play. In fact, Hamm is a mixture of Pozzo and Vladimir, while Clov is a mixture of Estragon and Lucky.

Certainly, very few who saw *Godot* could have suspected that the experience of the two central characters symbolized so literary a relationship as the one that obtained between Joyce and Beckett. Who could have imagined, when induced to pity for the two tramps, and to terror by the spectacle of the master with a whip, that Beckett was bespeaking his own literary friendship with the author of *Ulysses?* The core of Beckett's experience as revealed by *Endgame* can be summed up as follows: The worst thing that happened to Beckett was also the best thing that happened to him—his encounter with Joyce.

We can only speculate about their relationship, to be sure, but on the other hand we do know something about the two men. Beckett came to Paris as a young man interested in writing modernist poetry and fiction. Joyce was then the top figure of the whole modernist movement. He was the acknowledged master, the king of language, the great innovator, the destroyer of old forms, and the contemnor of old values. He had more pride than any other writer of the time, and he was more self-absorbed, too, being the very figure of a man dedicated to himself. For Joyce had little interest in other writers. Stephen Daedalus remarks in *Ulysses:* "His own image to a man with that queer thing genius is the standard of all experience, material and moral. Such an appeal will touch him. The images of other males of his blood will repel him. He will see in them grotesque attempts of nature to foretell or repeat himself." Now it is simply not true that all men of genius react in this manner toward other men. But Joyce did, no doubt of it.

And this was the man Beckett chose to be his literary father. Beckett did show Joyce his work. In fact, what I get from a study of the plays is that in Beckett's mind Joyce became Beckett's one family relation, his adopted father. And apparently it was Beckett who adopted Joyce—not Joyce, Beckett, though Hamm in *Endgame* claims to have adopted Clov.

Joyce wrote, and abundantly, of his own father and mother. Beckett—in his plays at least—only about himself and Joyce, and, in *Endgame*, of Joyce's father and mother. According to Richard Ellmann's book, *James Joyce*, the great writer once said to Beckett directly: "I don't love anyone except my family," in a tone which Ellmann notes suggested that he didn't *like* anyone except his family either. But if Joyce wrote of his own father and mother, and in every one of his books, Beckett never writes in his plays of his parents—only of Joyce's. Had they by then become Beckett's grandparents?

Perhaps it was because Beckett had adopted Joyce as his literary father that he did not want him for a real-life father-in-law. When, according to Ellmann's account, Joyce's daughter Lucia felt impelled to reveal to Beckett the passion she felt for him, "Beckett told her bluntly that he came to the Joyce flat primarily to see her father." (The effect on Lucia was catastrophic.) Maybe he meant to say, "*My* father."

To have adopted such a man as Joyce shows two things about Beckett which are evidenced in other ways throughout his work: first, a desire to be destroyed, and second, contradicting that desire, limitless self-confidence. When we consider how many men have been ruined because their fathers had too much power or personality, we can better appreciate what Beckett's daring must have been in adopting as his literary master and single human relation the mighty, coolly indifferent, and self-absorbed literary giant.

Beckett did, in fact, make many efforts to get away from Joyce. All of his novels are, I think, flights from Joyce—perhaps toward Franz Kafka. Beckett's essay on Marcel Proust is also a flight from Joyce, and an ineffectual one. Proust is not described personally in the essay, nor does Kafka appear as a character in *Malone, Malone Dies*, or *Murphy*. But Joyce is present in Beckett's plays; he is confronted and he is vanquished, though Beckett, whether as Lucky or as Clov, is never shown to be victorious. Yet Joyce as Pozzo is blinded; as Hamm, he is deserted by Clov and left to die. On the other hand, Joyce, whether as Hamm or Pozzo, is always more sympathetic and more human than whoever speaks for Beckett, be this Lucky or Clov.

Can we now say who Godot is? For those who saw the play performed, he may be a mythical being and stand for whatever unattainable thing they might be waiting for. My suggestion, though, derives from my first impression that Pozzo, whom I identified as Joyce, was, in fact, Godot: Godot would be Joyce if Beckett had never met him; Godot would be Beckett if Beckett had never had to admire Joyce.

Another question: Do these plays express despair or hope? This, too, has to be answered speculatively. The extraordinary thing about *Endgame* and *Godot* is that they are capable of moving people who have not the faintest conception of what the relations between two writers, one young and aspiring, the other world-renowned, could be. It does strike me that the plays are more despairing than hopeful; yet they induce an exhilaration we could scarcely get from pessimistic works. Are they tragic, then? Not quite. And yet . . . there is tragedy somewhere near the characters, not in them. Perhaps the tragedy has already occurred, and Beckett's figures, Hamm and Clov, Pozzo and Lucky, Estragon and Vladimir, are merely members of the chorus. Nell and Nagg are a chorus at a still further remove. It is the chorus which expresses the drastic pessimism of Sophocles' tragedies, never the protagonists who endure the agony. Beckett and Joyce were after all writers, scribes: Whatever happened between them could not be tragic except in the derived way discovered by Samuel Beckett, and which has made both of his plays authentic and extraordinary works. There have not been many such since *Finnegans Wake*, which was intended, I suspect, to make any masterpiece after it impossible.

THE THEATRE AND THE "ABSURD"

IS THE WORLD we live in "absurd"? And has it become so recently? And does our world, newly absurd, require a particular kind of theatrical art expressing "absurdity"?

If you are ready to answer "yes," then you are likely to be convinced by what Martin Esslin says in his book, *The Theatre of the Absurd*.[1]

Esslin says that our present sense of absurdity springs from the loss of humanly important realities. Of what realities? well, Esslin thinks we have lost God. I should like to know when this occurred. But Esslin probably means merely that we have lost a belief in God once natural to us. Now I confess to having very little nostalgia for those periods of history when it was "natural" to believe in God. Was such belief ever really natural? Sören Kierkegaard, for one, thought that Christian education, "natural" in the nineteenth century—this kind of education we have lost— was the main obstacle to Christian belief; for Kierkegaard, true belief was always possible, always miraculous.

Is the family gone? At least it is better understood. Is the State gone? But the State seems to require the efforts and adherence of the young, and more than ever. Is patriotism gone? If so, is the loss grievous? Yet the figure of Colonel John Glenn, so much with us at this moment, suggests that patriotism still has no little virility. The cosmonaut, who orbited the earth three times and saw four settings of the sun in a few hours, came back to earth to inform us that he is still thrilled by the sight of the American flag. Did he then go up into weightless space just for the sake of a fractious parcel of humanity confined to United States territory in the Western Hemisphere? If so, his

---

1. Martin Esslin, *The Theatre of the Absurd* (New York: Viking Press, 1968, reprint 1973).

226

exploit must frighten us, much as it thrills us. What a man can do so well, he still does not do for men. The world is not so different from what it was.

Is reason gone? Then who would infer anything from our loss of it? To say that reason is gone is to speak without any hope of being understood. An absurd world would be silent; it would not be plied with plays.

Esslin makes much of another loss: that of our formerly felt intimacy with the world. And in support, he quotes from Albert Camus's *The Myth of Sisyphus:*

> A world that can be explained by reasoning, however faulty, is a familiar world. But in a universe that is suddenly deprived of illusions and of light, man feels a stranger. His is an irremediable exile, because he is deprived of memories of a lost homeland as much as he lacks hope of a promised land to come. This divorce between man and his life, the actor and his setting, truly constitutes the feeling of absurdity.

I think it is absurd to take anyone—even Camus—for an authority on the "absurd." And, in fact, the quotation above, which Esslin has used to buttress his view, is fairly close to nonsense. Imagine: Camus prefers a world that can be explained by faulty reasoning—but why then use the term *explained?*—to one inexplicable by good reasoning. He wants the world to be familiar; Aristotle thought it should excite wonder. And how could the world ever be deprived of illusion, which is so large a part of it? Camus himself had plenty of illusions, one of them being that we are bound to have a feeling of absurdity if denied the memory of "a lost homeland" and of "a promised land to come." Is it absurd not to have had a good background or to be without real prospects? Sad, perhaps; but it is one thing to call the world sad, quite another to call it "absurd." The first statement is without philosophical pretension.

The world can no more become absurd than it can sin, starve, or fall down. There are many absurdities in the world; most of them were always there.

But was there always a Theatre of the Absurd? I claim there was not and that there is no such thing now. Esslin claims that (1) there was a Theatre of the Absurd in the past and (2) the group of contemporary dramatists whom he has singled out write the kinds of plays they do in response to a particular crisis the world is going through at this time. But the two claims refute each other. Esslin maintains that there is a particular spiritual crisis, and that a certain kind of dramatic art has been produced in order to express it; but he cannot maintain, then, that forms of theatre like those being produced now long antedated the crisis. Yet in a chapter entitled "The Tradition of the Absurd," Esslin ranges through past history for prototypes of the new kinds of plays now being written. The mimes of the Middle Ages, the court jesters, the clowns of Shakespeare, the harlequinades which entered into the British music hall and American vaudeville, the commedia dell'arte, the nonsense verse of Edward Lear and Lewis Carroll are all called on to account for the character of specifically modern works, which character, in turn, is supposed to be due to a special contemporary predicament. Esslin writes: "This is not the place for a detailed study of Shakespearean clowns, fools, and ruffians as forerunners of the Theatre of the Absurd." No, it is not.

But let us consider Esslin's main contention that there is a Theatre of the Absurd at this time, quite apart from his other contention that it preexisted its own *raison d'être*. Is it true that Samuel Beckett, Eugène Ionesco, Arthur Adamov, Jean Genet, Edward Albee, Fernando Arrabal, Günter Grass, Harold Pinter, and N. F. Simpson can be best understood if considered as investigators of a new theatrical art, the Theatre of the Absurd? Some of the playwrights listed above have, to be sure, written plays to Esslin's specifications, but only one of these, Ionesco, is really important. The three major figures, as I am sure Esslin himself would agree, are Ionesco, Beckett, and Genet. But of these three, only Ionesco fits Esslin's formula.

One individual, to be sure, if an artist of rank, has as much interest as a whole school. And Ionesco is a remarkable playwright with some five or six masterpieces to his credit. He has great invention and an exuberant humor; unfortunately, his ideas are topical, adventitious: the last thing one could say about them is that they are "new." One typically "new" idea of Ionesco's is that there are no new ideas, even in the construction of plays. Here he is quite wrong. He has written some plays that are really novel as structures. It is the ideas expressed in them that are all too familiar and which spring from the prevailing climate of political and metaphysical pessimism.

What is objectionable in Ionesco's theatre is curiously akin to what is objectionable in Esslin's whole concept. Ionesco thinks absurdity is something new;[2] Esslin wants to give us news of the absurd.

Esslin talks a lot about Beckett and Genet. But in the fairly detailed analyses he makes of their lives and work he is unable to illuminate much of their art or even to give us the feeling that he has judged it wisely.

Beckett he discusses under this rubric: "The Search for the Self." And Esslin searches accordingly in Richard Ellmann's biography of James Joyce (who knew Beckett) for such data as might throw light on *Waiting for Godot* and *Endgame*. Now Ellmann's book is valuable on Beckett as well as Joyce. For instance, it appears that Beckett is given to long silences and when he visited Joyce they often stared at each other for hours without uttering a word. This certainly tells us something about the kind of dialogue we have come to expect from Beckett. But what have the personal data about Beckett to do with a general cultural crisis, or with any modern feeling for absurdity? Beckett is a very strange man, no question of that. Even his handwriting, of which I have seen one instance, is peculiar in the extreme.

Esslin finds fault with my own view expressed in a piece I did on Beckett for *The New Leader*: "Samuel Beckett and James Joyce in *Endgame*," and in which I attempted to explain Beckett's play in terms of his attitude to James Joyce. Esslin says that my theory "surely becomes untenable"; not because there may

2. I don't think Ionesco regards "absurdity" as an *idea*, but as *anti-idea*. His theatre has been called "antitheatre."

not be a certain amount of truth in it (every writer is bound to use elements of his own experience of life in his work) but because, far from illuminating the full content of a play like *Endgame*, such an interpretation reduces it to a trivial level." Did I reduce the relationship between Hamm and Clov to a trivial level? I made the point that the *value* of recognizing the autobiographical material in the play was that by so doing, it was possible to absolve the author of the charge of pessimism. But never mind my own interpretation of the play. Here is Esslin's: "The experience expressed in Beckett's plays (including *Endgame*) is of a far more profound and fundamental nature than mere autobiography. They reveal his experience of temporality and evanescence; his sense of the tragic difficulty of becoming aware of one's own self in the merciless process of renovation and destruction that occurs with change in time; of the difficulty of communication between human beings; of the unending quest for reality in a world in which everything is uncertain and the borderline between dream and reality is ever shifting: of the tragic nature of all love relationships and the self-deception of friendship . . . and so on." Are Beckett's plays about all that? From this list of abstractions one would think that Beckett's plays had been written in the German language and not, exquisitely, in the French. Besides, what has Esslin's list of abstractions to do with the life of Samuel Beckett? And what has that life to do with a general cultural crisis? These are the connections Esslin is obliged to establish, and he does not.

On the subject of Genet, too, Esslin's concept of the absurd is little help. He turns to the data about Genet's life which we have from the playwright himself. It seems that Genet was abandoned as a child, and when accused of stealing, resolved to become a thief. Between 1930 and 1940, as Esslin notes, Genet led the life of an itinerant delinquent, among beggars and pimps; he made acquaintance with the French jails. Fortunately for the theatre, he never quite became "the hardened jail-bird on whom the prison gates shut forever."[3]

These facts show Genet to be a very strange person, too.

---

3. Arthur Rimbaud, *A Season in Hell*.

Should not his personal strangeness be related to his plays? But Esslin, out to prove his theory, disregards the personal facts and concentrates on the "absurdity of our historical epoch." He derives Genet's plays from the modern feeling of helplessness in facing a mechanized world. Esslin writes: "A feeling of helplessness when confronted with the vast intricacy of the modern world, and the individual's impotence in making his own influence felt on that intricate and mysterious machinery, pervades the consciousness of Western man today. A world that functions mysteriously outside our conscious control must appear absurd." Once again Esslin has trotted out fashionable and very misleading clichés. The world Genet describes in his plays is the product of a virile imagination, almost Elizabethan in its force and fancy. Genet could be compared to Christopher Marlowe, never to Franz Kafka.

Art, it must be admitted, is unable to occupy a central position in the modern world; thus, the artist cannot be in the very center of things. But Homer was certainly in the very center of things Greek when he wrote the *Iliad*, although he wrote it in Ionian Greek; and Sophocles was in the center of the Greek world when he wrote plays for the Athenian public. In the modern world, of course, no such privileged position is open to art. To look at all, the artist is probably condemned not to look all around him. Can anyone be in the center of things in our age? This is not sure. But this is sure: anyone who is will not be an artist. That is why a Homer is utterly inconceivable today. (Georg Hegel notes that there was not a single tool made by the Greeks which went unremarked in Homer's *Iliad*. Is it conceivable that any modern poet could sum up in song all the instruments manufactured in our society? Besides, to carry Hegel's point further, every tool Homer described was already an art object.) Very probably art requires, if it is to be practiced at all today, that its creator contribute to it his own personal oddity. I suggest that this is a logical consequence of the marginal situation of art as such. Political criticism of art, even when sensitive and cultivated, has proved utterly sterile and unable to instigate any sort of new creation. It was based on a fallacy: that politics was central (this is certainly to be questioned) and that being central, it had the right to insist that art be central, also; now two things cannot occupy the same place at the same time—perhaps they can if infinitely smaller than minuscule. But the political critics of modern art and literature were not thinking along the lines of quantum physics. They were thinking of the art produced in past epochs when art *was* central. In fact, the history of what we call modern art and modern literature has been the successive imposition on the public of bizarre standpoints, unexpected attitudes, peculiar effects. This has gone on for a fairly long time but it has only recently become a general trend in theatre. Of course, August Strindberg was as peculiar as Beckett or Genet; but he was more exceptional in the early part of this century. It is now to be expected that personally peculiar people will create the art which persons of sensibility are able to enjoy. Does this mean that a theatre created by "peculiar" persons should be called the Theatre of the Absurd?

I think the important point to make here is that this development in the theatre is belated, and follows some fifty or seventy years after personal oddity had vindicated itself in other fields—painting, poetry, and the novel—as essential to the production of authentic art. In fact, I would suggest that one reason good art has for so long a time been "advanced" art is that artists relished the freakishness attendant on being "ahead" of others. One way of being peculiar is to be in advance like the crane who, Le comte de Lautréamont says, flying first, forces all the others to look at its behind.

But for the theatre—and Esslin does not see this at all—the need to be bizarre, eccentric, individual involves the creator in a dialectic, as it perhaps does not involve any other type of creator—painter, poet, or novelist. Admitted that it is an advantage if you want to create to be personally strange; still, in the theatre your personal strangeness has to have an immediate effect on an audience composed of very different persons, who have to react to the play presented before they have had a chance to be converted to it by the intimidating force of cultural opinion. I do not think the dialectic I have indicated should come to an end. I think it is this dialectic which has made the plays of both Beckett and Genet more available to us than their novels were. If Beckett had not turned to the theatre, he would have remained the eccentric writer of morbid tales in monotonous, if good, prose. If Genet had not turned to the play form, he would have remained a writer of lyrical pornography. The dialectic imposed by the theatre has made it possible for these "strangers" to speak in a language pleasing both to them and to us. It is this dialectic which makes the new plays more interesting to me, at least, than the new poems or novels. Of all modern works it is the new theatre pieces which are, and have to be, I suggest, the least "absurd."

THE NOVELIZATION OF DRAMA

IN "EPIC AND DRAMA," one of Mikhail Bakhtin's seminal essays in support of the novel, the literary theorist shows himself to be anything but nonpartisan. " . . . the novel gets on poorly with other genres," he grants, and then goes on to spell out just what he understands by "poorly": "There can be no talk of a harmony deriving from mutual limitation . . . the novel parodies other genres . . . it exposes the conventionality of their forms and languages; it squeezes out some genres and incorporates others." All such effects of the novel are described not as criticism of it, rather, it seems, as praise. All the same, the theorist indicates that he is not quite ready to jettison the other genres, not even those the novel's power and richness may have rendered obsolete.

Is the stage play such a genre? The question is an important one, and I shall try to answer it. But first of all I want to compare Bakhtin's view of the novel with the views of others who also happen to have granted it premier status among the genres. Back in the thirties, Edmund Wilson brought pain to the many admirers of Charles Baudelaire, Rainer Maria Rilke and T. S. Eliot—notably to Delmore Schwartz—when he insisted that ever since the appearance of the novel, lyrical or narrative verse had to be judged of secondary importance. Much earlier, in 1908, Thomas Mann in *Versuch über das Theatre (Theatre Observed)* insisted on the stage play's thorough inferiority to the novel. I cite Mann's remarks from Kate Hamburger's *The Logic of Literature*, where she writes of Mann: "He considers the situation of the audience before the 'abbreviated' stage world symptomatic of the 'silhouette art' of the drama. 'In which play,' he asks, . . . 'is the modern scene which would excel the scene in a modern novel in the precision of its visual features, in intensive presence, in reality . . . The novel is more precise, more complete, more knowing, more painstaking and deeper than the drama in everything that concerns knowledge of man in body and character, and in contrast to the view that the drama is the true, plastic literary work, I profess that I find it far more an art of the silhouette. I find the narrated person alone to be rounded, whole, real and plastic.'" Unlike, I suppose, such less plastic, less whole, less real, less rounded persons as Macbeth, Hamlet, or Phèdre.

No doubt Mann was thinking only of characters in the prose plays of the nineteenth century, characters not energized by the rhetoric of the greatest poets of the West. But however that may be, my purpose here is not to argue against Mann's judgment of the stage play—of whatever period—but to compare it with Bakhtin's judgment of the genre, a judgment even more radically critical than was the novelist's. And I must add here that Bakhtin's opinion of poetry since the masterpieces of the nineteenth-century novel may be even more chilling to poetry lovers than was Edmund Wilson's. For Bakhtin contends that the stage play, and the poem, too, lyric or narrative, have already succumbed to the pressures of the novel-reading public; in fact, they have been "novelized." He writes: "In an era when the novel reigns supreme, all the other genres are to a greater or less extent 'novelized': drama (for example, Ibsen, Hauptmann, the whole of naturalist theatre); epic poetry (for example, *Childe Harold* and especially Byron's *Don Juan*); even lyric poetry (as an extreme example, Heine's lyrical verse). Those genres that stubbornly preserve their old canonic nature begin to appear stylized."

I am an admirer of Bakhtin; he may well be the finest literary theorist of the twentieth century. All the same it would be unwise to go along with his judgments when they are clearly wrong. *Don Juan* and *Childe Harold* are in no sense "novelized" epics. They are narrative poems quite without epic feeling or character, much less like the nineteenth-century novel than Homer's *Odyssey*, which Joyce was able to use as the mythic background for his twentieth-century novel *Ulysses*. To my mind, Shakespeare's sonnets have more of the qualities of the novel than can be said of the verses of Heinrich Heine, though the sonnets were composed long before the novel's greatest successes. Yes, the stage play has indeed been novelized; to some extent by Ibsen's realistic concentration on middle-class problems. But on the other hand, the novel was not uninfluenced by Ibsen's use of symbols. For in *The Wild Duck, The Master Builder*, and *When We Dead Awaken*, Ibsen mitigated with symbolism and poetry the realistic and prosaic style of his earlier plays, and Joyce followed his lead in writing *Ulysses*. We have it from the Irish novelist that he learned Norwegian to read Ibsen, whom he termed the greatest European poet since Shakespeare. So if Ibsen brought to the stage play a realism like that of the nineteenth-century novel, on the other hand he introduced the most realistic novelist of this century to the union of poetry with symbolism and myth.

Moreover, Gerhart Hauptmann was not as important in novelizing the stage play as was Anton Chekhov, who tried (with some success) to eliminate plot almost entirely from his plays. Certainly it is the case that if one wants to be fully realistic, dramatic plotting becomes a problem, since plot will require the intervention of the dramatist, and this can bring with it an element of the improbable. But as Corneille pointed out long ago, one needs the improbable to generate any kind of dramatic action. Tolstoy, who preached sincerity, and was against artificiality in art as in manners, was generally critical of stage plays dynamized by their plots. It seems that Chekhov took him to the opening night of his play *Ivanov*, (much admired on our off-Broadway stage), and when the curtain came down, Tolstoy (Chekhov reports) said to him, "You know that I don't care much for Shakespeare, but he's a much better dramatist than you are. And so is Ibsen; at least they tell a story of some kind, with a beginning, a middle, and an end." It seems when it came to spending an evening in the theatre, Tolstoy thought differently about plot than he did when reflecting on the value of plot in narrative art as such.

Had Chekhov's lead in trying to eliminate plot from the stage play been followed, all our theatres might have been closed down for good. I recall that during the sixties playwrights were regularly criticized by theatre critics for not having eliminated what was then called "the storyline" from their plays. Fortunately for our theatre, few playwrights obeyed these critics. What saved theatrical art was the revelation that theatricality as such is a permanent and irreducible aspect of life. This revelation was made first of all by Pirandello in those of his plays that I have characterized as instances of metatheatre (dealt with elsewhere in this collection of essays). But the value of theatricality as such goes beyond the specific expressions of it in metatheatre. Let me give an example of what I mean, for it may well be that my point cannot be made clearly if just stated abstractly.

At the Stella Adler school of acting, I witnessed the performance of two one-act plays that I think exemplified (1) the effect of the realistic novel on theatre, and (2) the resistance of theatre to realism. How? By the intensification of theatrical effects. One of the plays, titled *Margaret's Bed*, was by William Inge. The other, and much finer work, was Harold Pinter's *The Lover*.

Margaret's Bed is about a young woman's hesitation to have casual sex with a new acquaintance who is spending the night in her flat, and in which two beds are available. Should Margaret slip into the bed that she has offered her friend, or lie alone in her other bed, even if this means pounding her pillow? Certainly the matter could be dealt with interestingly in a short story. As certainly the staging adds no new element to understanding the difficulties and attractions of sex with a new person not yet longed for. On the other hand, the story in the theatre piece of Harold Pinter could be told only on the stage. We see a man about to take leave of his wife for work, and then later the same actor returns, differently dressed, and makes love to his spouse. Is he a lover or the husband? His clothes are different but the actor is the same. In Pinter's play the *The Betrayal,* it is adultery rather than marriage that is betrayed by the lovers (the dramatic reversal there is emphasized by the fact that the play begins with the ending of the affair and ends with its beginning); I think that Harold Pinter may in the *The Lover* be describing infidelity with, rather than to, one's spouse. The lovemaking is indicated by both the man and woman banging on a drum. This play, as I have indicated, is essentially theatrical, its mood entirely dependent on the play form; it could not exist off the stage.

I think the recognition of theatricality as a form of life has in fact saved the theatre—at least for now. And basically this is why the stage play is not yet obsolete; all the same, the main contention of Bakhtin that the stage play to a great extent has been novelized has to be granted. In fact, I would even add an argument to Bakhtin's contention, one he himself has neglected to give: There were two setbacks for the stage play in the nineteenth century: (1) its novelization, as Bakhtin has said, and (2) the fact that the greatest dramatist of the century was not a playwright, not Karl Georg Büchner, Albert de Musset, Victor Hugo, Edmond Rostand, Henrich von Kleist, Henrik Ibsen, or August Strindberg. What was great in nineteenth-century drama is to be found in Dostoevsky's novels.

It is interesting to note here that Dostoevsky was an admirer of Jean Racine, whom Tolstoy called "the wound of French poetry," and also Shakespeare, whose plays Tolstoy criticized so severely. Of all novelists, Dostoevsky was certainly the greatest dramatist, and in criticizing his books one thinks of comparing him first of all with the Greek writers of tragedy, and the Elizabethans, rather than with nineteenth-century novelists. So with the greatest dramatist of the nineteenth century a novelist, and with aspects of the novel entering into drama and tending to decompose its clear structure, the stage play has indeed suffered; my only claim is that it has not suffered mortally.

Having granted the competition dwelt on by Bakhtin between the novel and the stage play, let me now try to make clear the realities which seem more suitable to the one than to the other. A large list could be made of these, but I shall deal here with four, but these four are of great importance. They are life and death, sincerity and authenticity. In the novel life is abundant, and even the death of a character to whom the novelist is favorably disposed generally provides no brief for, or impulse to think better of, dying. The novel is like life itself, unfinished; thus the death scenes in a novel are never satisfyingly final.

Seldom are marriage scenes in a novel anticipations of a funeral soon to come. True, it was the novelist James Joyce who converted the word *funeral* into "fun-for-all"; but it was Shakespeare, with *Hamlet,* who may have suggested the pun to Joyce. In Shakespeare's play the villain Claudius speaks of "mirth in funerals and dirge in marriage."

I should like to assert that death is better dealt with on the stage than in the novel, which makes us yearn for still more life (generally, this is the case), yet there is no death in a stage play that quite equals the death of Emma Bovary in Gustave Flaubert's novel. On the stage it is true that death succeeds in finalizing. That is why it is so valuable in tragedy, in which for the protagonist, at least, it tends to be the very last occasion.

But then, death is more useful to the dramatist than to the novelist, which in no way implies that the former has to be the more gifted in handing out death sentences. Tolstoy, probably the greatest and most perfect of novelists—that is what Flaubert thought, and I cannot but agree with him on this—was as much "possessed of death" as John Webster, and his descriptions of dying—I am thinking of the deaths of Princess Bolkonsky, and of Ivan Illyich—are, with the death of Emma Bovary, among the greatest things in literature. On the other hand, Dostoevsky, whom I have characterized as a dramatist essentially, seems not to have been interested in death at all, not in his own, and not particularly in the deaths of his characters. Does this mean that my notion of death's serviceability in the genres is contradicted by the facts of literary history? I think not. The value of death on the stage is a purely technical one. It is conceivable, though, that had Dostoevsky presented his dramas in stage plays rather than in novels, he might have become more interested in the deaths of his characters and, possibly by reflecting on them, even in his own.

Now about authenticity. When Lionel Trilling lectured on *Sincerity and Authenticity,* he was undoubtedly aware that Martin Heidegger, whom he quoted in a note, was responsible for the distinction between the authentic and the inauthentic, and that this was a moral-ontological distinction, not a stronger formulation of the well-known psychological-moral distinction between sincerity and insincerity. I say that he was well aware of this, because in introducing his own discussion of authenticity he refers to "being," to the "sentiment of being" in Jean-Jacques Rousseau, and to the importance of the verb "to be" in William Wordsworth, but for all this his understanding of authenticity is, as far as I can make out, a psychological one, even at times belonging to journalistic "chatter," as when he argues that psychoanalysis is "authentic." But the term so used loses the ontological meaning Heidegger was careful to give it, and authenticity has no particular meaning as distinguished from sincerity in psychology. But it would make no sense to say of psychoanalysis that it is sincere—it is either true or false, strongly or weakly scientific; authenticity applies only to individuals, not to groups, peoples, nations, or doctrines.

It strikes me that sincerity and insincerity are proper notions for the novelist who does not have to bring his characters to a final occasion in which the meaning of their lives is summed up. It is an aspect of life, and life is more fully explored by the novelist than by the playwright. However, life, and that part of it which belongs to the theatre, are full of contradictions. While many novelists have dealt with sincerity and insincerity, one playwright, Molière, made of this distinction the theme of his unforgettable drama, *The Misanthrope*. And the interesting thing is that the hero of the play, Alceste, who insists on sincerity, exiles himself from society (one even wonders whether there is any place left for him in life). On the other hand, he never seems to me, at least, to be authentic, while Célimène, insincere throughout, is most certainly that. She will be insincere to her death.

All the same I will insist that sincerity belongs especially to the novel, and authenticity to the stage, certainly to tragedy. The sweep of action would be falsified by inauthenticity in a chief character. The remark in *The Red and the Black* that only people awaiting execution can speak sincerely is quite untrue as is the stagy ending of that wonderful novel. I think Stendhal who had always wanted to write plays fell into a theatrical mode which was untrue to his most inspired manner when he wrote the ending of his novel. I do not believe Julien

Sorel would have tried to kill Madame de Rênal, or would have looked forward to being beheaded for his deed. The whole theatrical ending is false to the great virtues of that most living of all novels. Stendhal was not adept at killing off a character — unlike any of the dramatists we are ready to call great.

Quite recently I came across Heidegger's *Fundamental Concepts of Metaphysics: World, Finitude, Solitude,* which has just appeared in English translation. Some regard it as a continuation of the philosopher's *Being and Time* (*Sein und Zeit*), in fact, as a second volume of *Being and Time.* In any case, in this opus Heidegger questions the nature of boredom, and what may be peculiar to it: Why people are bored, what bores them, and the further question, are they bored by what they are? In these analyses, some of which are masterly, Heidegger distinguishes three kinds of boredom, the last of which he calls "profound." And finally he asks this question: Is contemporary man bored with himself, with humanity? Is this the ultimate, the most profound cause of contemporary boredom?

All of this is certainly worth thinking about, but what I found disturbing is that Heidegger never asks, How does one stop being bored? How does one exit from boredom into interestedness? To excitement or adventure? And of course people do many things to stop being bored. Not a few take drugs. And Heidegger is quite right in thinking that boredom is a special problem in the present world. But as soon as one asks: How does one stop being bored? and tries to give this question a clear answer, one sees reasons for boredom which Heidegger has not discussed. One is never bored when one is in danger, especially when in danger of death. We have done much to make life safer, so that it is not dangerous nowadays to cross the ocean, but it is more boring to cross the ocean today, than when one had to go by ships that might not have been able to hold up in a great storm. Many of our activities are safer and more boring than they were when unsafe. And this has contributed to the boredom from which many of our contemporaries seek relief in drugs.

But I want to lift this discussion to a more positive level and I can do this by referring to drama. One is not bored when one is in dramatic situation one finds interesting, or when sitting in the theatre watching an interesting dramatic situation develop. One is not bored when one has been interestingly dramatized by one's convictions, one's religion, like Christianity or Stoicism. So I cannot agree with Heidegger's definition of profound boredom, which he thinks is the boringness of temporality as such. I think there would be profound boredom if even though caught in an interesting plot, or watching the development of an interesting play, one remained bored. There would be profound boredom in my view in watching a performance of *Oedipus* properly acted and directed and one were not lifted out of the boredom that sent one to the theatre.

So there we may observe the importance of plot, and with it the importance of the stage play, the value of which may be dependent on the plotting skill of the dramatist, as much as on his ability to present characters that, to use Mann's terms, are whole, really rounded, and plastic. Once more about Heidegger on boredom: he describes it as a "mood" to which we are "attuned." His image is that of the tuning of a musical instrument so as to produce a certain melody or, as might be the case, cacophony. Thus he thinks of the individual as an instrument. But to be played by what? By time? Here I would reject his word *attunement,* and substitute for it the word *dramatization.* For we are dramatized even in our idleness or boredom, by our taking up an attitude toward our circumstances, even by our failing to do so. One can dramatize oneself as a drug taker, or as a drug dealer, as a melancholic, as faithful or faithless; one is not played on altogether by events like a musical instrument. We are dramatized by others or by ourselves; if we do not like the plot we are in, we have the possibility at least of leaving the stage for a while and reappearing in another drama more to our own taste. May I repeat myself? What really would be profound boredom, in my sense of things, would be to find oneself in a profoundly interesting plot, and say, as Hedda Gabler does, in what I take was Ibsen's masterpiece: "I was born to be bored to death."

A further point about the stage play and clearly in support of it: The image of dramatization with which I would replace

Heidegger's image of attunement, comes, of course, from the language of the theatre and it implies that dramatization is universal—the world is a stage, rather than the background of a novel. Thus "novelization" cannot have the universal meaning that "dramatization" has, and that no change of stylistic fashion can rob it of. The stage play may have been novelized to a certain extent; but novelization does not describe our situation when, not in a novel but in life, we take up an attitude. We are dramatized even when not on the stage, and when there is no novelist at hand to describe our doings.

In arguing for the stage play, I am thinking of other values besides the formal virtues of the play as compared with those of the novel. I am thinking of values which Bakhtin does not even consider in his comparison of novel and drama. I am thinking of the fact that one cannot visit the theatre at any time one likes, that one has to make it a special occasion in going to see a play (I think, too, our standards were higher when we dressed up on going to the theatre). I think, too, that in the success of a play, many have to collaborate, the actors, the director, and others along with the playwright. So that in a great theatre piece, we must congratulate the whole of society, and not just the playwright. It tells us something positive about nineteenth-century Norway that Ibsen found a theatre for the new things he brought in his plays. Engels, in trying to defend Ibsen against those Marxists who attacked the playwright as "bourgeois," remarked that maybe in Norway one could be bourgeois and yet a man, even if this were, as he implied, not true elsewhere in Europe. But even beyond the special value I see in the theatrical occasion, I think there is something to be specially valued in the stage play as such, which Bakhtin also has ignored. It is devoted to dramatic conflict, which the novel can ignore altogether. I concede that Dostoevsky's novels gave us a dramatic system more profound that that of any nineteenth-century playwright; it is also the case that Dostoevsky's novels are very exceptional in that conflict is so central to them: the novel can do other things besides showing characters in conflict; it can depict the effect of the passage of time on people's character and on their appearance; it can analyze motives at length, all of which takes time, of which the playwright has very little at his disposal. He has to concentrate the action he is concerned with into two or three hours at the most. And the only way he can reveal his characters, as I noted, is to show how they react to challenges, which is to say, by relying on a dramatic plot. It should be recalled here that Aristotle considered plot to be the very soul of tragedy.

Afterword

Something about Dostoevsky's dramatic system: I have in mind a discovery of the novelist that Bakhtin was the first to point up. The theorist maintains that the characters of Dostoevsky—or in any case his chief characters—have two "voices," only one of which is generally heard. An exceptionally good character, like Alyosha in *The Brothers Karamazov*, can hear both voices of his brother Ivan; Ivan's illegitimate half-brother, Smerdyakov, hears only the voice of Ivan's cynicism. Now it will be seen immediately that a situation wherein one character can hear one of another's voices, others a different voice, and still a third both voices is something dramatically unprecedented and probably impossible of realization on the stage. The only thing like it that I know of was the effort of Eugene O'Neill, in his very interesting play *The Great God Brown,* to indicate that his characters had different voices by having them put on and take off masks they brought with them on stage. But this very stylistic device can hardly compare with the subtle and very realistic ways by which Dostoevsky in his novels was able to alternate his characters' different voices and the different receptions of their voices by others.

Dostoevsky invented something else, too, which I take to be of great dramatic value. And this discovery of his was not even noted by Bakhtin. In *Crime and Punishment* Dostoevsky manages to have his protagonist, Raskolnikov, meet a certain Svidrigailov who represents what Raskolnikov is certain to become if he does not confess his crime. Thus it is that when Svidrigailov commits suicide, Raskolnikov is both able to confess and genuinely wish to pay in suffering for his criminal deed. The confrontation of a particular character with another who in some sense represents his probable future should he not change his ways is something I have not found in any other dramatist or novelist. But this discovery of Dostoevsky, for I think he discovered it, could be immensely valuable in a stage play. It is because of these two original dramatic discoveries that I feel justified in calling Dostoevsky the nineteenth century's premier dramatist.

AUTHOR AND TITLE INDEX